Call Me
Counselor

J. B. Lippincott Company | Philadelphia and New York

Call Me Counselor

by Sara Halbert, Esq.

with Florence Stevenson

Copyright © 1977 by Sara Halbert and Florence Stevenson
All rights reserved·
First edition
9 8 7 6 5 4 3 2 1
Printed in the United States of America

With the exception of Joseph James,
Olga Cruz, Clarence Tucker, Sylvester Pendarvis,
Victor Rosario and others involved in his case, and judges,
lawyers, and police officers and other professionals
and associates, all names in the cases recounted in this book
have been changed to protect the privacy of living persons.

U.S. Library of Congress Cataloging in Publication Data

Halbert, Sara.
  Call me counselor.

  1. Halbert, Sara. 2. Lawyers—United States—
Biography. I. Stevenson, Florence, joint author.
II. Title.
KF373.H23A3   340'.092'4   77-21054
ISBN-0-397-01239-X

Contents

A Day in a Lawyer's Life

ONE EVENING A FEW MONTHS AGO, in the ladies' room of a restaurant, my sister, Bea, asked me what I had done that day.

"But, Bea," I said, "you know that Monday is always my murder day."

She answered casually, "Oh, yes, Sara, I forgot." In the mirror next to us I caught sight of a face, eyes goggling and mouth open; a second later, the woman standing beside me rushed out.

Bea picked up a lipstick, evidently dropped in mid-sprint, and laughed. "She's probably dialing nine-one-one."

"I should've said I stop work at six."

"Oh, come on, Sara, you never stop work. Anything interesting on your calendar today?"

"Today was a real workout," I told her. "I'm in the middle of preparing the Joseph James trial. . . ."

"Oh, my God." My sister rolled her eyes. "Do you think he'll get the chair for killing that correction officer?"

"If he's convicted of murder in the first degree, he must be sentenced to death. They won't let him cop out to felony murder with a sentence of twenty-five years to life. Those correction officers are determined to make an example of him." I sighed.

"I don't blame them. He didn't give a damn about his victim! That poor man and his family had rights too."

I was getting edgy. The subject of the death penalty always gets me aroused. "If it's wrong to murder, it doesn't become right when it's done in the name of the law. I don't

7

believe in an eye for an eye. James shot the officer as he was escaping from custody. That makes it felony murder. But don't let me get started on that."

"No," Bea agreed. "Best save your rhetoric for the court-room."

I was sorry that the nervous lady had not stayed around to ask what I meant by my "murder day." She would have been told that, as a trial lawyer, I preferred to schedule all my murder-case arraignments on Mondays, strictly for my own convenience. Brooklyn murder cases are heard by the judges who preside in the courtrooms on the ninth floor of the Kings County courthouse. In designating Monday as my arraignment day, I might be in court for eight hours straight, but at least I would not have to divide my time between those cases and my others—in the Bronx, Queens, and even Riverhead, Long Island. Many murder cases are court-assigned, given to lawyers on a special "murder list" who represent those people who cannot afford to retain their own private counsel. Generally the Legal Aid Society han-dles the indigent, but murder cases are outside its authoriza-tion.

At this writing, I am the only woman on the Brooklyn list. I am a criminal lawyer, based in Brooklyn. My office is on Court Street, and through my window I can see the great square outlines of the Kings County courthouse. I need to be within walking, even running, distance of that building be-cause I spend a great deal of my working day in it. Though I practice every possible type of law, including corporation, real-estate, civil, negligence, and matrimonial cases, I am primarily interested in criminal law, and my specialty is murder.

In the old gangster movies, criminal lawyers—or defense counsels, as we are also known—were termed "mouth-pieces." Their function was to provide largely fraudulent defenses for high-ranking gangsters. I have had very little to do with gangsters in my twenty years of practice. My clients are not Mafia types breezing back and forth in high-powered Cadillacs; they come from the ghetto areas, and they are the people most likely to be crushed beneath the juggernaut that passes for justice in New York City. Economically speaking, they might be called "the little man," but in my opinion that is a misnomer. To me, every man and woman in this city is the same size, just as in this country we are all free and equal. It was partly to preserve this freedom and equality that I became a lawyer.

But let me get off the soapbox and down to the specifics of that Monday, the Monday my sister asked about, which was in a sense a microcosm of my life in law.

On that day, I was involved with four assigned murder cases, two of them new clients and two who had been in jail for several months. I also had a private case to argue, that of a young Puerto Rican who had been accused of rape. In the newspaper headlines, he was called "the Brooklyn Heights Rapist." By coincidence, that very morning I had received a letter from yet another alleged rapist, Bill Foster, whom I had always called "the Bear."

The sight of that envelope in my morning mail had sent a whole series of images coursing through my mind. I had first met Foster at Matteawan, the state facility for the criminally insane. A heavy-set, powerful black man with a child's face atop an immense six-foot-six frame, he was in Matteawan because he was labeled a dangerous psychotic who, when irritated, destroyed everything in sight with his enormous shovel-like hands. Foster was accused of seven charges of rape which had taken place in different locations on the West Side of Manhattan. He had been arrested running wildly through the subway tunnels of Brooklyn some months after the rapes had occurred and he appeared to fit the description of the rapist, down to the extraordinarily large hands. After seven years at Matteawan, he was finally released to the court as fit to stand trial.

The minute he was sent back to the city jail, trouble

started. He had claustrophobia and hated being cooped up in small quarters; he had reacted like a punished child, exploding into violent tantrums. With his great strength, he was very difficult to control. I was told that he had once actually torn the toilet from the cement floor of his cell and hurled it against the bars.

Thinking about Foster always made me sad. He told the judge who presided over his case that he would let no lawyer represent him except me, that anyone else he was going to "smash up." I obliged. And I became part of the forces that had to grind this man through the wheels of justice. I treated him gently and he responded in kind. I was his momma, he was my child. With me at his side he behaved peacefully and was totally rational. But the role I was playing got to me. I felt I was somehow betraying him. "This man is like a big bear," I told the judge during the trial, "and I am leading him around by the ring in his nose. Forgive me for saying this about you," I said in an aside to Foster, who sat next to me, silent, trusting. "This man might be dangerous," I went on, "but he is dangerous the way a bear is dangerous, without evil intent. There ought to be some place for him other than a madhouse or a jail."

The judge nodded. He was kind and understanding. But he too was part of the system, and the time for Foster's trial had come.

Throughout the trial I would touch Foster's hand occasionally to keep him calm as he heard the women describe their terror-filled experiences. He kept murmuring to me, "I didn't do no such dirty thing." I cross-examined the women intensively on their identification—challenging their accuracy was the crux of my job. Six of the cases were thrown out by the judge. Foster was convicted, however, of the seventh charge, where the victim's identification was corroborated by an eyewitness. The jury rejected the defense of insanity.

Oddly enough, though he was convicted of a vicious crime, somehow everyone in the courtroom—the judge, the jury, the court reporter, and the correction officers who had guarded him throughout the trial anticipating explosive demonstrations—had become attached to the childlike giant. When the foreman stood up to pronounce the verdict, he literally blinked away tears and the other jurors seemed equally moved.

On the day of his sentence, the judge did not dare bring Foster into the courtroom. The proceedings were conducted in front of his jail cell in the notorious Tombs. While I pleaded for leniency, my client was running around wildly in his cell, shouting epithets, screaming, "I'm not an animal, I'm not an animal." The judge seemed as upset as I was. I could barely hear him as he sentenced Foster to fifteen years.

I tore open Bill Foster's letter and found a Mother's Day card. A touching gesture and in a way not surprising, since in the prison records he has listed me as next of kin.

I may be wrong, but I believe the Bear may very well be innocent. He had no recollection of the events. His mind was a blank for that period of time. I thought of him when I spoke to the alleged Brooklyn Heights Rapist later that Monday morning. This case also involved a problem of identification. The alleged victim had originally described the man who had raped her as in his middle thirties, dark-skinned and clean-shaven. She then altered her description, insisting my client was the perpetrator, though he was nineteen years old, fair-skinned, and always had worn a moustache, chin whiskers, and a goatee.

I was waiting in court to argue a preliminary motion on this case before Judge John R. Starkey, when the judge suddenly interrupted my whispered conversation with a colleague sitting next to me to ask, "Sara, do you want an assignment?"

"I'm very busy," I replied, "but if it's a murder, I might find time."

"It's a murder," the judge said. "You're assigned to a murder case." He grinned.

There was something about his attitude that I did not quite understand until I saw my new client, Beulah Williams, arraigned in court. She proved to be a tiny black woman aged about sixty-five. Looking at her, I was amazed. She certainly didn't look like a run-of-the-mill murderer.

The district attorney had another surprise for me. "Your Honor," he said to the judge, "we had a discussion at our office, and because of the special circumstances surrounding this case—she's never spent a day in jail—we're asking that she be paroled without bail." This did not mean that she would not stand trial, but that she did not have to pay bail money while awaiting her trial date.

"You have any objection to that, Mrs. Halbert?" asked the judge.

"Of course not, Your Honor, but do you mind if I faint?"

"No, you can faint right here," Judge Starkey allowed magnanimously.

He winked at the D.A., who said virtuously, "This will prove that the D.A.'s office really has a heart."

I was tactful enough not to comment on that one, but I could hardly wait to hear the woman's story. Early that afternoon, she came to my office. As she faced me across the desk, I was even more amazed at the murder rap. She looked like a law-abiding citizen, though there was a gleam in her eye that suggested she might be a bit feisty at times. Feisty is not murderous, however. I began my series of routine questions. "First, tell me, do you live alone?"

She shook her head. "No. I live with my dog and my cat."

Oh, God, I thought to myself. "Did you know the man who died?" I asked.

"His name is Morton, he's from my neighborhood. I knew

him to say hello, that's all. One day last March, he came to my apartment and knocked on the door. I looked through the peephole and saw who it was. I opened the door and I said, 'Come in and sit down. What can I do for you?'

"Well, he sat down and he pulled out a gun and he said, 'Give me your money.'

"Well, I was so surprised. 'You crazy?' I asked. 'What do you want my money for, man?'

"He said, 'Give me your money,' and he holds his gun at me."

"What did you do?" I asked.

"I disarmed him," she told me, "and I shot him."

I stared at her incredulously. "How big are you?" I demanded.

"I'm four-ten, and I think I weigh a hundred pounds," she said.

I put it at nearer ninety, but I didn't interrupt and she continued. "He was a big man. Weighed maybe two hundred pounds. And he got me scared. I said, 'Man, I'm scared.'" She fixed me with her bright, piercing dark eyes. "What would you do if a man pointed a gun at you and you're scared?"

"I don't know," I answered. "But how did you do it? You're going to have to show me." Taking a couple of pieces of paper, I rolled them up. "Let's pretend this is the gun. How'd you get it away from him?"

"Put it in your left hand," she instructed. "That's where he had the gun." As I obeyed, she said, "Now, do you want to see what I did?"

"Show me."

She took hold of my hand, and I thought she would break it.

"What are you?" I gasped. "A karate champ?"

"I had eleven brothers," she explained, "and we always practiced karate. Would you like me to flip you?"

"No, thanks," I said, unable to keep from laughing. "How many times did you shoot him?"

"Once," she said, "and he lay across my bathroom floor and I dropped the gun and I ran down the stairs and I ran to a telephone booth and I called nine-one-one and, would you believe it, by the time I got back to my building, the police were already there. I took them up and showed them. They brought me to the precinct and questioned me and let me go. They took me to the precinct three times, and I always told them what I'm telling you. 'Well,' they finally said, 'you've got to come to the D.A.'s office.'"

She had gone to the district attorney's office and demonstrated on six different cops how she had disarmed and shot the man who had come to rob her. Apparently they believed her, but since she was so good at karate and since she had taken a life, they decided that a jury must determine her guilt or innocence.

I decided I would not have her demonstrate her karate before the jurors at her trial; I would merely explain that she had disarmed him. Certainly she had a right to defend herself against a man who was going to rob and possibly kill her. Having explained my proposed defense, I sent her home and went over to the jail to see my two clients there.

One of them, Joe Chandler, was frightened, he told me. He wanted to take a plea. "But, Joe," I protested, "you said you're not guilty. You told me you were in North Carolina when the murder was committed. You said you have witnesses to prove it. You have no prior record. You can take the witness stand. If you're telling the truth, they'll believe you."

"I'm afraid to go on the stand," he said nervously. "I don't talk so good."

"You won't need to talk, Joe. You've got alibi witnesses who'll do the talking for you. And you've got me."

He nodded solemnly. "I know. They like you in jail. I guess I know why—a man can talk to you."

By the time I finally left Joe Chandler, I had persuaded him to stand trial. I could wish I had been as successful with Bill White, my other jailed client. He was due to be sentenced on his plea of manslaughter in the second degree, with the promise of a maximum five-year jail term.

His cop-out several weeks earlier had irked me. In common with Joe, Bill was black and scared. An alcoholic, he was illiterate and had an I.Q. of possibly 72. I had interviewed him earlier in the month, and at that time he had insisted, "I gotta plead, Mrs. Halbert. I gotta plead guilty. I done it. I killed her."

Cutting through his protestations of guilt was no easy matter, but finally I had pried the story from him. He and his lady friend had lived in a hole of an apartment somewhere in the Bedford-Stuyvesant area; they had passed their days drinking cheap wine.

"How did you live? How did you earn money?" I'd asked.

"I buy fish 'n' sell it on the street corner," he'd mumbled. "I make out."

I had already spoken with some witnesses and learned that he and the woman had had numerous arguments. According to his neighbor, he had hit her with a stick, causing her death. However, a stick would have made bruises, and according to the medical report there were no bruises; she had died of a concussion. "Tell me what really happened, Bill," I ordered.

He looked at me dully. "Neighbor says I hit her with a stick. Didn't have no stick. We was goin' up the stairs to our apartment. We was both drunk 'n' she was smackin' me. I push her away 'n' she falls down—falls all the way down the stairs." He became silent, looking blankly into space.

"And then what did you do?" I prompted.

"Went down 'n' got her 'n' carried her up the stairs 'n' put her on the bed 'n' she says to me, 'Go do the laundry.' So I go to the laundermat 'n' when I come back she's dead. I called the cops 'n' said she was dead 'n' she fell down the stairs."

"On the basis of what you've told me, Bill, it looks like it was an accident. You shouldn't take a plea. The truth will come out, you'll see. You have a good chance of being acquitted. You've got to get the courage to take the stand."

"Oh, no." He shook his head back and forth slowly. "Oh, no. I can't talk, see." He was right. He really couldn't.

I looked at him, noting that he was badly scarred. Possibly he was not telling me the truth. The neighbors had mentioned fights. He might be a violent man, and if that were true, he would not stand a chance on trial. Still, I could usually spot a liar, and I believed his version of the death. I said, "Where did you get that scar on your forehead?"

"She cut me."

There was another scar over his eyebrow. "And that one?" I asked.

"She cut me," he repeated.

"Where else did she cut you?"

"All over my body," he mumbled, opening his shirt. I could hardly believe it—his chest was a mass of cuts and scars.

"When did she hurt you last?"

He hesitated. "Day this happen . . . bit my finger 'most off." He held up his hand, showing me a mutilated finger with the nail gone. No wonder he had pushed her.

"Look, Bill," I said gently, "this sounds like an accident, pure and simple. You can still take the plea back. You can still have your trial."

He began to cry. "I can't talk, I can't talk," he sobbed. "The neighbor—he say I hit her with a stick. I don't know what to say back. I can't talk."

Argument accomplished nothing. That Monday, he was still insisting he wanted to be sentenced. I arranged there and then to bring him to the courthouse for a presentencing discussion with Judge Larry Vetrano, a kind and reasonable jurist. I said, "All this sounds like an accident to me, Your Honor. I don't care what the witnesses say they saw."

The judge studied Bill. "Did you hit her with a stick?" he asked.

Bill shook his head. "I didn't hit her with no stick, Your Honor, but I smacked her."

The judge's eyes lingered on Bill's mutilated finger, the origin of which I had explained to him. "It looks like an accident to me," he said. "Come back later this afternoon, around four, Mrs. Halbert."

When I returned to Judge Vetrano's courtroom and was waiting for Bill to be brought in, the judge told me that he believed that the woman had been killed by accident. He also said that both the probation officer and the psychiatrists had stated similar opinions in their reports. When Bill appeared, I said gently, "Everybody believes in you—the probation officers, the psychiatrists, everybody."

"You don't need to plead guilty," the judge said. "Go to trial."

Bill raised his dull, troubled eyes to the bench. "Your Honor," he said in a low voice, "I don't know what to do. I'm scared."

There was something in his demeanor that twisted my heart. I said, "Look, the judge says you can have a trial, even though you took a plea."

He remained silent, and the judge shook his head. "I'm very disturbed about this," he remarked. "We're all very disturbed," he told Bill. "You ought to have a trial. If you insist on taking a plea, you'll have to spend five years in jail when you could walk out of here a free man."

Bill sighed deeply. "What about those people who say I hit her with a stick?"

"Were they drunk like you?" I asked.

"Oh, yes, they were drunk, too."

"Your Honor, if I were to show the jury the cuts and bruises this woman inflicted on him—and the burns—they could not fail to be moved. I can't imagine why he stayed with her."

"Why did you stay with her?" the judge asked Bill.

As before, he answered slowly, articulating with difficulty. "I . . . stay with her . . . because . . . because I . . . I am alone and I . . . am dumb."

"I'm extremely upset about this man," Judge Vetrano said, "but if he insists on staying with the guilty plea, he has a right to make that decision. It's his life."

"Will you think about it a little more, Bill?" I begged.

The dull eyes looked a trifle brighter as he nodded and said, "I—I'll think about it."

The case was postponed for two weeks. Bill was taken back to jail, and I went out of the Kings County courthouse, down its broad stone steps, across its surrounding park to Court Street. As I stepped onto the sidewalk, I met two lawyers.

"Hi, Sara."

"Hi."

A judge passed me. "Well, Sara, how are you doing?"

"Good, Your Honor."

I feel at home on Court Street. It has a friendly atmosphere. Though Brooklyn has a population of two million, Court Street, flanked by its tall buildings and its courthouses, reminds me of a village square in a small town. It is a cozy place.

When I reached my office, I found a slender, lovely-looking black woman seated on my couch. She looked at me with distressed eyes and identified herself as the mother of Elaine Jackson, my fourth assigned murder case.

Elaine was in prison for allegedly beating her baby to death. Her boyfriend had been her accuser. Her mother, a well-dressed, well-spoken woman, startled me by saying,

"Elaine is partially to blame for the death of that poor baby. I told her not to live with that man. Her grandmother warned her, too. He did it, you know. She left the child with him for a while, and when she came back, it was dead."

I was inclined to believe the mother. I had seen Elaine Jackson in jail, and her wail, "I never killed my baby," still lingered in my ears. "I'll see what I can do for her," I promised. I was impressed by this woman's obvious intelligence, and her daughter had also seemed intelligent. I was glad I had taken the case. It meant a lot of work, but it was the sort of work I welcomed. It gave me a sense of accomplishment and fulfillment, made me happy that I had decided to leap the barriers and go into law practice—and believe me, there had been barriers!

Once I had stood at the foot of the courthouse steps I now mounted each day, enviously watching the lawyers, brief-cases in hand, whirl through the revolving doors. In those days I had wanted to be a lawyer, had known I had a special ability for the work—a real vocation. I knew, too, that I would eventually make it, but "eventually" seemed far in the future; meanwhile, I was poor. I had been poor most of my youth. If my clients and I had ever traded stories, I could have spoken with as much authority as any of them about steaming, overcrowded, bug-infested apartments, about going hungry, about working at anything I could find. I could have told how my present had been shaped by the deprivations and despairs of my past, for in fact my own life had been similar in many ways to the lives of the people I had chosen to defend.

1 | The Making of a Woman Lawyer

I OWE A GREAT PORTION of whatever success I've had in my career to my father, not because of his encouragement but because of the lack of it. I discovered long ago that I thrive on opposition, and I certainly received plenty of it from my father, Rabbi Ruben Maier.

My earliest memory of Papa is of a handsome man with dark, curly hair and a neat little Vandyke beard that he loved to stroke. He dressed elegantly, and he used to swing a malacca cane with all the cheerful insouciance of a Parisian boulevardier as he strolled down the streets of the city of Leipzig in Germany.

As a rabbi and a brilliant speaker, he was much in demand at synagogues all over the country. He was also called to lecture at universities and to preside over private gatherings.

On Saturday mornings, his seven children, all dressed alike in little sailor suits, filed into the synagogue to watch him conduct the Sabbath service. We were warned not to make a sound; not a sneeze, not a cough was tolerated by Papa. Even though I was a particularly active child, I could never utter a word while he was speaking. He had a beautiful, sonorous voice, and his oratory hypnotized me. It also hypnotized his congregation. No one could fail to be moved by his exhortations—except for my mother. She never seemed to be aware of his sermons; she sat quietly, her hands folded, her features composed, almost masklike.

Mama had been a beautiful girl, like Papa of Rumanian birth and from an Orthodox Jewish family. In common with him, she had loved learning, loved it so much that her father had actually hired tutors for her, an almost unheard-of procedure in a Jewish family of that era. She had learned to recite poetry in German and French; she had read omnivorously. Seemingly, she was the ideal wife for a scholar. Possibly she had thought so, too, and had dreamed of evenings spent reading poetry together. Any such hopes, however, must have been quickly forgotten once she entered my father's house as his wife. He might have been an ardent suitor, but he was an indifferent husband. In his world, women had a definite place—an inferior place. Not only was he totally uninterested in my mother's education and her poetry, he soon let her know that she had only two functions: sex object and baby machine. In ten years she bore him eight children (one boy died in infancy), and in the process her own personality was nearly submerged. From the moment she became a mother, she took on the mantle of the *Yiddische mama,* living only for and through her children. As we grew up, we heard very little of that poetry she could recite so beautifully.

By the time I was five or six, Papa's attitude toward women had filtered into my mind. I would be playing in the living room while he, draped in his prayer shawl, was saying his morning prayers. One of these began, "I thank thee, Lord, that I was not born a woman. . . ."

By that time, I had also learned that the Jewish man is blessed with 613 *Mitzvos* (good deeds) to carry out each day, while a Jewish woman has only three. One day I asked him about this strange and, to my mind, unfair distinction. "Why does a woman have only three *Mitzvos,* Papa, and why should you be so glad you're not a woman?"

Papa drew me onto his lap. He was always very loving with me, more so than with the other children, perhaps because I was the first girl after five boys, and he called me *Goldtöchterchen* (Goldilocks). Cradling me in his arms, he said gently, "Women have their place, *Goldtöchterchen.* They are the mothers of the race, they care for children, and they keep a good kosher home. Now, isn't that wonderful?"

Even then I could not agree. I did not see anything wonderful about doing housework—and was I to consider myself inferior to my brothers? When I said as much to Papa, he answered, "You think too much, little one. When you are older, you will see the truth of what I tell you. And one day you will marry a fine man and raise his children and be very, very happy." It sounded like the end of a fairy tale, but if that was how "happily ever after" was interpreted, I wanted nothing to do with fairy tales. But I said nothing. Papa did not like his women to speak out against the status quo. Outside his household, however, he was courtly and charming to women, lots of them. He loved variety.

He also loved to travel, and eventually his desire to see distant places drew him to America. I remember when we said good-bye at the train station before he sailed for New York. He embraced all of us exuberantly. "I will write every day; I will send you money as soon as I am settled," he promised. "And when I am established, you will all join me."

When Papa arrived in New York, the Jewish press hailed him as a renowned rabbi and scholar. He was praised and feted by various organizations, he reported in one of his infrequent letters. The news was welcome, but money would have been equally welcome and there was none in that letter or in those that followed. Though Papa had often been absent while he was in Germany, we had lived well. With an ocean between Papa and us, the flow of cash changed to a dribble. As the months passed, his letters became more and more scarce, and rarely did they contain anything more than his familiar protestations of love and longing, a longing he seemed to have under control since he never mentioned sending for us.

The situation at home gradually worsened. The quality of life changed drastically. At school, we looked enviously at our friends' thick sandwiches; our lunchboxes contained only thin slices of bread stuck together with margarine. Our suppers were starchy, too. Meat, vegetables, milk, and eggs were luxuries we could not afford. In time, my mother's brother, Abraham Safran, his wife Golde, and their baby came to live with us to share expenses, and our home no longer belonged to us. We were dependent on charity from other members of the family and from friends. It was depressing, especially for my mother, who had begun to fear that she would never see Papa again.

For us children, things were less gloomy. If we did not have enough food for our stomachs, our brains did not lack nourishment. My eldest brother, Joe, an earnest young college student, had taken over the education of the rest of us, and, in a sense, our father's place, dispensing discipline as well. Every Saturday after our sparse midday meal he gathered us together—my brothers Nathan, David, Emanuel, and even little Schillie, the youngest, as well as my sister, Rebecca, and myself. He gave us reading assignments which we discussed later. Unlike Papa, he did not consider girls to be his intellectual inferiors. Under Joe's tutelage I read nearly every book in my father's extensive library. By the time I was nine I was familiar with the works of Goethe, Schiller, Heine, and, most important of all to me, the German translations of Shakespeare. I adored Shakespeare, especially the tragedies. The more murders there were, the more I enjoyed them. I read them avidly—*Macbeth, Titus Andronicus, Julius Caesar, Hamlet, King Lear.* In common with most kids of my age, I wasn't troubled at all by the horrors and the gore—severed tongues and gouged eyes meant little to me. I found it all very satisfying, especially since, in the end, justice triumphed.

In 1929, when Papa had been gone for nearly three years, my mother grew tired of waiting for him to send for us. His letters were practically collector's items by then, and he had ignored her repeated questions about our joining him. Quiet and self-effacing though she was, Mama had a most persuasive way about her and she made friends easily. One of her friends was an American man of means who sympathized with her distress and translated his sympathy into the price of two tickets to America—two because Schillie could not bear to be separated from her. They left in November. Again there were promises to send for us as soon as possible, the only difference being that we trusted Mama. However, it was a very tense period. Though Mama's letters were reassuring, she did not enclose any passage money. We were all frightened and lonely.

If we had known about the chill welcome she had received from Papa, we would have been even more depressed. He had been functioning beautifully in New York. He had made a host of friends, male and, as Mama had probably suspected, female. He had been living the life of a happy bachelor. He let Mama know that he could not provide money for our passage. Perhaps he even cherished the hope that she and Schillie would return to Germany. However, Mama found new friends to persuade. In April, six dreary months later, she sent us our tickets and immigration papers. We set sail within the month.

Five of us made the voyage: David, Nathan, Emanuel, Rebecca, and myself. Joe, who was attending the university, stayed in Germany to complete his studies. We bade him an emotional farewell, but we did not mourn his absence long. The ship was so large—there was so much to explore—and we would be on our own for ten whole days! None of us has ever forgotten those ten days. Behind us were the overcrowded apartment, the wailing baby, the discipline maintained by our aunt and uncle. We were freer than we had ever been. We were looking forward to a new life, and meanwhile, between one world and the next, we were without any form of adult restraint.

Shortly after we were settled in third class, we made a

marvelous discovery—the dining room! There were some tastes we had actually forgotten in the last three lean years. We made a pact to eat only our favorite foods throughout the voyage. I concentrated on eggs and fish, Manny chose pickles and herring, and Nathan wanted only sweets. Three glorious meals later, shortly after our second lunch on board, we added a new word to our vocabularies: seasickness. Fortunately, we did not suffer long. We acquired sea digestions and sea legs and continued with our food binges.

On the tenth day, a fellow passenger knocked on the door of our cabin. "Hey, kids," he yelled excitedly, "come up on deck. Got something to show you."

We ran after him. The something, indicated by his trembling finger, was the Statue of Liberty.

Papa, who had become a dim memory, accompanied Mama to the boat. Characteristically, Mama, who had made it possible for us to rush down that particular gangplank, receded quietly into the background while Papa strode forward to greet us. His initial words were restrained, and his enthusiasm, if any, was muted. We, too, held back. In the thirty-six months of our separation, he had ceased to be a motivating force in our lives, nor would he ever again receive the love and admiration we had once given him. It was Mama we greeted most affectionately, kissing away her tears, and Schillie, too.

The following day, all of us were more relaxed, and Papa seemed eager to resume his role as paterfamilias. He took us to one of the most beautiful buildings we had ever seen, one larger and more glittering than any of the great palaces of our native Germany. It was the Roxy Theater. Seated far, far on the side of the house, we looked at strange, elongated figures moving across a huge screen and, incredibly, talking! It was our first talkie. It did not matter that we understood no English, this was a wonderful introduction to a new world.

The new apartment, in a place called the Bronx, actually

had hot and cold running water and a toilet that flushed. We were prepared to love America forever and ever!

Shortly after our arrival, however, we moved from the Bronx to Flatbush, Brooklyn, where Papa's new synagogue was located. Filing into it for our first Sabbath service, we experienced a sense of déjà vu. Papa had the same control over his American congregation as he had had in Germany; nothing had changed. In America, the free country, women were still restricted. According to the custom in Orthodox synagogues, my mother, my sister, and I were seated with the other females behind a curtain—so that the men would not be tempted to turn from the greater thought of God to the contemplation of our main function in their lives: sex.

Of course, this was symbolic, but to me it was particularly symbolic of a life in which I no longer wished to participate. I was not moved to worship a God whose beneficence was marked "Men Only." My father and the heavenly Father had excluded me from the active life of the synagogue; as a child, I could do nothing about that, but I was not willing in the future to emulate my mother and recede into female obscurity. If God were unwilling to smile on me, I would not smile at Him. I would function without His aid. It was a resolve I never forgot. Ironically enough, I had taken my cue from Papa. I, too, loved freedom in all its aspects, and I intended to be free!

Having formed my conclusions about my father's God, I found it easier to develop a new attitude toward my father. For three years he had been a stranger, and it was as a stranger that I appraised him, unemotionally, clinically—his selfishness, his lack of discipline, his cruelty. He had a dreadful temper, which was not sweetened by the presence of his unwanted family. Schillie, a frail, beautiful, golden-haired child, received the brunt of his anger against my mother for daring to join him in America. He used to strike the child unmercifully, and he would beat the other boys, too—particularly Nathan, the mischiefmaker. Papa used to strike him on the neck with the side of his hand. My mother felt these blows too, since Nathan had a rheumatic heart. She never wept, but we could see the pain in her eyes. Yet it was obvious that she loved my father; she was terribly jealous of the other women he visited. Witnessing my mother's misery, I was more than ever determined to be treated as an equal and to be in a position where I could work and prosper in a man's world.

The verb *to prosper* was one that particularly attracted me, for it was absent from our daily vocabulary. Much of our worry over money was, again, due to Papa. His angers were not confined to our household; he showed the same lack of control with the boards of the synagogues where he preached, with the result that he either left in a huff or was fired. He changed synagogues with monotonous regularity, and our moves were never for the better. By the time we had reached Brighton Beach, Brooklyn, Papa was nearly out of congregations and we were as poor as we had been in Germany.

It was the period of the Depression, but Papa made more money than many in his temple. He also spent it—on himself. He dressed beautifully and took wonderful care of himself. Every summer, on July 1, he went to Saratoga. He needed to restore his juices with the waters, he insisted. At that time there were many Jewish hotels in Saratoga Springs. He used to go as a rabbi; he did a little praying on weekends and in return received board and room.

In Brighton Beach, our life took on a pattern which, though I resented it at the time, proved immeasurably helpful when I started practicing law. It gave me an insight into the harried and frightening life of the poor that I never could have gained through research. For that insight, also, I had Papa to thank.

In those depressed years, the poor of New York moved regularly. We always owed so much rent by the time the summer came that the landlord would have to dispossess us. People did not pay rent in the 1930s, they just went hunting for a new apartment. We always tried to find one on a ground floor so we could hang up a sign: WEDDINGS PERFORMED. With so many apartments vacant, landlords welcomed new tenants. They gave concessions, usually two months' free rent. Little did they know what they were getting when, impressed by Mama's gentle, ladylike manner, they welcomed her into an apartment. They did not bargain for seven active, mischievous kids who were always wrestling and jumping up and down. Usually, by September, when Papa returned from Saratoga, we had been dispossessed and were settled in a new dwelling.

Meanwhile, the years were passing and we were growing up. I was ever more determined to break out of the family tradition. Money was what I needed, and I was never without the means of earning it. As a child, I was the most energetic bottle hunter in Brooklyn, *hunt* often being a euphemism for *steal*. I used to lurk under the boardwalk waiting for people to go into the water so I could descend onto their blankets and grab their deposit pop bottles. I also looked for bottles on and under the pier. I would take whole armloads of them to the neighboring grocery store. When I was older, I worked as a waitress, a baby-sitter, and a domestic; no job was too menial as long as it paid.

At school, I learned English quickly and had no trouble with any of my other subjects. I also loved athletics. Back in Germany I, a little Jewish girl, had actually managed to wangle myself into the turnverein, a gymnasium which until that time had excluded Jews. I never automatically took no for an answer from authority, and I had simply asked to be accepted. The turnverein had agreed, but my family had been less than overjoyed at this triumph. Both my mother and my Aunt Golde had wanted me to stop my exercises, which included performing on the rings, standing on my head, and doing splits. Splits might rupture my hymen, and then Sara would be thought to have lost that most precious of all possessions for an Orthodox girl, her virginity. I had laughed at them, and I laughed at the same protests in America. I continued demonstrating my athletic prowess, earning medals and other citations at school.

Scholastically, I was the equal of my brothers, but at home I was not an equal. In spite of all my outside work, Bea, as Rebecca was called, and I were expected to wash the dishes, make our brothers' beds, and do their mending. We were in training to be good Jewish housewives, to be behind a curtain in the lives of our men. By this time, at the age of eleven, I knew what I wanted to do with my own life. It did not involve curtains, it involved a career as a lawyer.

I had several reasons for making this choice. One of them was my experience with oppression. I knew it in many forms —through mother-watching and from my brother Joe, who, on finishing his schooling in 1933, had written a desperate letter to my father asking for a visa to leave a country where Jews were beginning to have a bad time. For once my father acted promptly; he had friends in the State Department, and a passport was quickly provided. A few years later, we heard that our Uncle Abraham and one of his sons had perished in a concentration camp. While there was no oppression of that nature in America, there was still discrimination against minorities. All injustice made me angry. I can remember seeing a little boy getting beaten up by the neighborhood bully, and though I was roughly the same size as the underdog, I rushed into the fray and pummeled the bully until he ran away.

Another reason for my wanting to be a lawyer was the high regard Jewish men had for the professions. They all hoped to be bankers, lawyers, doctors. That a woman could have similar aspirations brought condescending laughter, leers, and winks. I intended to be successful enough to plant other expressions on their faces.

Besides, I was good at arguing. I argued with my brothers. "Why should we do all your chores? Do you really agree with Papa? Do you really think your mother and your sisters are your inferiors?"

None of the boys wanted to be compared with Papa. In return for his three years of comparative freedom in the United States, he had forfeited their affection. Still, they had been raised in the Jewish tradition of male supremacy. Furthermore, it was very pleasant not to have to do anything except homework—to have the women darn socks, make the beds, wash the dishes, straighten the rooms, fry the bedbugs. These were perquisites my brothers were reluctant to forgo. Yet eventually they did, and we became a team.

Papa did not encourage their new attitude, and he alternately scolded and teased me. "You a lawyer, Sara? That's man's work. It does no good for a woman to be educated. What will you do with your fine education in the kitchen? Besides, you'll never get a husband if you are too brainy. Men don't appreciate bright women. Forget this foolish notion of college." His hand would stray to my hair. "Little Goldilocks," he would murmur, as he had all those years ago in Germany when I still revered him. "Once you are a mother, you will be fulfilled."

I had not quite arrived at the point where I was able to break all the ties that bound me to Papa. There was still an attachment, and perhaps there was even a small, lingering hope that I would be able to convince him that I was entitled to a place in a man's world, a place not determined by my sex. He was obviously fond of me; on occasion, I was aware that he might be too fond. I was not even a teenager when he began telling me, "Don't sit on the boys' shoulders, Sara. You might give them ideas, get them excited. Do not let them put you in front of them on their bicycles. You never know—at that age they have sex on the brain." On whose brain?

Papa was disturbed by the fact that I had matured so early. So was I. I had been a real tomboy, and when, at ten, my chest was no longer as smooth and flat as it had been the previous year, I felt chagrined and even ashamed and got strips of cloth to bind down my burgeoning bosom. It was only when I noticed the effect it had on the boys that I decided it was an asset. Anything that gave me power over men, I liked. When I was small, the old rabbis who were Papa's friends used to take me on their laps, smoothing my hair and tickling me gently.

"How can you let them touch you, Sara?" my sister Bea protested. "You know what they'd really like to do."

I laughed at her. "Sure I know, and they are demonstrating their weakness. I am stronger. And when they give me little presents—candy, a gold necklace, a bracelet—I profit in two ways—materially and in my self-esteem. I am in control."

I maintained this philosophy through the years. When I was working as a legal secretary, some of my bosses gave me pats and squeezes, but instead of candy or jewelry, I received invaluable instruction about the law.

Papa never minded my being a favorite of his friends, but he did mind my popularity with boys of my own age. By the time I was eleven, I had a steady boyfriend. Gone were my tomboy airs. In those days, Jean Harlow was everybody's favorite blonde; I emulated her arched eyebrows, and everybody told me I had her swinging walk. I didn't wear a brassiere, and everything bounced.

"You're torturing the boys, Sara," Bea would hiss at me.

"Let them suffer." I would shrug. "And if they dare get

fresh, I'll kill them. I'll kick them you know where."

When I entered Lincoln High School, I met Morris Halbert, star soccer player and all-around athlete. He was my ideal, built like a Greek statue, dark, wavy hair, smooth olive skin, bright-green eyes—very handsome and the strongest boy in the school. He could pick me up and bounce me around as if I were a Ping-Pong ball. I weighed only 110 then. Since I was the best female athlete in the school, all our friends began calling Morris and me "Tarzan and his mate."

Papa liked Morris; in fact, the whole family liked him. He and his eight brothers and sisters had been born in Israel, as had their father. When Morris was seven, the family emigrated to the United States, and subsequently both parents died. His brothers and sisters had had to raise him. He was shunted from one household to another and felt the lack of parents deeply. My parents welcomed him into our home, where he was like another brother, playing chess with Papa and helping Mama and me hunt for apartments when our periodic moving day came around.

However, Papa did not encourage my dating Morris. Possessive and domineering, he considered that his commands were to be obeyed without question. I kept my questions to myself and did what my conscience dictated, which was often at variance with Papa's commands. But I had not entirely lost my respect for his word, which meant I was not entirely free of him. The final break occurred when I was fifteen.

"You are not to have a late date with Morris on the pier," Papa said to me one evening. "You are to be in the house by seven thirty at the latest."

"Um," I said, signifying that I had heard him. Seven thirty indeed! Children had to be in at seven thirty! I was full grown. I worked after school and on weekends and contributed to the household expenses.

I did not say good night to Morris until eleven thirty. The

house was very quiet when I returned. I was tiptoeing toward the stairs when Papa suddenly emerged from the living room.

"Come here, Sara," he ordered in a soft but menacing voice as he unfastened his heavy trouser belt.

I followed him into the living room. The fact that he had removed his belt meant trouble, but though he had often beaten my brothers, he had never struck me. Perhaps he was only trying to scare me. I was wrong. He brought that belt down across my shoulders again and again and again until my skin was crisscrossed with welts and he was too exhausted to lift his arm.

"Go," he said roughly. "Go to your room and stay there."

I went silently. I had been silent throughout the entire beating. I would not give him the satisfaction of hearing me utter so much as a whimper. On reaching my room, I still did not cry, even though my back hurt dreadfully. My sense of justice had been aroused. There had been no reason for Papa to treat me so cruelly. Possibly he had hoped to break my spirit, but I was not Mama and his beating had had the opposite effect—it had broken any hold he had ever had over me. Mama suffered more than I. For the first time, she cried openly. From that night on, I had only contempt for Papa. I showed the marks on my back to everyone in the family and explained what had happened. Papa writhed under their scorn, but he could offer no excuses for what he, a holy man, God's anointed, had done.

Morris and I continued dating. We were very much in love, a fact we did not flaunt at home. We made love on the rocks at Brighton Beach and also met beneath the boardwalk and in front of the big square pails in which the beach workers collected the garbage. When we came home, my sister would say knowingly, "I know where you and Morris went tonight—I can smell bananas."

By the time we graduated from Lincoln High, Morris and

I had our future planned; he intended to be a microbiologist, and, unlike Papa, he encouraged me to become a lawyer. After graduation, we went looking for jobs, which were very difficult to find in the 1930s. My brother Manny, who now holds two doctorates, worked as a toilet cleaner in an old-age home after his graduation from City College. Morris and I were luckier. He found a job as a lab technician, and I as a legal stenographer. I had learned to use a Stenotype machine.

Papa had ceased to protest about my plans; he just wanted me to get married. He repeated his usual formula: "Wait until the children come, Sara. Then you will think differently about your life."

The wedding that he gave Morris and me took place in a synagogue on the Lower East Side of Manhattan near the Williamsburg Bridge. Twelve rabbis presided, among them some of the old men who had so fondly stroked my golden curls. At the time, it seemed as if their collective congregations were also present. The synagogue was so packed that Morris and I, with our respective family escorts, had to squeeze up the aisle sideways.

Our wedding night also had its comic elements. By this time, Papa had a congregation in Washington Heights in upper Manhattan, where the family was now living. Morris and I had rented an apartment in the vicinity, where we proposed to spend our honeymoon. However, my brother Manny had persuaded us to let him use it the night of the wedding. He was dating a new girl.

"Okay, okay, but be out by the time we get back from the wedding party," I said.

"You'll be a while getting back," he replied, obviously thinking of the twelve rabbis.

He was right, but when we returned, he met us at the door, feverishly begging us to wait. We spent the greater part of the night sitting on the stairs.

Papa came to see us only a few hours after we had finally fallen asleep in our own apartment. I answered the door to his importunate ringing. "Papa, what are you doing here?" I gasped.

"You forgot your marriage certificate." He waved it up and down in front of me. "You'll need it, Sarale."

I looked at him incredulously—twelve rabbis to usher me into wedlock, and I needed a license, too? "Why, Papa?" I demanded.

He had no answer.

Over the next few years, Morris and I were growing up and maturing together. We worked six days a week and attended college at night. We hardly saw each other weekdays, and the weekends and vacations were precious. We were free from parental control, and we made enough money from our respective jobs to provide for our then humble needs. World War II was going on, with rationing and a fuel shortage. Morris had to work very hard at the hospital; eventually he was the only bacteriologist there. Three times he was scheduled to be inducted into the military. Each time the hospital managed to get him deferred on the grounds that, if he left, the bacteriology department would have to shut down.

We decided to have kids despite the war and the draft notices; we wanted children while we were young. I did not give up my professional ambitions, but I did not want to be a lawyer at the expense of excluding motherhood.

Our first child, Judy, was born in 1944. I quit my job, and Morris worked at two jobs, spending an eight-hour day at the hospital and five nights a week and all day weekends as a soda jerk, a regimen he followed for five years.

"When the children come, Sara, you will forget all this business of wanting to be a lawyer," Papa had said, but his words did not prove prophetic. Eight months after Judy's birth I went back to work. Armed with my Stenotype machine, I became a per diem public stenographer, and I continued attending college at night. A neighbor, who was a divorcée with children, baby-sat with Judy.

Some of the neighbors were shocked. As one of them put it, "Your husband's a very tolerant man to let you go to school and to work. Only a mother should raise her children."

Two years later, I had a son, Jackie. Morris and I had amassed a little more money—out of every paycheck we managed to save something. With my sister's husband, Sidney, Morris bought a candy store–luncheonette located in our own building. Continuing his work at the hospital, he worked harder than ever at the candy store, but at least I could see more of him. To be able to talk with Morris, who always understood me and my aspirations, was one of my few pleasures during that period.

Our two-room apartment—we lived in Brighton Beach, now, six steep flights up, sweltering in the summer, freezing in the winter—was like those of my childhood. All the spray and paste in the world did not keep out the armies of cockroaches; all my shouting did not drive off the pigeons that sat cooing on our windowsills. Everything in the apartment was old—the walls, the fixtures, and the appliances. The refrigerator groaned through the night, often keeping us awake, so that we were tired and irritable through our long working days.

Furthermore, my parents, now based in Minnesota, where Papa had gone in search of a new congregation, came for a brief visit, ostensibly to help out with little Jackie. My sister and her husband also moved in with us temporarily, and two of her friends from California, having no place to live, were put up at our apartment for a week—with their seven children. For 168 hours there were nineteen people in that two-room apartment!

Later I understood only too well the clients who suffered through similar conditions without the promise of surcease, clients who throughout their lives knew only overcrowding, dirt, insects, and top-floor aeries. After standing over a machine in a factory for eight hours, they would have to pull themselves by the banisters up steep flights of narrow stairs, then collapse in the hallway, panting a few moments before crawling into the kitchen to fix supper, care for children, or minister to elderly, indigent relatives. There was often violence in these walk-up apartments. From such apartments came drug addicts, members of juvenile gangs, thieves, murderers. I understood their plight, their volcanic rage.

But my own life was different—I had hope, they had none.

In 1952, when I was thirty years old, my two children and Morris watched me graduate cum laude from Brooklyn College. Earlier that year I had taken a job with a law firm, as a secretary for Leo Salon of Salon and Romanelli. I had started as a temporary replacement, but Salon, impressed by my eagerness, my meticulous work, and my determination to be a lawyer, had hired me full time. Since I could not afford law school, I persuaded him to give me a law clerkship. Such clerkships, especially with a man of Salon's ability, were hard to find. He was a brilliant lawyer, and I learned a great deal from him. But I was kept busy with secretarial duties; I did not have a chance to read law books, and I was working for my M.A. at Brooklyn College at night.

"I'll never be a lawyer this way," I groaned to Morris.

"So go to law school," he advised. Morris could make crossing the Atlantic in a rowboat during a thunderstorm sound as easy as sailing a toy boat on the Central Park lake.

Actually, I got to make that particular voyage. My brother Joe had married a girl named Alice Heumann, whose brother, Ernest, was in real estate and very prosperous. He knew about my problems, and when I won a partial scholarship to Brooklyn Law School, he paid the other half of the tuition fees. However, there was a condition attached: "You must consider it a gift, Sara, not a loan." I was too grateful to be proud. I now needed only the money for my textbooks, which I could provide out of my salary.

In 1954, I enrolled at Brooklyn Law School.

I used to call my schedule a rat race, but I don't think any sane rat could have kept up with me. I attended law school in the morning; afternoons, I spent six to seven hours in Leo's office. I hurried home to prepare dinner and put the children to bed. I would then nap for a half hour and, at the sound of my alarm, rush to my law books and start studying, finishing around 3:00 A.M. Eating became a matter of popping candy for quick energy.

I read those law books with delight, savoring the knowledge between their covers, the brilliant writings of the great judges. I was thrilled by their reasoning, their wisdom, by the logistics of the law. It was everything I had thought it would be.

At the end of my first semester at law school, I had a week off. I was delighted. I loved being with Jackie and Judy. Morris and I felt as if we were growing up all over again. Thanks to our combined incomes, we had moved to a better building and were able to give the children more security than either of us had ever enjoyed. During this particular vacation, we decided we would all go ice-skating in Prospect Park. Though it might be said that for the last sixteen years I had been figuratively skating on thin ice, I discovered the literal meaning of the expression when, in the midst of a beautiful and complicated swirl, I fell through some honest-to-goodness thin ice and broke my leg.

At the hospital, the doctor put me to bed and sent my family home. It was, he told me, a bad break. I could echo that. It was a very bad break, especially with my busy schedule. I talked him into giving me a cast and crutches and checked out of the hospital. Morris and the children were amazed to see me come swinging through the door. I had willpower enough, but I had a dreadful time manipulating the crutches, though I was determined to return to class.

"You can't go, Sara. Work and school will wait," Morris stated during one of the numerous arguments we had been having since I had hobbled home. In fact, in all the years of our marriage we had never had such heated discussions, and though I was a professional arguer, Morris had right on his side. We were living in a building with an elevator, but there were still the long stairways to the subways, yards of them, and, in that particular February, coated with ice.

"If you climb up and down those damned stairs, you'll break the other leg, and then what will you do, huh?" Morris glared at me.

I felt like Job in the Bible. I retired to my bed and wept. I did not speak to anyone in the family for the next three days, but on the fourth day, accompanied by a still-protesting Morris, I went back to the doctor. "Do something about these damned crutches," I growled. "I have to go to work and to school, and they're in my way."

"Will you please tell her she can't go?" Morris begged.

"Look," sighed the doctor, "your wife's crazy. Let her go."

He built a heel on my cast. Though I practically had to turn myself inside out, I managed to discard my crutches and to climb the subway stairs. Furthermore, though my five toes were exposed to the winter breezes, I did not even get frostbite. At school I sat for four months with my immobilized leg in the lap of my patient friend Blossom Heller, who later became the first female assistant district attorney in Kings County, Brooklyn.

Just before the beginning of my second year at Brooklyn Law School, I decided nothing was happening fast enough for me. I went to see my adviser, who was also the dean of the law school. I told him I wanted to do third-year work instead of second. "I haven't the time to wait," I explained.

He gave me a dubious look and ran a hand over his head. "It's never been done before."

"I'm eligible to take the bar examination because of my law clerkship," I said confidently. "I want third-year work."

"It can't be done," he protested.

"Is there a law that says I can't skip my second year?"

"No, there isn't," he admitted reluctantly.

"Then let me do it," I begged.

His name happened to be Prince, and he lived up to it. He granted me permission.

I soon learned that I had been too smart for my own good. Time was against me. I needed a forty-eight-hour day, but my clock stubbornly ticked out the regulation twenty-four. A few months before the bar examination, I groaned to Morris, "I can't do it. It's not humanly possible."

He gave me a cool, appraising look, and in his best cross-the-Atlantic manner he shrugged and said, "You'll do it."

"But Morris," I moaned, "I'll never pass. I haven't even read fifty percent of the law, much less studied it."

"Try," he urged. "You can't throw away all those years of clerkship. Quit work for a while and try. If you don't pass, you can always return to law school and take the year you missed."

"But we need the extra money I bring in," I objected.

"Not that much," he said gently. "Not that much, Sara."

Strengthened by his faith in me, I left Leo's office and settled down to serious cramming. I rose early each morning and prepared breakfast. Then I studied until midafternoon, when the children came home from school. Jackie and Judy were pleased to see me in the afternoons. It was a novelty they really enjoyed, and I did, too. We talked about their studies, we discussed their daily problems. It was all very companionable. After dinner, I started studying again, usually finishing at two thirty or three in the morning.

After two weeks of this routine, I was full of renewed hope. I was beginning to think I had a chance to pass that bar examination after all. Then, suddenly, the past was in my present again, in the person of my parents.

Papa decided to leave Minnesota and with Mama returned to Brooklyn and to us for a visit that promised to be permanent. They had six other children, each with a home, but they preferred mine.

"Papa, I am studying for the bar examination," I told him.

"Don't worry, little Goldilocks," he said affectionately. "We won't be in your way." Running through those soft words was a vein of iron. To him, my years of study meant nothing; I was merely a daughter obeying the Fifth Commandment as God had relayed it to Moses on Mount Sinai: "Honor thy father and thy mother."

They moved in with us. Morris had no more to say about this arrangement than I. He had always been fond of them; they had been kind to him in his lonely, orphaned youth, and he had looked upon them as his parents, too. But it was not an easy situation. They took over my home, my children, and my husband. Our apartment became a mini-synagogue, and we my father's captive congregation. We were expected to join in his long daily prayers, observe all his strict religious rituals, those Orthodox customs we had never adopted in our own household.

Furthermore, my mother had finally learned to speak up to my father. They argued incessantly, he loudly and she with the quiet but never-ceasing persistence of water over stones, wearing him down, wearing all of us down. Her years of having to live only for and through her children had imbued her with a devouring need to possess them—especially me, and of course my children. She felt fulfilled in our home, but I was increasingly nervous and tense, and Morris had no relaxation, either.

One particularly hot Friday evening a few weeks after my

parents' arrival, there was a minor upheaval. My father's rules were in full force: in accordance with Orthodox custom, which forbids manual labor on the Sabbath, the oven, lighted at sundown, would remain lighted until the following sundown. The heat it generated was augmented by a kettle boiling furiously on the back burner.

Sundown, Friday; sundown, Saturday. It was a crazy litany in my head as, drenched with perspiration, I stood in the kitchen. "If I don't get out of here, I will go berserk," I muttered to myself.

"What did you say, dear?" Mama inquired mildly.

"Never mind," I answered, not caring that my voice sounded loud and ragged. "Never mind!" I fled into the living room, where Morris and the children were seated. "We're leaving for the weekend," I announced breathlessly.

Before they could protest, I had a suitcase packed, and the four of us rushed out the door and into an air-conditioned movie. We remained there until the theater closed, and in the middle of the night, we arrived at my brother Dave's place in Washington Heights and slept on his floor. We did not return to Brooklyn until after sundown, Saturday.

The statement implicit in our exodus went unheeded by my parents, and the situation did not improve. Instead, it grew worse. At the end of two months, I was sure I would have a nervous breakdown. An explosion was imminent, and it was Mama who lit the fuse. One afternoon, she came into my bedroom, where I was huddled on the bed, feverishly trying to read. It was the first moment I had managed to snatch for myself since early morning.

"Sarale," she said.

Pulses were pounding in my head, as I said, on an ascending scale, "Ye-es?"

"I don't see how you can study here." Mama gave me a commiserating smile. "So much going on."

I looked at her in amazement. It was the first reference

she had made to my predicament. Could she actually be suggesting that she and Papa might visit another member of the family? "It is difficult," I agreed.

"It must be," she murmured. "I have a good idea for you, dear. Why don't you go to a hotel and study there?"

It took a moment for the full import of her words to penetrate. She was suggesting that I leave my home and go to a hotel? I could not afford a hotel. My parents had made no contribution to expenses but had lived on our earnings. It was too damned much! For the first time in my life, I did not give her a soft answer. Leaping from the bed, I screamed, "This is *my* home and *my* husband and *my* children. I am not leaving them to move into any hotel. *You* move out of here. *You* move into a hotel!"

The walls were thin, and Papa heard my angry words. He came in, eyes flashing, looking like Jove about to hurl a thunderbolt. "Sara, what dreadful thing are you suggesting? You, a daughter, ask us, your parents, to go to a hotel? May God forgive you, may God not punish you by having your own children turn against you and throw you out onto the streets in your old age!"

"I'll chance it," I yelled back.

In the midst of this altercation, Morris came home, and he, too, lost his temper. He could not tolerate their telling me, his wife, to leave his home. Though he did not argue—he never argued with my parents—he made it plain that he was on my side. When my father announced grandly, "We will leave this house immediately," Morris replied, "As soon as you've packed, I will drive you to a hotel."

I have never forgotten standing in the doorway of the apartment watching my parents silently walking to the elevator—Adam and Eve expelled from Paradise, and by a daughter! "But I had no choice," I murmured to myself. "It wasn't only my studies—Morris and the children were unhappy, too." It was true; they had found my domineering parents very hard to take. For two months we had had no peace, and they were as edgy as I. Yet, though I had freed us, I regretted the price I had had to pay.

Fortunately, I had no time to dwell on it. I had hundreds of pages to read and only six weeks to complete a whole year's work. That very night I hit the books again.

Twenty days before the bar examination, I received a notice from Albany stating that I was not eligible to take the bar examination. I had not had enough law clerking. I was ready to kill myself, but instead I called Albany and protested.

A voice on the other end of the line said tersely, "You want to be a lawyer. There's a way. Find it."

I wrote a long, pathetic affidavit explaining that if I were not allowed to take the bar examination, my husband and I faced financial ruin. I told how much I had sacrificed to become a lawyer. If the authorities would let me take the examination, I would make up the remainder of the clerkship afterward.

I returned to my books, studying harder and longer than ever. The date of the examination came closer and closer, but I heard nothing. Finally, when there were only three days between me and the examination, an order with a big official red seal arrived from the New York Court of Appeals, the highest court in the state. It read: "Permission granted."

I had won my first case.

Three months after the bar examination, at 6:00 A.M. on Yom Kippur, there was a telephone call. Giuseppe Gianfortoni, a childhood friend, was on the line. An insomniac, he rose at five thirty every morning and walked to the nearest newsstand to buy *The New York Times,* which always publishes a list of successful bar applicants.

"Congratulations, Counselor," he said. "You've made it."

I started to cry, but the kids and Morris laughed. Between laughing and crying, I said, "You know what? I'm going on a diet."

I was ready to practice law, but there were other official procedures to follow before I could become a full-fledged attorney. I had to pass under the scrutiny of the Committee on Character and Fitness, and I needed to be sworn in before the judges of the Appellate Division of the Supreme Court of the State of New York. Both events would take place about three months later, during December of 1956. Meanwhile, I filled out various forms and bided my time, not patiently.

We had moved again and were living in a two-story, semidetached private house in a different and better part of Brooklyn. Our economic situation had improved to the point that we had a part-time maid to see to the housework once a week. One evening two weeks before I was to be interviewed by the Committee on Character and Fitness, I bent over to open the bottom drawer of a cabinet and felt a stab of pain so excruciating that I could not rise. I had a slipped disk.

Our doctor taped me up and gave me an antispasmodic injection. He also prescribed a wooden board for my bed. I was in agony. I could not move. "How long will it take to get over this?" I groaned. "How long?"

"A few weeks, maybe six." The doctor shrugged. "It's hard to gauge."

Morris took me home. I was in a panic. I had to be back on my feet in time to appear before the committee. "You must rest," Morris emphasized. "When you're sick, you're worse than a child. Relax."

"I can't relax," I said mutinously. "If I don't do it this month, I'll have to wait until June. I can't wait until June."

"You can if you have to," he replied. "How can you be sworn in if you can't even lift your right hand?"

"Morris!" I exclaimed. "Can't you understand? I've worked so hard. All these years . . . do I need to tell you? All our sacrifices. I'm so close now. How can you ask me to wait?"

"I'm not asking you to wait. It's your spine that may ask you to wait."

"Well, I won't!" I cried defiantly. "I won't. I am going to do it on schedule."

I wrote the Committee on Character and Fitness and explained what had happened. I asked for a postponement of the interview and was told I could have it and that I should call when I was ready. The hearing was required to take place, however, before the date the court had set for the swearing in of lawyers. As the days passed, there was no improvement. I was totally immobilized, and every unnecessary movement sent arrows of pain shooting through my whole body.

Two days before the last day I could appear at the hearing, I was still in agony, but I could not bear the thought of missing my chance. "I am going to get out of this damned bed and go," I swore to myself. "If it kills me, at least I'll die a lawyer."

Closing my eyes and taking a deep breath, I inched up toward the head of the bed. I had learned to lift myself up by using my arms and keeping my body rigid. Ignoring my pain, I said, "I will do it. If I can get to the bathroom, I can get to the committee."

I managed to get out of bed. Pushing myself along the wall, I gained the bathroom. I gulped down two aspirins. I could have used twenty-two more, but I restrained myself. Still using the wall for leverage, I went to the closet, selected a dress that buttoned down the front, and slipped into it. Buttoning each button was sheer agony. I thrust my feet into my shoes and managed to get both a sweater and a coat around me. Inching my way to the bedroom door, I tottered to the stairs.

At the top of the stairs, I stopped. Though there were only sixteen steps, they seemed to stretch before me into infinity. The thought of negotiating each one was appalling. Mumbling a fast prayer, I clutched the balustrade and took one slow step down, then another and another. I do not know how long it took, but I reached the bottom.

Picking up the telephone on the sideboard was another challenge, but I met it and called the committee. I was assured they could fit me in, and I ordered a taxi. Holding onto chairs, tables, and the wall, I got to the front door and propped myself against it, waiting for the cab. Just as I had pushed myself into position, the telephone rang. I knew who it was—Morris. Occasionally he could be telepathic. Occasionally I could be, too. This was one of those occasions.

The cleaning lady was there that day. She hurried into the hall to answer the telephone. As she picked it up, her eyes fell on me and widened. She said into the phone, "She's at the front door."

"Get her on the telephone," he shouted, so loudly that I could hear him from where I stood.

Rubbing her ear, she held out the telephone. I inched back to it. "Hi," I said in a small voice.

He was too angry to observe the amenities. "What in hell are you doing at the front door?"

"You know I—I'm nuts, Morris," I said, trying to speak steadily and swallow my groan as the pain coursed up and down my back. "I wanted to go through with it. I wanted to get to the other side of it, Morris."

"You get to bed," he ordered. I was defeated. I had to admit I would not have been able to manage it, anyway. I canceled the appointment but made one for the following day. The cabdriver was paid off, and I dragged myself back to my room.

Naturally, Morris and I had another argument that night, and the next morning he left with a suspicious, "Now don't do anything foolish."

"I won't," I promised, but he knew I could be a liar. After all, it wasn't foolish to make an appearance before the Fitness Committee, not when you wanted to be a lawyer as badly as I did.

My trial run had given me courage. It was easier this time to get out of bed, get dressed, and go downstairs. Though I was as rigid as a store-window mannequin, I climbed into the cab. I shall never know how I got to Borough Hall without passing out, but finally I was ushered into the boardroom and was facing the members of the committee. They had my request for a postponement on the table in front of them, also a bulging folder of forms and letters from people who knew and had worked with me.

"I am in great pain," I said between stiff lips. "Please ask me whatever questions you want, because I must be sworn in tomorrow."

"We don't need to ask you any questions," said the spokesman. "All the answers are in this folder. You come back tomorrow. You'll be sworn in. Good luck, Counselor."

Counselor! It was the most beautiful word I had ever heard!

I expect I had more of the same pain the next day when, accompanied by Morris and proud Mama and Papa, in unison with some three hundred other hopeful lawyers, I took an oath to abide by the principles and statutes of the lawyer's code. I remember only the repeating of the beautiful words that finally made me a lawyer.

Afterward, people crowded around to congratulate me. I barely heard them. I was thinking about the future, when I could put all the theories I had learned into practice, when I would try cases in the courtroom. Again, I grew impatient; I felt a sense of destiny—and then I felt a knife stab and remembered my back. Clutching Morris's arm, I muttered, "Better get home."

He looked at me fondly. "Okay, Counselor," he said, beaming.

2 | A Lawyer Needs Clients

"SARA HALBERT," the license read, but where was I going to hang it? At first, with my new status, I had no doubt that Leo Salon, my mentor and my boss, would welcome me into his firm. He knew—none better—how persevering I had been. The qualities that had enabled me to get my degree would stand me in good stead as a lawyer. Furthermore, if I were attached to the firm of Salon and Romanelli, another hurdle would have been leaped. I knew that women had a very difficult time acquiring the sort of recognition that brings clients. But the Romanelli half of Leo's firm answered to the name of Marilyn, and she was a most successful attorney.

As I had anticipated, Leo was in a congratulatory mood, and he took me back into the firm. However, my expectation that he would be dumping cases in my lap was not realized. He gave me plenty of work, but it took the form of letters and briefs to be typed. After a few frustrating weeks, I had a talk with him. To my dismay, he said that, while he had a very high regard for my acumen, "I see you as a secretary, Sara."

Naturally I had arguments, and he listened patiently, but it was obvious that his mind was made up. Finally I said, "Maybe I'd better go out on my own." I'll admit that I was hoping for a change of heart. He had always called me indispensable.

There was regret in his eyes and in his tone as he agreed. "Maybe that'd be best, Sara." A trifle wistfully, he added, "I

49

won't say I'm not sorry to see you go. You're a great secretary."

"I'll be a better lawyer," I told him.

My next move was to my own "office," rented from another lawyer. I was not a partner, I was a lodger, occupying what had been an oversized supply closet. It proved to be an extremely undersized office, especially when furnished with the beautiful new desk and chairs provided by Morris, my parents, my brothers, and Ernest Heumann. The view consisted of four walls and a door.

In order to pay my part of the rent, I had an agreement with my landlord to type up complaints in negligence actions. Every day I came in and knocked them out at twenty dollars each. That's all I did. I was making considerably less than in my secretarial days, and money was still tight.

I started checking want ads in the *Times* and *The Law Journal* and found that one of the big law firms wanted a per diem secretary. Armed with my Stenotype machine, I got the job. By midafternoon, the head of the company had evidently been told that I was not only fast and accurate but a self-starter who knew all the legal forms cold. He called me into the kind of office I hoped to have—wood paneling and ceiling-high bookcases. A tall, broad-shouldered, handsome man wearing an expensive suit and fairly breathing success, he sat behind a huge oak desk. He smiled and in the words of Leo Salon said, "You're a very good secretary, Mrs. Halbert. How'd you like to work for us on a permanent basis?" The salary he offered me would have been tempting to even a very good secretary.

"I'm ashamed of what I did today," I told him frankly. "I'm a lawyer. I worked many years to become one. I can't be your secretary but"—I gave him my most bewitching smile—"I'd be very happy to work for you as an attorney."

His own smile remained as he said, "Not here. You're going to find it tough, Mrs. Halbert."

"I know," I said.

"Do you intend to specialize—family, civil cases . . . ?"

"Criminal cases."

"You're going to have a tough time," he repeated. "Who'll hire a woman lawyer?" It would be some years before the term "male chauvinist pig" found its way into popular parlance, but an equivalent flashed through my mind. "Look," he continued genially, "I'll put you in charge of the steno pool." He named an even higher salary.

"No," I said. "I'm not going to do this again. I'm a lawyer now, and I mean to work as a lawyer."

He did not need to repeat himself, but he did. "We have no openings for women lawyers in this firm."

"Thank you very much," I said politely.

Coming out of the building, I resolved that even if I had to starve, I would never be a secretary again. Out loud, I muttered, "I'm going to be the best damned lawyer in New York!"

A man next to me gave me a startled glance. "You talking to me, lady?"

He was even more startled when I shook my head and said, "I was talking to the world."

The next day I sold my Stenotype machine.

I spent the next few weeks trying to get cases. Each morning I took the subway to Schermerhorn Street, where what was then the Magistrates Court is located. Now known as the Criminal Court of the City of New York, it is the preliminary court to which a defendant is brought after having been arrested and booked on criminal charges. Escorted by a police officer, he is arraigned on formal papers prepared in the court clerk's office and sworn to by the complainant before a judge. The charges are read out by a clerk in open court. The defendant is officially told that he is being held on a felony or a misdemeanor. A felony is a serious crime: murder, felonious assault, robbery, or burglary. A misdemeanor is a minor crime, such as petty larceny, simple assault, or unlawful entry.

In the 1950s and early 1960s, the lower court assigned unpaid counsel to handle the cases of indigent defendants, a matter now taken over by the Legal Aid Society. After indictment by a grand jury on felony charges, the defendant was again arraigned in what was then called the County Court (now the Supreme Court, Criminal Term). In the indictment, specific degrees of a particular felony were spelled out: murder in the first degree, murder in the second degree, manslaughter one, manslaughter two, and so on.

Many aspiring lawyers came to this court hoping to be selected as "unpaid counsel." I would sit at the back of the room watching as the judge assigned case after case to these volunteers. Yet, though I fixed my eyes on the bench, practically willing the judge to call on me, my signals were not received. Evidently the judges were not interested in assigning cases to women lawyers. To them, we were all strictly bush league. The big ball park was still marked "Men Only."

Unfortunately, people do not advertise for lawyers, but in a sense I got my first case from a newspaper, *The Law Journal,* which ran an ad from the Brooklyn Bar Association asking for members of the bar who could sing and dance to audition for a show lampooning judges, politicians, and well-known lawyers. The production was scheduled for that spring of 1957. Judge Hyman Barshay, one of the stalwarts of the County Court, was listed as a coauthor.

My shriek of joy brought Morris up from his newspaper blinking at me and asking, "What happened?"

"Opportunity, that's what!" I thrust the paper under his nose. "Look. This is how I am going to meet Judge Barshay and all the others who haven't let me near a case. I am going to sing my way in."

"You can't sing," Morris objected with a laugh.

"Can Ethel Merman?" I demanded. "I can dance and I can belt out a song just like she does. I don't need to be Kirsten Flagstad. I just need chutzpah."

"You've got plenty of that," Morris said.

I auditioned for one of the skits and, much to my joy, was accepted. Furthermore, my number was a catchy tune with the sort of lyric you might think a judge too sober to write, dealing with the aspirations of another lady lawyer, considerably my senior, who wanted a judgeship. To the tune of "Hey, Look Me Over!" the words went something like this:

> "Hey, look me over, lend me your ear,
> I'll be a judge from the front to the rear,
> Though justice is lovely, justice ain't blind,
> Control your nerves,
> While you look at my curves,
> And never mind my mind."

And never mind the sexism of its message, Sara! I sang it, with a couple of bumps and grinds thrown in for good measure, and I got a lot of applause, plus my coveted introduction to its author, Judge Barshay. He looked far less intimidating than he did on the bench. He was a mild-mannered man with a pleasant face and very bright blue eyes. There was a twinkle in them when he spoke to me.

"You have a lot of bounce," he said. "You really put it over."

"Thanks," I said.

"I haven't seen you around," he continued. "You practice in Brooklyn?"

"I've seen you around, Judge," I said. "In County Court. I'm there every day. I want to practice criminal law."

"What on earth for?" he demanded.

"Because I think that the poor deserve the same kind of representation as the rich."

That twinkle remained in his eyes, but his voice was dry. "That's very noble of you."

"I mean it."

"Women aren't easily accepted in criminal law."

I bit down an angry retort. "Do you go along with that?" I said. "Do you really have such a low opinion of women's capabilities? You're a judge, you see what goes on in your own courtroom with assigned cases. Do you think those men are doing such a great job? Half the time they don't even bother to investigate a case. Don't you think a woman could do just as well, if not better?"

He was silent, considering me, assessing me, judging me. Finally he said, "All right, young lady, if you want a criminal case, you'll get one. Be in my court at ten o'clock tomorrow morning. I'd like to see what you can do."

I was there at five minutes to ten, and this time I sat at the front of the courtroom. A case was called. As it happened, I had read about it in the papers. Everyone had; it was a headline maker about a woman who had cheated on welfare. Her name was Olga Cruz, and as the words resounded through that crowded courtroom, every hopeful lawyer tensed and a bevy of reporters sat with poised pencils. There were more potential headlines in the Olga Cruz case, enough to keep a lawyer's name in print for weeks.

"Sara Halbert assigned."

Startled, I looked toward the bench.

"Come forward, please, Mrs. Halbert," Judge Barshay said.

His voice sounded faint and faraway in my ringing ears. Dazedly I walked forward, leaving all my theories behind me. I might never have stepped inside a law school, much less out of one and into a courtroom. I was terrified. In despair, I whispered to the court clerk, "What do I do now?"

"Whatever the judge says," he whispered back, "you say, 'Not guilty.'"

"How do you plead?" Judge Barshay demanded.

"Not guilty, Your Honor." I was so nervous, I was not even sure I had spoken aloud. I had suddenly realized the magnitude of my responsibility. This woman's entire future was in my hands. The fact that the *Daily News* interviewed me that day and published my picture only heightened my feeling of inadequacy. Yet, when I read the article, I found I had managed to keep my qualms to myself and that my answers to the reporter's questions had sounded knowledgeable and even experienced. However, if I failed, everyone would know it.

My terrors were momentary. The next day, I felt much calmer, even though I was making my first visit to a jail. It was the Women's House of Detention in Greenwich Village, a sagging red-brick building, an eyesore outside and in, with pimpled plaster walls of a bilious green, dark old woodwork, dim halls, miserably overcrowded. Still, to be in a position to command jail doors to open and close was reassuring.

Olga came to the interviewing room. She was a dull-eyed, heavyset woman in her middle years, dressed in the regulation gray prison smock. Her olive skin seemed to have taken on some of that gray hue. She looked frightened and hopeless. I spoke gently to her. "I'm here to *help* you," I emphasized. "I want to help you. Tell me all about it."

She sighed, opened her mouth only to close it again, and shook her head despondently. It took a while to obtain her confidence, but finally, after much persuasion on my part, she was able to tell me about the vicious drunk of a husband who beat her and their children senseless unless she gave him money for alcohol.

"He go away. Then, when there is no more money, he come back. The kids are scared all the time. When he beat me, it is hard for me to work. I work in city hospital as laundress. So finally I apply for welfare because all the time he ask for more money, more money. I don't tell them about the job because they don't give me nothing if I do."

I left the jail filled with anger. I believed her, but she was up against the city, and nobody would care about her reasons, only that she had cheated the Welfare Board. Of course I did not rely on her testimony alone. I researched her background, interviewed everyone with whom she had come in contact. I collected mountains of corroborating data, and in the process I discovered that she had actually minimized the hardness of life in the small, drab, walk-up apartment with its dark rooms facing an air shaft, the only touches of color huge prints of a suffering Jesus and the Madonna and Child, each with its votive candle flickering in a cheap glass holder beneath. Walking down the narrow, garbage-strewn halls of the tenement, I wished that I could have brought the judge there. But at least I had plenty of material and I could try to convey to him a very real picture of her daily life, which I did.

Today, those who commit welfare fraud are rarely imprisoned. They are indicted, but usually they are permitted to make restitution if possible, and then they are placed on probation. In 1957, however, Olga Cruz could have received a ten-year sentence. Because there was no way for her to extricate herself from her predicament, I advised her to plead guilty to a lesser charge. As an example to other would-be frauds, she received a sentence, but because of the list of mitigating circumstances I was able to produce, she was given a one-to-three-year term.

Naturally, my family had been following the story of Olga Cruz with breathless excitement. Jackie, then ten years old, had been particularly fascinated. Shortly after the newspapers headlined her sentence, I heard him arguing with the boy next door.

"My mother won the case," he said proudly.

"Yeah?" his skeptical pal said. "If she won it, how come Olga Cruz went to jail?"

"You don't understand," Jackie replied loftily. "The lady was guilty. She could've gotten ten years. My mother got her off with a one-to-three. She won it, you jerk!"

Much to my delight, Judge Barshay, who had followed the case, agreed. While I was grateful for the congratulatory messages I received from friends and a growing list of colleagues, my real gratitude was reserved for Olga Cruz. In defending her and in seeing the circumstances in which she lived, the dull hopelessness of her life, I began to see a direction for myself. I had told Judge Barshay that I wanted the poor to have the same representation as the rich. After Olga Cruz, I narrowed my sights. In defending her, I had become acutely aware of the existing prejudices against the dark Hispanics and the blacks. Judges and lawyers alike looked askance at them; the cops treated them with contempt. While I wasn't ruling out any client that came my way, I felt they needed my services the most. With that need in mind, I started studying Spanish.

Whenever I had the opportunity, I would sit in on the trials of older, well-known lawyers. The more I saw, the more I was convinced that I was heading in the right direction. Lawyers assigned to indigent black or Hispanic defendants did little, if any, investigation on their clients' behalf. If the defense is to be adequate, investigation is essential. Possibly this apathy was partially based on the fact that the lawyers were not reimbursed for their work and experience, even though a case might require weeks or even months of labor. The Legal Aid Society had not then entered the defense picture in New York City, and the poor, guilty or innocent, often had scant hope of receiving more than token legal counsel.

Even when money was forthcoming from the state, as in

murder cases, assigned lawyers were often dilatory, mainly because there was never enough money to do the job thoroughly. In those early days, I was often amazed by the injustices in justice. The prosecution had almost unlimited funds, but defense attorneys were allotted only a flat two thousand dollars, which was divided four ways. On arraignment day, the presiding judge assigned a senior attorney, an experienced lawyer, to supervise a murder case, with three other lawyers to assist him. Often this trio did nothing more than appear in court, looking important as they sat at the defense table. The major share of the work fell to the senior attorney, but he received the same amount of money as the other three. (Today, one experienced attorney usually handles a murder case at the state's expense, with reimbursement for expert testimony and investigatory services.)

Since five hundred dollars was a sizable sum in those days, the competition for assignments was fierce. A political affiliation helped. Each judge had a patronage list, furnished by the leader of the local political club. Arraignments were held once a week. (Now they are held daily.) I used to call it "Roman circus time," with the courtroom as the Colosseum, each judge as Nero, and the lawyers as gladiators or lions battling one another for the prize—the alleged murderer, who meant all those precious dollars to the winner.

If the financial setup was bad, the psychological effect was even worse. Unless the senior attorney was a crusader, on fire to better the lot of his fellowman, he would pass on responsibility to his colleagues, and as one domino fell on the next, there were predictable results. At the trial, all four were likely to be badly prepared, and if, as happened all too often, there was a vindictive judge on the bench, the innocent as well as the guilty could be convicted.

"A wise and upright judge . . ." praised Shylock. To me, as to many law students, the title "judge" had a special meaning; in reading law, I had always been impressed by the great judicial decisions. In theory, judges were all "upright." In practice, they were not necessarily clever lawyers or scholars, but rather were astute politicians, or they had a "rabbi" who sponsored them from the local political clubhouses. While some were as honorable as their title indicated, others abused their position to vent their malevolence on those who came under their jurisdiction.

Early in my legal career I came before one of these, Judge Samuel Leibowitz. I had once read about George Jeffreys, who, during the reign of James II in England, had caused about three hundred people to be hanged for treason, often on extremely doubtful evidence. To my mind, Leibowitz might have been his present-day incarnation. Jeffreys had been known for his sarcastic tongue and sadistic practices; Leibowitz was similarly inclined. He was the terror of the accused and of their lawyers as well. In his courtroom, attorneys had been so intimidated by his scathing tongue that some had fainted and one had actually had a heart attack. Needless to say, the Honorable Samuel did not like women lawyers, and we locked horns practically at first sight.

"You'll never get an assignment from me," he barked at me one arraignment day.

Primed by the assignments I was beginning to receive from Judge Barshay, I replied as calmly as I could, "I don't need them. When I come before you, Your Honor, it will be on a retained case."

"And I'll dismiss you for incompetence," he said with the poisoned sweetness for which he was so justly famous.

"You'll never have cause," I said with equal sweetness.

It was not only on my own account that I grew to loathe Leibowitz's courtroom presence, it was because of his attitude toward those I had sworn to defend. He seemed to revel in goading the blacks and Puerto Ricans. When they appeared for arraignment, he would demand, "Are you on welfare?" or "How many illegitimate children does your mother have? And where's your father?"

My dislike of him was so intense that I actually developed an allergy in his presence. Whether his insults were direct- ed at me, another lawyer, or an alleged criminal, the result was the same: I came out in spots—big, ugly, red, itching splotches appeared on my chest and neck. I did not scratch them. I would not let him or anyone else know that he was getting to me. I simply wore special accessories in his court- room: a turtleneck in winter, a scarf in summer.

However, I had a way of retaliating. Swinging my hips, clicking my high heels, I would approach his bench, coming to a halt directly in front of him. In those days, he was about sixty and far from impervious to women, however much he might deride their legal abilities. "Yes, Your Honor," I would say, shaking my shoulders so that everything bounced. Much to my private satisfaction, his eyes would widen and he would twitch. The inevitable verbal assault would begin. Under its onslaught, I would stand ramrod straight at military attention. "Yes, Your Honor. Yes, Your Honor. Are you finished, Your Honor?" Before he could reply, I would turn and walk back up the aisle.

"Don't you walk away from me!" he would yell furiously.

I would swivel on my heels. Dulcetly, I would croon, "Yes, Your Honor. Oh, excuse me, I thought Your Honor was finished." Sometimes I even saluted him.

Leibowitz considered himself omnipotent, and he was right. He ruled with absolute and tyrannical authority. Many attorneys avoided him like the plague carrier he was, but much as I despised his methods, I enjoyed the challenge he offered. Only one other woman lawyer in the Brooklyn courts agreed with me. That was my old friend from law school, Blossom Heller.

"Blossom," I said to her one day, "we've got to talk to that man or he'll destroy us both. I'm going to his chambers. You want to come?"

"Sure thing." She smiled fiercely. "I'm with you." Together we marched into his office.

"Well?" he rasped.

"Your Honor," I said, "what do you have against me? I am young and I am here to stay, no matter what you do. You might as well learn to live with the idea."

"Mrs. Halbert," he began sweetly, "I've nothing against you. You're a very nice lady, a nice Jewish lady, but"—his voice hardened—"you don't belong in a courtroom. Go home and cook chicken soup for your husband."

I surveyed him coolly. "What makes you think, Mr. Justice Leibowitz, that the only approach to another human being is the male approach?"

Out of the corner of his mouth he growled, "Go home, Mrs. Halbert."

"I always go home, Judge—after work, and then I come back the next morning. That's my routine. I'm not changing it, and if you're cherishing any notions of trying to remove me from your courtroom, forget them. Any time I come before you, I'll be well prepared. I might add, Judge, that I am always well prepared."

By that time, I could speak with some authority. I was getting more work. Most of my early courtroom assignments came from Judge Barshay, but he, in turn, had introduced me to his close friend, Judge Nathan Sobel, one of the finest legal scholars I have ever known, a man respected throughout the United States. These two judges became my guides. I have always said that they were my mentors and Leibowitz my tormentor.

Several months after I started taking assignments, I moved from my depressing little closet into the next building, where I rented a larger office from a friend, the lawyer Robert Garvar. I had wall-to-wall everything, and I was beginning to build a reputation. The world of the courts is small and interlocking. I was becoming known as a lawyer who worked hard whether she was paid or not. Satisfied clients recommended me to their friends, and actually most of them did manage to give me some retainer. I had as many as five assigned cases a day.

When I walked into Brooklyn's Raymond Street jail—a dank, creaking dungeon of a building—the prisoners, and the correction officers, too, would welcome me. "Here comes Sara," they would say, or "Sara's here, have no fear." More often than not, when I faced a prisoner across the wired cage through which we had to communicate, he or she would mutter, "They tell me you work hard. They tell me you don't stop—even if a person gets convicted."

"That's right," I would reply. "If I believe in you, I never stop fighting."

I had been in practice some seven or eight months when I got my first murder case. It was not assigned; I was retained. My client was lodged in the Raymond Street jail, and it was his father who had called me.

"You handle murders?"

"That's my specialty," I lied, never having handled a murder case.

"Like I hear good things about you. I want you for my son's lawyer."

"Come and tell me about it," I invited him.

A few days later, he came, a thin, nervous black man. "My son didn't kill nobody," he stated belligerently. "You get him off." He admitted, however, that he didn't really know the facts in the case. Leaving me a modest retainer, he departed.

I went to see the son. He would have made two of his father. Well over six feet in height and with bulging muscles, he looked like a contender for the Mr. America title. He also looked capable of anything, but I did not form any conclusions. "Talk to me about the killing," I said. "Tell me everything you did that day."

"Everything?" he inquired, with the suspicion of a swagger. "Wanna know what I had for breakfast?" Throwing his head back, he laughed, displaying a set of white teeth with some molars missing. "Had myself six eggs 'n' half a pound of bacon for breakfast. I needs to eat good for my job as a longshoreman." He went on to describe a hearty lunch and a series of bouts with the bottle before, during, and after meals. "When I quits work, which was 'bout six, decided I'd get me some cunt." He rolled his eyes at me. "Oh, 'scuse me. I mean I wanted to get laid—all that drinkin' 'n' stuff made me feel sexy."

"Then what happened?" I inquired.

"So I went to the cathouse and honked the door."

That was a new one to me. "*Honked* the door? What does that mean?"

My ignorance seemed to surprise him. "Mama lawyer, don't you know nothin'? It means I smash the door down— kick it in."

"Go on."

"This whore was in bed with this guy, see. He was on top of her, humpin'. I tol' him to git. Las' time I tol' a guy to git, he dove right outa the window, naked ass 'n' all, but this cat, he say to me, 'I ain't gittin'.' I tell him again, 'Git, you mothafucka,' 'n' he say to me, 'I don' wanna git.' He was in the middle of fuckin' her 'n' he didn't wanna to git off'n her till he come."

"Then what happened?"

"Well, I wanted to fuck her, too. But she starts screamin' she don' wan' me to fuck her 'n' so this otha guy pull a knife on me 'n' we start wrestlin' on the bed on top of the whore."

"Yes?"

"So the fuckin' knife goes into her 'n' she's killed." He looked at me blandly and shrugged.

"I'll see what I can do," I promised, and left him.

My investigations led me to the "cathouse," actually a run-down, sleazy hotel with a management that demanded payment before it handed out a key and was frankly uncurious about the names and addresses written in its register. I did not find out much about the dead woman there, but I did track down the interrupted lover, who had total recall spiced by anger.

"This cat knew her," he told me. "She was scared of him. Din' want no part of him, so he stuck a knife in her."

Further investigation into Mr. America's background brought forth a criminal record. He had a reputation for violence, and he had been convicted for practically everything except murder. Undisciplined and amoral, he gained from his strength a power which he had never hesitated to employ. If I were to help him at all, he would have to exercise considerable restraint upon his incendiary temper. I was not sure he would be able to achieve the necessary self-control, mainly because the judge presiding over his arraignment would be none other than Samuel Leibowitz.

On the day he was arraigned, the courtroom was packed. There were always more interested spectators when Leibowitz sat on the bench. A bevy of lawyers was eagerly awaiting assignments, and, armed with his famous patronage list, the judge was ready to oblige. He was in fine fettle—eyes agleam and tongue sharpened. His caustic sallies sped like arrows into their designated targets. Under my turtleneck sweater, I was beginning to itch. Then the court officer called my case. The other lawyers, unaware that it had already been given out, leaned forward, licking their chops in anticipation.

My client entered the courtroom, big, black, brawny, and handsome, white teeth highlighting the jaunty smile on his face. I walked beside him, trying to match his long-legged stride. When Leibowitz saw me, he howled, "You! What are you doing in my courtroom, madam?"

"I am *retained* counsel, Your Honor," I said smoothly.

"Who retained you?" he snarled.

"I was retained by the family, Your Honor."

"What do you do, Mrs. Halbert," he questioned sarcastically, "run around the jails giving out your card?"

"I get retained like every other lawyer," I said evenly, hoping that the blotches on my neck would not spread as far as my face. I was shaking with fury.

"You're not qualified to try a murder case," he snorted.

"I'm as qualified to try a murder case as anybody else in this courtroom. Do I have to pass a special bar examination to practice before Your Honor?"

My reply brought his interrogation to a sudden halt. I had caught him off guard. Behind me, I heard a lawyer whisper, "Boy, that Sara has balls!"

Leibowitz abruptly changed targets, concentrating on my client, barraging him with insults. I held my breath, waiting for the moment, even hoping for it, when my client would shove his fists into the judge's face. It did not come. Much to my surprise, the volatile he-man held his head high and kept his mouth shut. I grabbed his wrist and held it tightly, aware that his powerful arm muscles were clenching and unclenching beneath his sleeve. A nerve was throbbing in his temple, but he stared straight ahead at a point about two inches to the side of the judge's nose. He had learned how to ignore the white man.

"With your long record, plead guilty and you'll get a hundred years," Leibowitz threatened. "Plead not guilty and I'll see to it you get the chair."

Mr. America was arraigned, and the charges of murder in the first degree and lesser charges were read to him.

In those days, after the accused was arraigned, his case was placed in a wheel and assigned to one of the five judges sitting in the County Court. Fortunately, my client's case fell to Judge Carmine Marasco, who practiced another sort of justice in his courtroom. He was fair and impartial.

Since I knew Mr. America was responsible for the prostitute's death, I could not allow him to stand trial. With the evidence against him and his bad record, he could have ended in the electric chair. Though he had been intimidated by Leibowitz's threats, I pointed out to him that Marasco was a different judge, one who lived by the letter of the law rather than any subtexts. Finally I persuaded him to plead guilty to a lower murder count, and he received a ten-to-twenty-year sentence.

After this case, my confidence increased. I had met the enemy, and while he was not precisely conquered, some of his venom had been drawn. I would not have so many qualms about facing him again.

There are many ways for a lawyer to get the contacts necessary to attract clients. One is to join a political club. When I was starting out in law, I joined a Democratic club presided over by a small-time Irish politician named Frank Nolan. He was really the compleat politician—fat, expansive of personality, a born hand-shaker and waist-squeezer who was always either running for office or in office. He had quite a bit of clout in his district, and his club was thronged with judges, lawyers, and other politicians. There were different affairs practically every week. I attended many of these, and I did get some work from my affiliation, mainly estate cases. However, as soon as I felt I was well enough known, I got out. Lawyers remain in these clubs only because they hope for an eventual judgeship. I never wanted to be a judge. From the bench, I would never have been able to accomplish all I had set out to do.

Meanwhile, I was getting more assignments, but though I was achieving a certain reputation, I still had a dearth of private clients. Leibowitz was not the only man to be prejudiced against women in the courtroom.

"Let's get rid of the women first; they're a pain in the neck." I heard that remark or variations of it often when,

with one or another assistant district attorney, I was selecting a jury. Generally my rejoinder was, "Wait a moment,
you son of a bitch. I am a woman, or had you forgotten? You
know I never excuse anyone on a categorical basis."

I selected jurors by personality rather than sex, race,
creed, or professional background. To be fair, however,
many assistant D.A.s had begun to realize that the women
on my juries identified with me.

"You really fought for that client with no holds barred,"
one said to me. Another exclaimed, "Mrs. Halbert, you made
me feel ten feet tall." Even male jurors were complimen-
tary. "You fight like a man, Mrs. Halbert." I really had a
laugh when one D.A. came up to me at the conclusion of a
hard-fought court battle to say, with more than a trace of
anger, "You are taking advantage of being a woman, Mrs.
Halbert."

Yet, though I could score in a trial, I was still bucking a lot
of prejudice. It was apparent in the attitude of the judges,
too. "Madam," they would begin.

Before they could proceed, I would interrupt, "Don't call
me 'madam' unless you call my opponent 'mister,' Your
Honor. I'm not a madam, at least not in the courtroom."

My retort would leave the judge confused. "Sorry," he
would say. "What should I call you, then?"

"Your Honor, why don't you just call me 'counselor' if you
don't remember my name."

However, if I made my point in one courtroom, there was
always the next one and a different judge; furthermore,
their memories were extremely short. Invariably, it would
be "madam" again.

I was not only fighting for a client when I came into court,
I was fighting for recognition. I got a little tired of wielding
two swords. Eventually it occurred to me that if I were going
to be really successful, I had better link up with the opposition. I had reached this conclusion at about the time that a

fiery young Puerto Rican lawyer named Manuel Nelson Zapata tangled with Leibowitz.

Zapata and I had a lot in common. We had both been poor, and we had both struggled to become lawyers. He had dropped out of school at thirteen to support his mother, younger sister, and three brothers. At twenty-one, he had joined the Navy. Four years later, at the end of World War II, he was discharged. Married and the father of three children, he had worked as a waiter by day and completed high school, college, and law school at night. It had taken him seven and a half years.

I first met him at a friend's office. He gave me a real Latin greeting—a kiss on the hand that threatened to proceed all the way up to my elbow. "Don't," I growled. "I'm a lawyer, too."

"But a charming lady," he replied gallantly.

At the time, I was not impressed by his suavity. It was only when I met him in Leibowitz's courtroom that I began to feel a certain empathy with him. I also managed to save his legal life. Furious at what he termed a double cross on the part of the judge, he was determined to leap to the bench and strangle him. With another lawyer, I held him back. "You'll be disbarred," I warned.

Sinking back in his chair, he muttered, "I am a man—I'll show that son of a bitch I am a man."

"He knows that," I muttered back. "Better show him you're a man with self-control."

Gradually he subsided and murmured a reluctant, "Thanks. Want to have coffee afterward?"

Later, we adjourned to a drab little luncheonette in the vicinity of the courthouse, settled down in a booth at the back, and had coffee, plus three hours of conversation. I found out that we had more in common than our backgrounds of grinding poverty and struggle; we were both dedicated people. He spoke earnestly, if a trifle pontifically, about his beliefs and his ideals. He described the miseries of the Puerto Rican community, the inequities of the judicial system, and he also mentioned that he felt he had a God-appointed task to right these wrongs.

That was the beginning of our friendship. A few weeks later, I was retained to defend three young Puerto Ricans in an assault case. My Spanish was still limited to a few words, and I asked Zapata if he would help me prepare the witnesses. He, in turn, asked if we might try the case together. I agreed. As luck would have it, the presiding judge was Samuel Leibowitz.

A Puerto Rican lawyer provided as much grist as a woman lawyer for Leibowitz's mill. Sarcastic taunts spewed from his lips, most of them directed at Zapata. By the time he had uttered half a dozen off-the-record "spics," Zapata, sitting at the defense table with me, was white with anger and minded toward mayhem. Again, he had to be forcibly restrained from attacking the judge.

"I am going to kill that son of a bitch," he growled.

"Not here," I begged, holding him down. "Wait until you can confront him in a dark alley."

When Nelson Zapata is angry, he clicks his jaw and the muscles on the side of his cheek pop in and out. He was doing considerable clicking and popping as he hissed, "That son of a bitch, I'd like to push his teeth down his throat. That would stop him talking."

"He'd love to disbar you," I whispered. "You don't want to give him that satisfaction. Be a successful lawyer, that's the best revenge."

After that trial by fire, Zapata and I worked together on a case he brought me. Our client, Maria Peralta, a thin, undernourished girl of fifteen, was in her fifth month of pregnancy when she was arrested. Incredibly, she was a gun moll. Zapata thought she would be more inclined to talk to a woman.

At first I had trouble with her, for she was sullen and silent.

But finally, under my gentle probing, she began to speak. As I listened, I mentally exonerated her from any complicity in the crime for which she had been arrested. A member of a street gang, she had carried the guns for some boys who had committed a murder.

Maria Peralta herself could be termed a murder victim, doomed before she emerged from her mother's womb. Her father was a drunk who had abandoned his common-law wife. To support herself and her daughter, the mother had become a prostitute. At three, little Maria, lying neglected near an open window, had fallen out. Impaled by the leg on an iron fence, she had survived to eke out a miserable existence in their fetid hole of an apartment. At twelve, she was inducted into a street gang. She had no steady boyfriend; everybody slept with her, and as a loyal member of the gang that had given her the only status she had ever known, she carried its guns tucked into her bra. Eventually she pleaded guilty to possession of a weapon.

I felt a little sick when I finally had her whole story. In my plea at her sentence, I cited her youth and contrasted her with my own daughter, who was just her age. Had Judy been subjected to the same pressures as this child, who knows what might have happened to her? "These people are not born criminals," I told the judge. "Environmental forces beyond their control have shaped them."

Maria had turned sixteen and had just given birth when her sentencing came up. I remember holding that newborn child in my arms and pleading that she be allowed to keep it; it was all she had. Eventually it was decided that the child would be placed in a foster home, where Maria could see it once she was released from prison. She might have received a stiff sentence, but the judge was lenient; he gave her three years.

Zapata was pleased with my handling of the Peralta case; he had a lot of kind words to say about my understanding of his people. I liked working with him, and a warm friendship was developing between us.

Our next case brought us even closer together. It was one that had been assigned to me by the court. We were representing Sarah Warren, a black prostitute of some forty winters, accused of throwing lye at two clients. Ordinarily I would have tried for a plea, but she insisted she was innocent and a trial was scheduled.

I had visited her in jail and found her to be an unprepossessing woman whose gray prison smock hung in deep folds over a gaunt body. Her appearance promised little in the way of sexual rewards, but she must have had attractions that did not meet my eye, for she insisted that one of the two men she had maimed with the lye would testify in her defense.

"They call him Joe Palooka; you find him in my building."

"I've got bad news for you, Sarah," I said. "That building's been abandoned since you've been in here."

She shook her head. "No, you find people in it still."

"Okay, if you say so," I replied doubtfully.

The building in question was in the Bedford-Stuyvesant section of Brooklyn, and I was heartily glad that Zapata would be accompanying me. We decided to go after work, but as we started out, rain splattered against my windshield.

"Want to turn back?" Zapata asked.

"It has to be tonight," I said.

"Good girl."

By the time we reached our destination, the storm had increased in intensity and, in lieu of streetlights, flashes of lightning illuminated a dreary waste of broken buildings and pitted, trash-strewn streets. When we arrived at the address Sarah had mentioned, we looked at the place in disbelief.

Most of its windows were boarded up and the rest were empty wells of blackness.

"Nobody can live here!" I exclaimed.

"You ought to know better than that," Zapata commented grimly.

We left the car and went up a moldering flight of stone steps to a door which, when pushed, opened with the traditional screech on what had to be a vestibule. We couldn't see anything, but we could hear the splashing of water. There were huge holes in the roof, and the rain was pouring in.

"We need a flashlight," I said. "I'll get it."

I went back to my car and fetched one from the glove compartment. It was raining harder than ever when I ascended the steps a second time, and it was with a certain reluctance that I rejoined Zapata. He, on the other hand, was calm and even laughing as he took the flashlight. Under its glow we saw that a large puddle had formed beside a narrow flight of rickety stairs that seemed to rise straight into darkness.

"Come along, Sara," he invited gaily as we sloshed through it. Under our feet the stairs, broken in some places, slanting in all, creaked.

Clutching the slippery, splintered balustrade, I giggled nervously. "We've got to be crazy, the two of us."

"Rats!" Zapata replied. It wasn't a retort. The beam of the flashlight had picked out a couple of big ones, which ran from the sudden illumination, squeaking loudly. By that same light we saw that the doors on the first floor were barricaded with strips of wood nailed across them.

"Nobody home," I remarked.

"No?" Zapata whispered. "Take another look." Gesturing with the flashlight, he pointed out one door innocent of the sealing boards. A thin, wavering light was visible beneath it. Since there was no electricity, someone had to be using a candle. Zapata strode forward and pounded on the door.

"What you want?" demanded a woman's voice. Her heavy Jewish accent surprised me. I had thought the neighborhood solidly black.

"Listen," I said, speaking through the door (she never did open it), "we're looking for a man who goes by the name Joe Palooka. You ever hear of him?"

There was a pause before she said, "I wouldn't know where to find him, but there's an old man up there could help you, maybe."

"What floor?" Zapata inquired.

"Top," she said.

"It's too much," I groaned as we started up. Moments later, I was tempting fate and unfurling an umbrella indoors as a barrier against the rain pelting through the holes in the roof. Each time the thunder rolled, the house seemed to shake to what was left of its foundations. The flashlight kept revealing and scattering rats that scampered down narrow halls flanked by more boarded doors. As Mrs. Anonymous on Floor One had predicted, there was an unbarricaded room at the top, but no reassuring line of light greeted us.

This time it was Zapata who admitted, "No one home."

"Let's see," I panted. "I haven't come all this way for nothing." I trudged down the hall on floorboards that sagged, slanted, and groaned. I could only hope that I would not speed the demolition process by falling through. Reaching the door, I knocked tentatively.

"Who's there?" a man demanded in a drink-slurred voice.

Zapata did the explaining.

"Sarah Warren," the man in the room repeated. "Sure, she do good on her back until that thing happen. I was there in her kitchen that night. I seen it all." Unsteady footsteps came toward us, the door was jerked open, and a man stepped into the hall.

Zapata thrust the flashlight into his face, and I swallowed

a cry as I looked into two mad eyes which seemed larger and wider than any I had ever seen; a nimbus of white bushy hair framed his high forehead. He looked like something out of a horror movie. However, in another second I realized that his expression was not mad, merely startled by the sudden light. A glance into his apartment revealed that he had been sitting alone in the dark and, by the smell on his breath, drinking cheap wine.

"Yeah, I know Sarah," he mumbled. "She didn't mean to throw no lye. We was—the four of us, we was sittin' 'round this table 'n' she was stirrin' lye—Drano, to open her sink. Man, it was all clogged up! So somebody say somethin' 'n' somebody else, he say somethin' back 'n' first thing you know, there's a fight 'n' Sarah gets nervous 'n' somehow that stuff gets thrown. She don' mean to throw it, swear to God. You gotta talk to Joe Palooka, he got hurt, but he don' hold nothin' against her."

"Where do you find him?" I asked.

He shook his head slowly. "Don' rightly know."

"Look," I said, "she needs somebody to speak for her. How's about you coming along to testify?"

"Don' remember much . . . was drunk, but I go, only how I get there?"

"Mrs. Halbert will take you," Zapata said grandly. As I had noticed on more than one occasion, he had a habit of volunteering my services. My car was better than his.

"Not only will I take you," I said, even more grandly, "but I'll give you breakfast."

The old man grinned. "Okay, I come."

Accordingly, I called for him the next morning. He looked much better than he had the night before, and he put away a hearty breakfast.

The case was being tried before my old enemy, Judge Leibowitz, but for once he did not bait my witness. Indeed, he seemed utterly enchanted by him, especially when the old man said, in answer to one question, "I has my fun and I minds my business."

"What do you has as your fun?" asked the judge, grinning.

"I likes to drink," the old man said. Because of that drinking, his mind was not entirely clear as to what had actually happened in Sarah Warren's kitchen on the night the lye got thrown, but since he did remember a few particulars, the judge allowed his testimony to stand.

Later, when Sarah described the scene in the kitchen, Leibowitz, who always liked to instill dramatic action into the proceedings, resorted to an old courtroom technique and had four actors portray what had taken place at her table.

Meanwhile, I was confident that we might get her off, even without the corroborating evidence of Joe Palooka. The D.A. disagreed. He, too, was eager to bring Joe into the case, but as a witness for the prosecution.

"If you find him," I said, "remember she insists that he's on our side, and she ought to know."

Eventually, investigators from the D.A.'s office found Joe Palooka and brought him to court. As Sarah and the old man had insisted, he was willing to speak on her behalf. On the witness stand he said, "Don't matter what happen to me. I love Sarah—always have 'n' always will. She didn't mean to do me no harm."

Unfortunately, his words had no weight with a jury which, to a man, shuddered away from the sight of a human gargoyle. The lye had eaten into his face, and half of it was gone. That horror was compounded by a look at the mutilated arm of the fourth man to sit at her table that night.

Sarah Warren got five to ten years, but without our painstaking investigation she could have received a twenty-five-year sentence.

It was shortly after Sarah's trial that Zapata and I decided to go into partnership. My decision was based on several factors. We were a good team, both fighters. As a woman, I was afraid I would never make it big alone. The theme "Who'd hire a woman lawyer?" was still resounding through my head, and whenever my telephone failed to ring for a few days, it seemed to me that I was receiving corroborating evidence that I needed male support. Furthermore, Zapata had a large Spanish practice, which meant that I would be working right in the center of the group I had decided to represent.

At the end of 1959 we formed our partnership and celebrated the event at a correction officers' party, at which we were also part of the entertainment. We surprised the assembled guests with a rumba that proved us not only well matched in our law experience but damned good dancers, besides.

We got a big hand, and the guest of honor proclaimed, "I have to toast you with champagne." Facing the assembled officers and their wives, he continued, "They surprised you on the dance floor, didn't they? But that's nothing to what these two do in the courtroom."

The guest of honor was Samuel Leibowitz. Once off the bench and in a social gathering, he was Mr. Charming in person. The fact that he could doff his courtroom personality as easily as his black robes annoyed me. It suggested that his daily performance was just an act to him, while it was only too real for his supporting cast. Still, it was better to have at least some of him on our side, and with his unofficial blessing we were on our way—Zapata and Halbert, out to oil the scales of justice.

③ | Zapata and Halbert, Partners

DECISIONS ARE ONE THING; reality is another. Between the two there can be quite a gap. A significant gap in our new partnership was the great divide between my office in Brooklyn and Zapata's Manhattan quarters. At merging time, I was located in the large, comfortable suite rented from my friend Robert Garvar. Three other lawyers, all Italian, were also in Garvar's office; they've subsequently become judges.

Bob Garvar really helped me. So did another lawyer, Sol Vladimir, a wonderful fat, balding character with a twinkle in his eyes who liked performing as much as I did and used to appear with me in a lot of the Bar Association shows. Those two taught me the ropes when I was starting.

When I was still operating out of the closet in the building next door, Vladimir brought me supplies—paper, pencils, pens, even a stapler which I still use. He and Bob also introduced me to judges and politicians. They saw to it that I got to the gatherings at Nolan's club nearly every week, and they gave me minor cases. They were great. I had real ties to Garvar's office and to Court Street, where it was located. Thanks to my sponsors, thanks to my appearances in the Bar Association entertainments, thanks to my growing reputation, lots of people said "Hi, Sara" every time I went out for lunch or across the street to the courthouse. Naturally, I was highly reluctant to leave that friendly atmosphere, and at first I even planned to stay where I was. "We'll be partners," I told a protesting Zapata, "but I'm still going to work out of Brooklyn."

Two weeks after our partnership decision, I took on as law clerk a radio announcer named Santiago Grevi. He was well known in Spanish-speaking circles and had a wide audience for his programs, but he had a feeling of being unfulfilled, and though he was well into his forties, he was studying at night to become a lawyer. It was Santiago who said to me one day, "You know, Sara, this is all wrong. If you have a partnership with Zapata, you two should be sharing the same office."

By that time I had reached the same conclusion; I crossed the divide and went to Manhattan. Grevi moved with me.

Zapata's office was also shared with two other lawyers, men he had met in law school. It was a large loft, two floors above a luncheonette on East Twenty-third Street in Manhattan, next to a branch of City College. He had made partitions between the offices, but they did not reach to the ceiling and you could hear everybody talking. Zapata wanted me to share one large room with him. Smiling beatifically, he said, "Sara, we will have two desks side by side, and we will talk."

A vision of Nelson at the telephone rose before me. He always spoke as if he were trying to bridge distances by sheer lung power. The conversations were generally in Spanish, a language I was only beginning to learn. I did not relish its rapid rat-a-tat-tat in my ear. Furthermore, since I had slept in the dining room of every place my family had inhabited since our arrival in America, I had a passion for privacy. I said defensively, "No. I'd prefer to have my own office. Let me make a few rearrangements of your space."

There was a reflective gleam in his eye but a protest in his mouth. "There's only one free room—it is the garbage room, Sara."

"You don't have a collector?" I demanded incredulously.

He shrugged and replied vaguely, "It is the way it has always been handled."

The garbage room was by far the best and largest room in the suite. I arranged for regular garbage collections, cleaned out the space, and moved in my own possessions. I also installed a typist for the whole office, the first they had ever hired. Somewhere along the line, I thought I identified the gleam in Zapata's eye. He had known of my years as a secretary, known me to be a good organizer and office manager, and I was being just that. Had that been one of his reasons for offering me the partnership? It was a less than welcome thought, and I began to think in terms of the future, when I might set up my own office and practice. By that time, I hoped, I would have the reputation that would bring in the clients. Meanwhile, working with a man would help me achieve it. Office organizer or not, I was in a law partnership, and shortly after my files were in order, there was a case to be tried, our first as partners.

The case in question had been given a title by the newspapers—"The Case of the Two Cigarettes"—and it was a lawyer's dream. In addition to being challenging, it would receive the newspaper coverage all lawyers covet, the sort that can build a reputation. In fact, it had been brought to us by a newspaper, New York's prestigious Spanish daily *El Diario*. The editors made it their business to look into the problems of the Puerto Rican community, and they had been informed of the plight of two young workers who had been employed on a Poughkeepsie farm. The boys had been arrested on what they contended was a false charge of robbery. In effect, they had received a twenty-five-year sentence for stealing two cigarettes.

Of course, the case had ramifications of assault with intent to rob. Charges had been brought by their alleged victim, a man named Bryce Hager. Late one night, in front of a Greek restaurant on Main Street in Poughkeepsie, Hager had supposedly been accosted by Carlos Sotomayor and Dario Gallo.

They had demanded two cigarettes, and in the course of an attempted robbery, they had inflicted knife wounds on his chest. When Hager had informed the police of this encounter, the cops had rounded up all the Puerto Rican farmhands in the district, among them Sotomayor and Gallo. Hager had positively identified them as his assailants.

Both boys had indignantly denied his charges, asserting that they had never seen him before. However, since they had been absent from the farm that night and could produce no alibi witnesses, they had been arrested. A court-appointed lawyer had handled their case. Unfortunately, he was a real-estate lawyer and had never acted for the defense in a criminal case. With only a week to prepare his case and no knowledge of Spanish, he had made such a poor job of the defense that the pair had quickly been convicted and sentenced.

Zapata, alerted by *El Diario,* had appealed the case, and the Appeals Court had ruled that the previous lawyer had been so ill prepared that the conviction could not stand. A new trial had been scheduled, and Zapata and I were hired to defend the boys. By this time, they had been in jail for three years. *El Diario* provided bail, and they were released.

Every day during the period preceding the trial, Nelson, myself, the two defendants, and the reporter from *El Diario* piled into my car for a three-hour drive to Poughkeepsie. During these journeys I got to know the two boys quite well. They were pleasant-spoken, charming young men. I had no trouble believing them when they insisted they had been railroaded into jail via that makeshift trial and the prejudice of a jury chosen from that almost all-white community.

In addition to the attention the case was receiving in *El Diario,* it was extensively covered by the local press. One night when we stayed over for a late meeting in Poughkeepsie, we took a taxi back to our hotel. The four men were in the back, and I sat in front with the driver. I noticed a newspaper on the seat beside him, and our story was on the front page. I asked him if he had been following the case.

"Oh, yes," he said. "I know the guy who accused them. He's been in my cab."

I had been doing a lot of thinking about Hager's story. Though he had accused the boys of stabbing him, and ostensibly he had the knife slashes to prove it, no one had ever asked if his shirt had been cut. A slashed shirt would have been a valuable piece of evidence for the prosecution, but it had not been offered. Furthermore, he had received five wounds on his chest, and from their appearance, it seemed to me that they could have been scratches from five fingernails. On impulse, I said to the driver, "I've a funny feeling about this case. I have the impression that there might have been overtones of homosexuality here."

"Of course there were," the driver said casually. "More than once I've driven him to one fag bar or another."

Trying to subdue my excitement, I duplicated his casual tone. "He goes to that kind of bar?"

"Yep," the driver said. "He's one of the boys, all right."

"Look," I said, "let me introduce you to the people in your cab. I'm one of the lawyers for the farm workers—the defendants. They, my partner, and the reporter from *El Diario* are in your back seat."

There were introductions all around. The driver was really impressed. "I hope you two get a fair shake this time," he said.

"Maybe you could help us," I said. "You mentioned those bars—you suppose you could drive us around to some of the places where this man goes?"

"Sure thing," he agreed heartily.

He stopped near a bar on Main Street.

"You people stay in the cab," I advised my companions. "You all have heavy Spanish accents, and that can be damned off-putting in this community, as you know. Let me go in alone."

"Alone?" Nelson questioned, his Latin chivalry evidently aroused.

"If I need help, I'll yell," I assured him.

In those days I was slim and my blond hair was natural. When I sauntered into that bar, I don't believe anyone thought me a lawyer looking for evidence. Since I've never had any trouble talking with people, I soon struck up a conversation with some men at the bar. I found that the clientele was mixed—some straight and some homosexual. I was talking with a couple of the straights, and one was particularly informative.

"Sure, Hager goes with the fags," he said, not troubling to lower his voice. "He's well known in here. I know a couple of other places where he hangs out, too."

I gave him one of my best smiles and said, "Here's a subpoena. Do come and testify for us at the trial." I named the date.

He laughed and said he would. He even wished me luck.

By the time I had visited the other two bars, I was feeling a little high—I am not a drinker. However, I also had a fund of useful information. Hager was not one of the town's more popular citizens. He was a troublesome drunk, and, furthermore, someone mentioned that he had a bad service record. After leaving the bars, I got the driver to take us to the Greek restaurant Hager had been patronizing just before the assault allegedly took place. Though it was reasonably early in the evening, the owner was just closing for the night.

"Don't you usually stay open longer?" I asked.

"No," he replied. "We always close about now."

I discovered that this policy had been in effect for more than three years, yet Hager had told the police he had emerged from that restaurant late at night.

The following day, I went to the electrical appliance store where Hager worked. The owner told me that he was not reliable. "He has a habit of calling in sick," he affirmed.

Meanwhile, the reporter from *El Diario* had visited the local military station and learned that Hager had been dishonorably discharged from the army because of homosexual misconduct.

My final interview took place at the farm where the boys had been employed. The owner, a very nice German woman, spoke highly of them. She could not believe them guilty of the assault, and she was willing to testify on their behalf.

By the time I concluded my investigations, I had formed a picture of Hager and I also had a pretty good idea of what had probably taken place. In the course of a homosexual encounter, he had had an argument and a fight; hence the marks on his chest. Possibly the person or persons involved had been Spanish, but Hager, being drunk, could not remember them. When asked to make an identification from the lineup, he had picked Dario and Carlos at random. A prejudiced police force had subsequently arrested them.

When we came to court, the nature of the proceedings had changed completely. It was now a problem of mistaken identity and the boys were exonerated. The case was the subject of editorials in the *New York Post,* the *Daily News,* and, of course, *El Diario,* and Zapata and I got some valuable publicity.

"I'm certainly glad you had the hunch about the shirt," Zapata told me afterward.

During the 1960s I became especially concerned over the plight of those people accused of a crime and too poor to pay the high bail set against their release. Because of crowded court calendars, those individuals were only too often literally "lost in jail." As in the case of the Poughkeepsie farm workers, they could be detained for as long as two years even though they might be innocent of any crime. I learned of these injustices when I started visiting jails.

The bondsman is a middleman, a sort of unofficial liaison between judge and accused. After a defendant is arraigned, the judge sets bail—the more heinous the crime, the higher the bail fee, the object being to keep the accused in prison. However, the bondsman is concerned only with profit and security.

Since very few defendants have the ready cash to post bail, the bondsman supplies money for the accused in return for a premium fee, which is usually about fifty dollars for the first thousand, forty dollars for the second, and thirty dollars for each additional thousand. In order to safeguard his loan, he generally demands collateral in the form of savings bank passbooks, jewelry, a deed to a house—whatever is available. If there is no collateral, the bondsman usually refuses to grant a bond.

When it comes to doing business, the bondsman prefers the well-heeled gangster to the poverty-stricken petty offender, with the result that the obviously guilty rest at home while the innocent poor languish behind bars.

This miserable situation reached crisis proportions for me at the time that my friend Blossom Heller became Brooklyn's first female assistant district attorney. When she received her appointment she had been handling several cases, two of which she passed on to me. My new clients were two court-assigned defendants, Sylvester Pendarvis and Clarence Tucker, both black. It was September 1962, and they were nineteen and eighteen years old, respectively. Each had been in the Raymond Street jail, awaiting trial, for the better part of a year.

After I received their cases, I spoke to Judge Barshay. "Your Honor, when are these two men going to get trials? They've been in jail over ten months!"

"They'll get it, they'll get it," he assured me.

Though I kept pushing during the next several weeks, all I got was more promises. Meanwhile, about six weeks after my original plea for a trial, there was a big, splashy arrest—that of Palma Vitale, a well-known gangster. He was immediately released on twenty-five thousand dollars' bail. Three weeks later, the district attorney came into Judge Barshay's courtroom and demanded a trial for him. I had been in the back waiting to be heard on behalf of my two boys. Listening to him, I was furious. I stormed up to the bench. My face was red with anger as I said, "Judge, it's revolting what's going on in this court. Here we have two men who are in jail over a year begging for a trial, and the D.A. wants to put this gangster on trial right away! What is happening, Your Honor?"

"Calm down, calm down," soothed Judge Barshay. "They'll get a trial soon."

"No," I said loudly, "I'm not interested in soon. I want that trial now."

The district attorney, who was also present, said, "We're not ready on this case."

I said, "Well, I am doing something about it and you will hear from me tomorrow."

I knocked out four habeas corpus writs, two for my young black men and two for a couple of Hispanics who had also been in jail for a long time. That afternoon, the D.A. was served with the habeas corpus papers. In movies and television plays, a lawyer is usually shown handing in a paper at police headquarters and blithely ushering his client out of jail. That is not the way it is done. It takes three days to get the work through. After preparation of the paper, you need a judge to sign it, and he sets a return date. You then serve the district attorney and the jail; then, one to two days later, depending on the judge who has the habeas corpus papers, a hearing is scheduled. That's how it happens.

When I had presented the papers, I called a friend on *The New York Times* and told him what I had done. "Those fellows deserve some publicity," he said excitedly. "I'm going to get the reporters there, Sara."

The hearing was scheduled for eleven in the morning of a day in November. As luck would have it, I had a bad toothache that morning, and a nine o'clock dentist's appointment. It was only after one side of my mouth became immobile that I realized I would have to give a speech. "Do something!" I groaned to the dentist. "I can't go in there with a crooked mouth."

He shrugged. "I can't make that stuff wear off any faster."

With visions of all the reporters and photographers who would be present, I stood in front of a mirror and practiced trying to get my crooked mouth straight. It took some doing before I was ready to join Zapata in the courtroom.

Though Zapata had not originally shared my anger over the unfairness of the bail system, he was aware that the newspapers would be giving the case and its lawyer a big play. He wanted a piece of that action, and, accordingly, he asked me if he could represent the two Hispanics since they had come to me through him. Naturally, I agreed.

By the time I reached the courthouse, I had largely forgotten about my crooked mouth. I was on fire with all I wanted to say about the bail issue. When finally I stood in front of the bench, I said, "Your Honor, there's only one difference between a person in jail and a person on bail—money. These boys are poor, and that's why they've been ignored. I've seen too many of these cases in the last five years. I'd put the number at five hundred to a thousand. Personally, I would like to see the court's bail policy completely revised. I think it's unrealistic. In some states, if you can't bring a case to trial within six months, the defendant must be paroled.

"Why should they be kept in jail because they're poor, without even being convicted of anything?"

I pointed to Sylvester Pendarvis. "Look at this boy, Your Honor. He is supposed to have ridden in a stolen car. He's not accused of having stolen it; he rode in it as a passenger. He needed only fifty dollars for the bondsman, but he had no money and so he's spent a year in jail. How long, Your Honor, how long is enough?"

The judge looked concerned. "I'm going to release these two men," he said to the D.A. "I give you one week to give them a trial."

The first trial was accorded to Pendarvis. The district attorney stated the case against him in its entirety: he had been found with three other boys riding around in a stolen car. That was the beginning and end of it.

Judge Barshay was visibly upset. "Make your motion," he said to me.

"I move to dismiss the charges as a matter of law."

Judge Barshay dismissed the case.

There had never been a legal case against Pendarvis. But no one could make up for that wasted year.

The Clarence Tucker case was more complicated. He was accused of joining another boy in committing a robbery at gunpoint. Tucker insisted that he had not been present at the time the robbery took place.

In the course of the trial, his alleged colleague took a plea, but Tucker still contended that he was innocent. It seemed to me that I was making some headway in proving his innocence, but I had no sooner reached this conclusion than a policeman who had interviewed Tucker after his arrest took the stand to say that he had an unsigned confession taken down verbatim from Tucker.

I was extremely upset. Taking my client aside, I said, "Why didn't you tell me about the confession?"

"I never made any confession," he exclaimed. "I never, never did! That cop is a goddamn liar."

I had heard that only too often, but I believed him. "May I see that confession?" I asked the witness.

It was handed to me, and, looking at it, I saw that it was dated November 1962. Putting the officer back on the stand and glancing at the confession from time to time, I began my interrogation.

"Officer, you took this confession?"

"Yes."

"The same day the boy was arrested?"

"Yes."

"That was in November 1961?"

"Yes."

"As he talked, you wrote it down?"

"Yes, that's right."

"And you kept it all this year?"

"Yes."

After I had buried him in a heap of his own lies, I thrust the confession at him. "Officer, look at this confession. This is what you wrote. Look at the date."

He obeyed and turned pale.

"What does it say on this confession—the date? Give me the date!"

In a small voice, he said, "November."

I screamed at him, "What year, Officer? Tell the jury the year of that confession."

Barely articulating, he said, "1962."

"Let me see that confession!" thundered the judge.

It was obvious to all that the cop had manufactured a confession one year after the defendant's arrest.

The jury found my client not guilty. Afterward, I discussed the case with Zapata, whose two clients had also gone free. "That officer perjured himself," I said. "He wrote out of habit 'November 1962' because that was when he made up that confession. Something ought to be done about him. I'd like to start proceedings."

"No," Zapata said quickly, "that is the way it is. We have had a victory. Leave it at that, Sara."

"But—" I began, and stopped. It would have availed me nothing to tangle with the cops, who in those days stuck to one another like glue. I did nothing more about it, and that lying cop was home free. But, as Zapata had said, I had won my point.

The trials of Pendarvis and Tucker inspired *The New York Times* to do a series of articles on bail abuses, and subsequently Attorney General Robert Kennedy organized the National Conference on Bail and Criminal Justice. Participating were law-enforcement officials, judges, and legislators. Though neither the reporters from the *Times* nor members of Kennedy's staff consulted me directly, my two cases were cited as prime examples of bail abuse.

Out of this furor came the Vera Foundation and its Manhattan Bail Project. The founder, Louis Schweitzer, a chemical engineer and leading New York philanthropist, stated, "No system of equal justice can tolerate this discrimination between rich and poor." I am very proud that Schweitzer, who before establishing his foundation had consulted some of the top legal minds of the country, including U.S. Supreme Court Justice William O. Douglas, also came to me for my views on the subject.

The project was established in cooperation with the New York University Law School. Its office is in the Manhattan courts and is staffed with a director and a team of NYU law students. It investigates the backgrounds of defendants in all the city's court cases. The purpose is to provide a substitute for high bail fees. This substitute is in the form of a promise that any defendant sponsored by the project can be released on his own recognizance in return for his personal guarantee that he will be present to stand trial. Naturally, before receiving such aid, each person sponsored by the project is thoroughly investigated. No one accused of rape, narcotics charges, or any other major crime is eligible. In the years since its inception, the project has been highly successful. There are still problems with overcrowding in the jails, but considerable progress has been made.

4 | The Vampire's Victim

AFTER THE "TWO CIGARETTES" and the young gun moll cases, our practice picked up considerably. Yet, in spite of what I had contributed to both cases, I was still inclined to agree with Zapata when he said, "We are getting more clients, true, Sara, but do not forget that it is me they are coming to see."

He did create a marvelous impression in the courtroom as he made his impassioned pleas. I used to say to Morris, "He's going to be one of the great lawyers. You'll see."

He made an equally good impression outside the courtroom, attracting clients by the sheer force of his personality. He was handsome and flamboyant; women adored him. Men liked him, too, because he was a great drinking companion and spent money lavishly. "Drinks all around" was one of his favorite phrases.

Yet, even in those early days, I was not quite the little shadow he had envisioned. I had my own way of handling a case, and when he would say, "Sara, I don't agree with what you are doing in such and such a trial," I would answer, "Look, Nelson, you have your way of doing things and I have mine, and that's how it has to be."

Though he admired my show of independence, in his world, as in my father's, women stayed in the background. They were attractive furnishings intended to enhance men's surroundings and men's self-esteem. It took Zapata quite a while to realize, reluctantly, that I was not going to be a member of the worshipful entourage that he loved to gather about him. We nevertheless remained on very good terms.

Because of those two early successes, we were getting a lot of mail from the inmates of jails. One such letter, post-marked Beacon, New York, came from the State Hospital for the Criminally Insane, known as Matteawan. Its sender, a man named Victor Rosario, had followed the "Two Ciga-rettes" case in the Spanish-language newspapers of Pough-keepsie, which is not far from Beacon.

Rosario's letter was addressed to Zapata, but its source put Nelson off. Lawyers get a lot of mail from crackpots as well as from desperate inmates of prisons and mental institutions, and he was quick to shove such mail into the "nut file." I, too, have a tendency to believe that people in mental institutions are there for the reasons stated in their certification papers. Still, I do read their letters, and if they make sense, I answer them. Occasionally I hear from relatives of the patient. A few weeks after I decided that Rosario's letter was coherent enough to warrant an answer, his aunt and uncle flew from Puerto Rico just to see me.

Their visit surprised me; I had not expected a personal call. They were good-looking, well-spoken, and well-dressed. "We are so grateful," the aunt said. "In all the time that Victor's been at Matteawan, he has written to hundreds of people—lawyers, judges, politicians—but he has never before received a reply. You are the very first person who has shown the slightest interest in his plight. We want to assure you that we do not believe he is insane."

"No," affirmed his uncle, "he is not. We can't understand why they have kept him there for so long."

"Four years." His aunt sighed, her eyes filled with distress. "I wish to impress on you that Victor is a good man, a kind man, a responsible man."

I was more influenced by the fact that they had come all the way from Puerto Rico to see me on behalf of their nephew than I was by what they said of him; relatives are apt to be prejudiced. But these two were willing to act on their belief, and as further proof of their sincerity they left me a two-hundred-dollar stipend to cover some of the cost of my investigations. I made arrangements to drive to Matteawan and interview Rosario.

Matteawan! It was a name I had heard all my life. It was the place where you sent the crazies. When I was a kid in Brighton Beach, we made jokes about it. "Aw, you're nuts. They oughta tie you in a straitjacket and put you in Matteawan." When I grew older, I knew better than to joke about Matteawan. There was nothing funny about being shut behind its walls. I had a vague idea of the shock treatments and the lobotomies that were part of the therapy for the insane, but, as I learned later, no one outside that prison could realize what it was like inside. In letters from former inmates, I read reports of youthful prisoners being raped; of cruelly protracted punishments—prisoners locked in cells for twelve hours or longer and refused water, or bound in straitjackets and forced to defecate in their clothes; of constant sedation and medication whether needed or not. It was a place that the Marquis de Sade might have described in a novel, but Matteawan was no fiction—it existed in upstate New York, only three hours out of Manhattan.

In those days, the facilities of Matteawan were limited to several badly overcrowded buildings, three or four stories high. Squat and brick-red in hue, they cast a blighting shadow on the rolling green hills of the surrounding countryside. As I drove through the hospital gates, I was as much intimidated by the ugliness of the institution as by its significance. Even though I was not yet fully aware of the horrors lurking in its cells, I was uncomfortably reminded of Auschwitz, Belsen, and other concentration camps. The idea of spending even an hour in it appalled me. Victor Rosario had been there four years. I could almost hope he was mad. To be sane and shut behind those gates was a fate I preferred not to imagine.

I had arranged for an interview with the doctor in charge

of the institution before I met Rosario. My depression increased as I followed a guard down an ill-lighted corridor, the walls of which were painted bile green. In the eerie stillness the click of my high heels sounded preternaturally loud. I was very glad to see the door of the doctor's office. I was even more pleased when, on being ushered into a small white chamber, I was greeted by a pleasant, middle-aged man. He was introduced to me as Dr. John Lanzkron, assistant director of Matteawan.

"I knew you were to meet with Dr. Johnston, the head of the hospital," he said in heavily German-accented English, "but he is away. *Und so,* you must speak with me, yes?"

Though he had addressed me politely enough, he had looked at me a trifle warily. When I answered him in German, he thawed considerably, and we continued our conversation in that language.

In answer to my inquiry about Rosario, he shrugged and smiled. "Quite frankly, Mrs. Halbert, if you could induce him to stop telling a certain story, he could be released."

Considerably startled, I said, "What story would that be?"

"It is that he insists that his wife's lover drank his own blood, Mrs. Halbert." Lanzkron rolled his eyes upward and smiled.

Naturally, I was taken aback and depressed. I also tended to believe the doctor when he added, "He's a typical paranoid schizophrenic. He insists he was framed by his wife and her lover. All paranoids believe they were framed. That's why they're here."

Reaching into his desk drawer, Lanzkron brought out a document. "This is Rosario's order of commitment," he explained. "I will read you part of it. Rosario must stay at Matteawan 'until he shall no longer be in such a state of imbecility, idiocy, or insanity as to be incapable of understanding the charge against him or of assisting in his own defense.'"

He put down the paper and said, "If he could help his lawyer in his own defense, we'd release him to the court to stand trial. It's a pity, you know. Aside from his delusion, he is perfectly lucid." A buzzer sounded, and he rose suddenly. "If you will excuse me, please. I must attend to something. I will be right back."

After he left, I noticed that the Rosario file was still on the desk. I was learning not to be backward about examining material, confidential or not, that might be important to a client. Snatching it up, I quickly scanned the reports of the psychiatrists who had interviewed Rosario over the past four years. Each report stated that the patient persisted in his story about his wife's lover's drinking blood. Discouraged, I returned the file. It seemed to me that the doctors were right—my client was unfit to stand trial. Still, when Lanzkron returned, I asked if anyone had ever checked out Rosario's story.

"No," he told me.

"Has he ever had any visitors?"

"Oh, yes," he asserted. "Many—once seven in one day. His wife brought the children to see him last year."

That surprised me. Had she broken up with her lover? Had there, in fact, ever been a lover? Perhaps the whole story was in Rosario's mind. That seemed a logical explanation, certainly more logical than the blood drinking. Most likely I had made the long drive to Matteawan for nothing, but since I was there, I would see Rosario—I owed him the courtesy of an interview.

"If he'd stop insisting on this blood drinking, we'd recommend his release. It is to our interest to release patients," Lanzkron said.

"Well," I answered, "at least he's not saying he's Jesus Christ. I think I'll look into his story."

"As you choose, Mrs. Halbert." Lanzkron made a notation in his file, evidently recording my statement.

Rosario wasn't as easily accessible as Lanzkron. Accompanied by a tall, tough-looking guard, I went through so many steel doors I stopped counting them. Finally I found myself in a small room with walls painted that ghastly green color and barred windows facing one of the dreariest courtyards I had ever seen. It was a vast space of bricks and mortar without even a touch of greenery. Sunshine only accentuated its dingy reaches, and I shuddered to think how it must appear on a rainy day.

In a few moments, Victor Rosario was brought in. He was dressed in the drab gray pajamas and heelless slippers that comprised the prison garb. A well-built man of middle height, he had dark, wavy hair and big brown eyes. His broad smile revealed that his front teeth were missing. He was very excited. "You are the first person who comes to see me," he said. "I've written to judges and lawyers and the Bar Association and the mayor and government officials and the governor, but nobody answers. Only you have answered. I hope you will help me."

Questioning him was difficult. Language wasn't the problem—since my Spanish was still rudimentary, we conversed in English—but he wanted to say everything at once, and his tongue balked. Words piled up and turned into gibberish. It took a while to extract even a partial account of what had happened. But before we got down to these facts, I said, "Mr. Rosario, your doctor told me about your insistence that your wife's lover drank his own blood. If you'd stop saying that this statement is true, they'd release you."

His huge brown eyes glistened with tears. "But it's true," he asserted. "It's true. It's true. He did drink his own blood. I saw. I saw it."

"All right," I said hastily, soothingly. "Tell me what happened."

The story I finally got from him was the familiar, the eternal triangle—two men and the woman both coveted.

Rosario came to New York from Puerto Rico in 1946 and settled in the Bronx. In the early 1950s, he met a woman named Carmen Ortiz, who had one daughter from an earlier marriage. He established a common-law relationship with her, and another daughter, Martha, was born to the couple.

Since Rosario had had little formal schooling either in Puerto Rico or the United States, his grasp of English was more limited then than now, but he was ambitious and industrious. He worked as a waiter, dishwasher, handyman, janitor, and eventually as a longshoreman. Sometimes he held several jobs at the same time, making as much as six thousand dollars a year, a good salary in those days. He did not squander his earnings; he banked them in a joint account with his wife. They had an apartment in the Bronx and, he believed, a good life. When their daughter was about four, Carmen bore him a son. The godfather of the boy was Robert Perez Castro, a friend of the family. He had been the superintendent of the apartment house in which they had previously lived. A frequent visitor before, he continued his visits at the new place, and Rosario soon realized that he was interested in Carmen.

Castro didn't try to hide his feelings. He taunted Rosario, declaring that he wasn't man enough to deserve the affections of the hot-blooded Carmen. One afternoon when they were all in the kitchen, Carmen at the ironing board, the baby in his crib, Martha playing on the floor, and the two men at a table drinking beer, Castro decided to give Carmen a demonstration of his devotion and his masculinity. Taking out his knife, he calmly cut his upper arm, squeezed some blood into his glass, and drank it.

This savage act may have impressed Carmen, but Rosario was angry. "I told him it was an ugly thing to do in front of my children. I told him to get out of my house."

Castro refused, and a fight ensued which Carmen, still

clutching her sizzling iron, tried to stop. Pushed aside by the men, she got burned on the nose. Then Castro, grabbing the iron, thrust it against Rosario's bare arm, inflicting another burn. Carmen, frightened, called the police, but when they arrived, she did not defend her injured husband. Instead, she and Castro accused Rosario of having provoked the quarrel and of inflicting wounds on each of them. When the police found the bloody knife, Castro insisted that it belonged to Rosario, and though the latter protested his innocence, it was two against one. Rosario was arrested for assault and battery and taken to jail. Bail was set, but Rosario could not pay it. His checkbooks were in Carmen's possession, and she refused to free him. He pleaded innocent to the charges and spent the next sixty-five days in jail awaiting trial. Finally, in desperation, he secured the services of Martin Gallin, a Spanish-speaking lawyer.

After a discussion with the district attorney, Gallin explained to Rosario that the judge would free him if he pleaded guilty to assault in the third degree.

"But I am innocent," Rosario insisted.

"Yes, yes," agreed Gallin, "but you've already been in jail the equivalent of the time you will have to serve for the reduced charges, and if you don't plead guilty, you'll have to stay in jail. The court calendar's so crowded it might be at least a year before you could get a trial."

"But that will give me a criminal record," Rosario said. "And I didn't do anything wrong."

"You want to stay in jail?" Gallin asked.

Rosario was weary of his long incarceration, and reluctantly he pleaded guilty. More than a month later, after an investigation by the Probation Department, he was released, the report to the judge noting that he was probably not guilty.

Loaded with presents for his two children, Rosario started home. He met Carmen on the street near the house. She greeted him coldly. "You're not supposed to come here," she said.

"But I have presents for the children," he protested.

Finally, reluctantly, she agreed to let him see them, and he went home. Castro was in residence there but left immediately. "He just walk away without a word," Rosario told me.

Though it was clear that Carmen and Castro had been cohabiting in his absence, Rosario settled back into his home and commenced living with his wife as if nothing had happened. I found this part of his story extremely surprising, given my knowledge of the Latin temperament. His psychiatrists had commented that he had limited intelligence, and, of course, this might explain his easy acceptance of that situation. But I gradually learned that though he was a simple, uncomplicated man, he was not unintelligent; he simply had a very passive disposition, and what might have incited another individual to fury made little or no impression on him.

Delighted to be home again, Rosario started back to work on the docks. Life was reasonably calm, and he saw nothing of Castro until an evening five weeks later when the doorbell rang and Rosario, peering through the peephole in his door, recognized Castro and a companion. Looking angry, Castro rang again, but Rosario, scenting trouble, did not open the door. "I did not want to be arrested a second time; that would have been bad."

But Rosario could not avoid trouble. It came in the form of an argument late one day with Carmen, who had been drinking for seven and a half hours in a girl friend's apartment. Rosario came to fetch her and angrily kicked her in the leg. Once back in their apartment, he scolded her for leaving the children and slapped her. The infuriated woman, waiting until he left the room, climbed down six flights of fire-escape stairs to the street. He was not even aware she had gone until the doorbell rang. On answering it, he found Carmen accompanied by two policemen.

"They come running up the stairs saying, 'Here is the guy.' They push me into my apartment and knock me down. They break my false teeth and push them halfway down my throat, then they start beating me with their sticks."

He wasn't aware of much that happened after that initial attack, but he thought he heard Carmen yell, "I wanted you to arrest him, not to kill him."

Bleeding and unconscious, he was carried out of his apartment and taken to the police station, where, on being revived, he was told he was once more charged with assaulting Carmen. As for his own wounds, the police told him that if he would blame them on his wife and her boyfriend, they would leave him alone.

"I told them I would not lie. I begged them to get me a doctor. I was in great pain."

Bundled roughly into the patrol car, Rosario was taken to two hospitals that night and X-rayed for possible fractures. He was given nothing to relieve the pain. Instead, he was put in jail.

Arraigned before the judge in Criminal Court the following morning, he was a pitiable sight. His face was bruised and swollen, his mouth cut and torn. His head was bandaged and his clothes bloody. His throat was raw from contact with the shattered dental plate. Part of the plate had been found by someone and thrust into Rosario's pocket. Speaking with difficulty, he mumbled to the judge, "I—I need a doctor. The cops beat me up."

Behind him, the arresting officer, James Clifford, twirled a finger to the side of his head, signifying that Rosario was crazy, and told the judge, "He kicked his wife in the stomach and she fled down the fire escape and called us. This guy has a record of assaulting her, so we came up to see what it was all about and he goes after us with a bailing hook. Got me in the hand." He held up the bailing hook, which Rosario remembered as having been on top of the refrigerator. The officer continued blandly, "I had to use necessary force to subdue him, Your Honor. This guy is dangerous—last time, he was pulled in for going after his wife with a red-hot iron. He pleaded guilty to that charge, so they let him go. I hope they're not going to be so easy on him this time. This time, he's charged with assault of his wife, resisting arrest, and assaulting a police officer."

"It's not true!" the terrified Rosario protested. "It's not true. None of these things did I do. They beat me without asking any questions." Piteously, he added, "I am still in great pain. I got to see a doctor."

"You'll see a doctor," the judge agreed. "I'm sending you to Bellevue for treatment."

He did not mean medical treatment, but Rosario did not understand that. When he was taken to the psychiatric ward, he was sure that the judge's orders had been misinterpreted, and said so to Dr. James Reilly, the first psychiatrist to examine him. Reilly listened, then, instead of giving him the medical treatment he requested, turned him over to a second psychiatrist, Dr. Theodore Weiss.

Weiss and Rosario had problems communicating with each other. Weiss spoke with a German accent so heavy that Rosario could not understand him, and Rosario's Spanish accent confused the psychiatrist. However, he seemed sympathetic enough when the man protested, "I am not crazy. I need medical attention. Look at me. You must see that I need it. I am *not* crazy!"

"Of course not," Weiss assured him. "Tell me what happened."

Once more, Rosario explained about being framed by his wife and her lover, a theme which must have had many variations in that ward. "Um," the doctor commented. "You ever hear voices? Do you sometimes see things?"

"I am not crazy!" Rosario cried. "If you want to know who's crazy, it is Castro, my wife's boyfriend. He wants to kill me and also he drinks his own blood. That's what I call crazy!"

It was also what Weiss called "crazy." He had heard about Castro's penchant for corpuscle cocktails from Reilly, and he agreed that it was a delusion. Coupled with Rosario's present and previous records for assault and battery, it formed the basis for their diagnosis: dangerous paranoid. On July 29, 1958, Reilly and Weiss filed a report that read, in part:

> This patient is very circumstantial, confused and has a probable paranoid system, involving some man who is out to get him and maybe out to kill his wife, also. States that police officers have beaten him, knocked his teeth out, etc. He is in such a state of insanity as to be incapable of understanding the charges, proceedings, or of making his own defense. In summary, the individual is suffering from a mental disorder diagnosed as Schizophrenic Reaction, Paranoid Type. He is a suitable case for commitment to a mental hospital.

After that report, Matteawan was Rosario's next address despite numerous protests on his part. Again he hired Martin Gallin to represent him at a sanity hearing, but Gallin, having talked to the police and the psychiatrists, did not believe his client's assertion that he had been framed. His reluctance to defend Rosario may also have had a connection with the fact that he had once represented Carmen Ortiz. Rosario hired another lawyer, Louis Raybin, to represent him at a sanity hearing on October 9, 1958. Three judges of the Criminal Court presided, but all proved to be in accord with the personnel of Bellevue, and on their findings Rosario was certified insane and remanded to Matteawan.

His account was moving, and I could agree with Lanzkron that he did seem lucid except on that one point about Castro's blood drinking. "Look, Victor," I said gently, "if you'd stop telling that weird story about Castro drinking his own blood, you could get out."

Once more, tears welled in his eyes. "It's true, Mrs. Halbert," he sobbed. "It's true. It's true."

"Listen to me, Victor," I said. "I'm going to check it out, but if I can't find any corroborating evidence, I want you to promise me you'll do something for me. If I write a letter to you and tell you to stop insisting that Castro drank his own blood, I want you to stop."

He shook his head and sighed. "It's true."

"Victor," I said gently, "I am here because I want to help you. If I tell you to say you made it up, whether it's true or not, say you lied, please."

Very reluctantly he said, "I will say I lied because I want to get out, but I swear to you that it is the truth."

Before leaving the hospital, I spoke with Lanzkron again and learned that Rosario's frenzied attempts to free himself had not been limited to writing letters. He had also compiled three writs of habeas corpus, presenting one a year at court hearings held in the Matteawan gymnasium. At each session he had been questioned by the presiding judge as to Castro's blood-drinking activities. He had always reaffirmed the truth of his statement, adding that he was innocent and had been framed. Three different judges had subsequently declared him unfit to stand trial.

Back in my office, I asked my clerk, Santiago Grevi, to write to Carmen Ortiz, asking her if she would come to see me. A few days later, she appeared with Martha, her little girl. Santiago interviewed her first. Known as "La Voz de Borinquen"—"The Voice of Puerto Rico"—to a large Spanish-speaking radio audience, Santiago was a wonderful surprise to my Puerto Rican clients. He was their Johnny Carson, their Merv Griffin—a real celebrity—and they were thrilled to discover him in, of all places, a lawyer's office. In middle age, he became a law clerk in my office until he passed the bar. After he became a lawyer, he worked for the Legal Aid Society for several years and was then appointed by Governor Nelson Rockefeller to the prestigious position of Commissioner of the Narcotics Addiction Control Commission, where he remained for nine years. Ironically enough, Matteawan Hospital became one of the hospitals under his supervision. He is currently in private practice again and is my associate.

Carmen Ortiz really opened up to Santiago, so much so that when he escorted her into my office, he whispered, "Hold on to your hat, Sara, you've got a surprise coming to you."

Primed by my conversations with Victor Rosario, I had half-expected to see a Carmen like the gypsy heroine of Bizet's opera—fiery, sensual, magnetic. The woman who entered my office was heavyset, with a muddy complexion. She dressed neatly and was very well groomed, but certainly she was no femme fatale—in my opinion, anyway. Somehow I could not see her engaged in any torrid romance. Once again I wondered: Had the episode occurred only in Rosario's imagination?

Martha had a dark complexion and wore her brown hair in braids. She, too, was neatly dressed and seemed alert and intelligent. At my invitation she sat down in a chair and, folding her hands in her lap, listened quietly and intently as I questioned her mother.

Explaining that I had met her husband at Matteawan, I asked Carmen if she had visited him over the past year.

"Yes," she said.

It was time to corroborate Rosario's story. "Did your husband make a good living?"

"Yes, he gave me money and furnished a nice apartment. He was very good to the children. He is a kind man," she told me.

"Why didn't you tell that to the police?" I demanded.

Carmen shrugged. "They didn't ask me. They spoke only with Victor."

"You know a Robert Perez Castro?"

"He was my—uh—boarder," she answered, avoiding my eyes.

"Do you still see him?"

"I got rid of him," she replied, a spark of anger in her eyes. "He was no good. He beat me up. Drank too much and beat me. I threw him out."

"Did Victor ever beat you?"

"No," she said. "Castro, he make me say these things. Victor never hurt me at all."

"Really." A trifle hesitantly, I continued. "Victor tells me your—er—boarder drank his own blood."

The little girl suddenly sat up straight in her chair. "Sure he did," she declared.

Her words went through me like an electric shock. I had to fight to keep my tone level. "Did he cut his arm and drip the blood into a whiskey glass?"

The child shook her head solemnly. "No, he did not do that," she said. "He dripped it into a glass of beer that make it turn red, and then he drank it. Also he make a big sign on the wall with his blood—it is still there."

I whirled around to Carmen. "Is this true?"

"Oh, yes," she said calmly, "it is true. Two–three times he cut his arm and he drink the blood and he make signs on the wall."

I almost fell out of my chair. Glaring at her, I yelled, "Get down on your knees, get down on your knees and pray for forgiveness, Carmen Ortiz! They have kept Victor Rosario in that madhouse for four years because they thought he was crazy for saying such a thing."

Her big dark eyes grew even rounder as she exclaimed, "Is that why they keep him there? I didn't know that."

"You didn't know?" I repeated.

"I didn't know. Nobody ever tell me."

It seemed incredible to me, but it was true. None of the policemen, lawyers, psychiatrists, or judges had ever bothered to let Carmen know why Victor had been committed. No one had ever checked out his statements with her or other members of the family or spoken to his friends or with the men who had worked with him on his many jobs. There had been no investigation. Everything had been accepted at face value. If they had investigated, they might have uncovered Castro's lies and extracted the real truth from placid, pliable Carmen. But then, Victor Rosario was only another Puerto Rican in trouble, one of a group whose members were always fighting among themselves, a "spic" whose presence in New York aroused the same resentment once incurred by newly arrived Italians, Irish, Jews, and the great mass of blacks. Poor, seemingly insane Victor Rosario had been convicted by his very presence in jail. He had been assumed guilty, and on that assumption he had spent four terrible years in Matteawan.

I got Carmen to sign an affidavit corroborating her statements. Now all I needed to do was take it to the doctors at Matteawan and Victor Rosario's long ordeal would be at an end. They would have to free him.

I wanted to leave immediately, but it was impossible. I had another long-standing commitment—to my family. In the last few years, Morris and I had both been doing much better in our professions. Before my first trip to Matteawan, we had planned our annual two-week vacation. We were spending it at a lovely resort hotel in the Catskills called Sha-Wan-Ga Lodge. It would be our first time at such an elegant place. Our reservations had been made months in advance, and our children had been talking about nothing else for weeks. They were also looking forward to spending two weeks with both parents, without their mother running away to tend to the needs of her many demanding clients.

I could not disappoint them. I wrote to Rosario, explaining that I would see him as soon as I returned.

Though I had been just as excited as my family by the prospect of our vacation, I couldn't get Victor Rosario's plight out of my mind. I talked about that affidavit to every guest I could corner at Sha-Wan-Ga. I told his story over the dinner table; I dreamed about it at night and got up the next morning still thinking about it. I had the key to unlock the doors that confined poor, misunderstood, misused Victor Rosario in the madhouse, and I could hardly wait to turn it.

Finally our vacation was at an end and we drove back to Brooklyn. I would be exaggerating if I said I threw my suitcase into the front hall and raced straight off to Matteawan, but it was almost like that. Armed with my affidavit, I made the three-hour trip in something less than the allotted time, slowing to a crawl only when I reached the outskirts of Beacon. I admit to being a trifle nervous. A trifle! I felt as though I were about to open Pandora's box!

I had made an appointment with the director of the hospital, and this time, when I was ushered down those depressing halls, Dr. W. C. Johnston met me in person. Silently I handed the papers to him. He read them carefully. When he finally looked up, he was considerably paler than when he had started reading. Summoning an orderly, he said tightly, "Pull out the Rosario file."

Leafing through that file took Johnston a long time, and the silence was heavy in the room when I finally said, "Dr. Johnston, I give you twenty-four hours to release this man."

He blinked, spluttered, and stuttered. "He could have been insane on—on other grounds."

"Oh, no," I retorted. "He was found to be insane because he insisted that he was framed, that he was innocent, that he was sent to Bellevue's psychiatric ward by mistake, and finally that his wife's lover drank his own blood—and the lover's the one who's crazy. After all these years, you can't start to invent new grounds to keep him here. I'll tell you this, Doctor, if you don't release him within twenty-four hours, I'll see that Matteawan gets publicity that will blow it sky-high!" I was really angry. I could feel a flush on my face, and my hands had knotted into fists, as if to punch him in the nose.

Having made my point, I asked to see Rosario, and since they could not refuse my request, I was escorted to that dreary little chamber off the courtyard. A few moments later, he was brought in.

"Victor," I cried, "you're going to be freed."

He stared at me and turned away quickly to gaze through the barred windows into the bleak bricked courtyard beyond. Finally he said quietly, "At least I shall never have to walk out there again."

The doctors did not act immediately on my ultimatum. A day later, Victor was still in Matteawan, but an entry was made on his medical record. In essence, it read: On the basis of reliable and recent information supplied by his lawyer, this man is cured.

It was amazing how a hopelessly insane patient could be cured overnight, and by a mere piece of paper. It took another twenty-four hours, a staff meeting, and some more red-tape snipping before Rosario was remanded to the court, where, being judged of sound mind, he could aid in his own defense and stand trial for beating his wife, resisting arrest, and assaulting a police officer. He was returned to the same Bronx Criminal Court from which he had been committed four years earlier.

When I arrived in court, the assistant district attorney, a man with the appropriate name of Tiger, took me aside and whispered, "Why don't you just let him plead guilty to a misdemeanor and we'll let him go."

I was incensed, but I did not let him see my outrage. I said coldly, "I don't like that word 'guilty.' He didn't commit a misdemeanor. He's innocent. Throw the case out. There are only two positions you can take. Either he was insane when he committed the alleged assaults and cannot be held responsible, or he was not insane and should never have been sent away. Why don't you speak to the parties involved, the wife and the cop who says Rosario resisted arrest?"

Interrogated by the D.A., Carmen admitted that Victor had never harmed her. Clifford, the arresting officer, preferred to state that Rosario had swung at him with the famous bailing hook but missed. But the outcome was the same; he had not been "assaulted."

The D.A. announced to the court, "In the interests of justice, I move to dismiss the charges against Victor Rosario."

That was one motion the judge did not deny. In September 1962, Victor Rosario went home.

The story was duly reported by *The New York Times* and then was picked up by nearly every paper in the United States and even some in Europe. I received clippings and letters from people in England and Hungary. The case became the subject of lectures in law schools and in nursing and psychiatric courses. I was invited to speak on television and radio panels. Lurid sensation-seeking magazines wanted to interview me and my client, especially after one banner headline proclaimed: FOUR YEARS' LIVING DEATH IN AN INSANE ASYLUM ARE OVER! Dr. Thomas Szasz, the famous psychiatrist, used this case in his book *Law, Liberty and Psychiatry* as an example of psychiatric mishandling of a patient.

When I appeared in courtrooms, the lawyers and judges invariably asked the same question: "Why didn't the doctors check out Rosario's statements?" The question was elementary, and so was my answer: "I don't know."

Dr. Johnston was also asked that question by the judge who finally released Rosario after the criminal charges were dismissed. Johnston's answer was full of words that added up to very little. I never told that judge, however, that he had been one of the original trio of magistrates who had found Rosario insane four years earlier. It would have been too embarrassing. I contented myself with having won my client's freedom and vindication, with the stigma of insanity erased.

By coincidence, however, I met another judge in a restaurant a few days after the Rosario case had been reported in the newspapers. Calling me over to his table, he congratulated me on my great success and laughingly inquired, "Tell me, Sara, who was the stupid judge who had him committed in the first place?"

"Listen," I said, "there were three judges who committed him to the nuthouse, and you were one of them."

He was stunned. "Well," he said, after a pregnant pause, "the doctors must have convinced us."

I relented and agreed. "Sure, they can be damned convincing with all that double-talking gibberish in a German accent. That's the trouble."

Rosario's troubles were not entirely over. Despite the publicity his case received, the officials of the Longshoreman's Union were not quite ready to accept his version of his four years in an asylum. However, after I met with them and explained what had happened, he was accepted back into the union with all seniority rights intact. Though he was extremely grateful, he was still unhappy.

"Sara," he said, months after his release, "I have lost four years out of my life; four years when I could have seen my children growing up; four years when I could have earned money to buy a house; four years of shame and torture. Isn't there something that can be done about that?"

"Victor," I said, "nobody can replace those four years. However, you can sue the State of New York for the neglect you sustained at the hands of its employees. Would you like to do that?"

He hesitated. "Well," he said slowly, "I think it would be only right."

I knew such a suit would be costly and the chances of winning it slim, but I was outraged, too, and I started proceedings through my firm. The charges against the State were: subjection of client to shame, humiliation, hospital- and prison-type routine; damage to reputation; destruction of morale, family life, employment; unusual and severe mental anguish over a period of approximately four years.

The suit was tried at the Court of Claims in Poughkeepsie, New York. It was there that I got the full picture of Victor Rosario's past sufferings and of the Bellevue and Matteawan psychiatrists' participation in his case. The whole story was obtained through direct and cross-examination of all the people involved. In my own mind, I had a caption for those proceedings: "Trial of Errors."

Nelson Zapata tried the case. I assisted him at the counsel table. I was needed as a witness. We had precious few to speak for Rosario. Seemingly, the State held most of the cards, the psychiatric cards. Appearing for it were all the fine medical brains from Matteawan, and James Clifford, the arresting officer. Appearing for Rosario were Carmen, whom he had finally married; their daughter, Martha; Dr. Lawrence Kaplan, a psychiatrist; and myself.

The lawyer for the State was Assistant Attorney General Maurice Goldberg, acting for Attorney General Louis J. Lefkowitz. Judge John Carroll Young of the Court of Claims presided; there was no jury.

Rosario was called first. He hobbled to the chair on crutches, for he had recently been injured at work on the docks. In spite of that, he looked very good. He was neatly dressed for the occasion in a dark business suit—seemingly a very different man from the bedraggled creature I had first encountered at Matteawan. But in fact he was not different, he was the same man, had been the same, sane man all the years of his life, and I prayed that we would be able to establish that fact officially.

Under Zapata's careful questioning, Rosario told the court of his early life, his arrival in New York, and his various jobs. He also testified that he had never had any mental problems, never had visited a psychiatrist until he had been sent to Bellevue at the behest of arresting officer Clifford.

According to the testimony, on admitting him to Matteawan the doctors had found that Rosario "smiled inappropriately" and at times seemed "tearful and downhearted"—as if such behavior were completely unrelated to the confusion and disorientation of an incoming patient. They prejudged him insane and monitored all his actions on that basis. This attitude prevailed throughout his incarceration, even in the face of evidence to the contrary, such as the description in the nurses' notes that Rosario was "neat and clean, sociable, interested in his surroundings, and conducting himself normally."

The overall picture that emerged was of a sane man in a madhouse. Yet, in spite of the known facts, in spite of the corroborating testimony of his wife and daughter, the psychiatrists who appeared for the State all defended their actions on the grounds that he was a schizophrenic with a persecution complex. Possibly this was predicated on the erroneous reports that Matteawan had received from Bellevue, but how easily it might have been altered had the doctors looked into his background, as they should have done. The only effort they made was to send a questionnaire to Rosario's brother Rafael; receiving no answer, they relied solely after that on "direct interview with the patient."

The trial made it clear that Rosario had been defeated

partly by persistence in the blood-drinking statement and partly by language difficulty. No one had ever fully explained to him in Spanish the reasons why he had been committed, even though the nurses' notes acknowledged a "partial" language barrier. Consequently, the psychiatrists, measuring him by their own inexorable standards of sanity, continued to consider him "lacking in insight"—"insight" meaning, in their terms, an acknowledgment of guilt.

The verbose and confused testimony of the Matteawan staff almost made me believe that the patients at the institution were not the only crazy ones. I had the feeling that the judge agreed; certainly he showed considerable impatience on hearing some of those statements.

Dr. Solon Wolff's answers were typical. Wolff, attached to the staff since 1941, had been in practice since 1910—half a century! Bringing that vast experience into play, he insisted that Rosario had been insane during his confinement. The fact that Rosario had ultimately been proved innocent of the charges brought against him did not alter Wolff's thinking in the least.

After listening to much of his testimony, Judge Young finally demanded sharply whether Rosario might not still have been in Matteawan had not his lawyer checked into the case. "No, Your Honor, we are always on the alert to release patients; we have a committee that is especially interested in release," Wolff replied, and he went on to explain that the committee considered discharges at the request of the doctors, and that this was a "regular routine."

Referring to the notes on Rosario's consistently good condition, his amicable social relationships, his lack of aggressiveness, the judge asked a final question: "Is it your judgment that four years is a reasonable time to keep a man there?"

"Well, Your Honor," Wolff replied, "our judgment depended on the nature of his illness, and our conclusion was that this situation in which he was involved on the outside was instrumental in bringing out the type of mental illness he showed. At the hospital, he was free from the tensions, stress, fear that was caused in him by his environmental factors—the marital problems, the rivalry."

Listening to him, my incredulity increased. By the time Rosario's suit came up for trial, I had been to Matteawan many times, and I knew just how "free from tension and stress" it was: about as soothing as Dante's Inferno.

The judge commented to Wolff, "You wouldn't keep a man in the hospital because he was afraid of someone on the outside."

In answer, Wolff simply restated some of the same old double-talk about Rosario's disturbed emotional state. The judge commented that a man incarcerated for four years might naturally be disturbed, but Wolff had an answer for that, as for everything else; he absolutely refused to acknowledge that Rosario had been sane. The good doctor pointed to the fact that as late as June 1962, Dr. Marcel Friedman, the ward physician, had noted no change in Rosario's thinking.

Yet, after I had presented the affidavit to Johnston in August 1962, the psychiatrists, interviewing Rosario at a specially scheduled staff meeting, noticed that in the two months since Friedman's examination he had shown marked improvement. He still made the same claims, but they were uttered in a "different tone of voice" and he seemed to be in much better spirits. Unanimously, they declared him fit to stand trial. Was a change of voice all they needed to indicate the change in his mental condition? If so, it certainly shed a new light on psychiatric thinking.

That thinking was evident through the entire trial, revealing clearly why Rosario's numerous protests had been ignored. The reason the three writs of habeas corpus he had presented at the hearings in the Matteawan gymnasium had failed was also obvious. All patients at Matteawan were allowed to make these presentations, defined in this instance as "the right of a citizen to obtain a writ of habeas corpus as a protection against illegal imprisonment." Hearings were held once a month.

In order to render such a procedure truly effective, a "citizen" needs the assistance of qualified counsel; at Matteawan most patients presented their own arguments, often from ill-prepared papers. Ranged against them were the staff psychiatrists; it was a pitifully unequal contest.

I remember those hearings as scenes out of Kafka—the great gray gymnasium, the prisoners milling around in its basement waiting restlessly until they were led up a flight of narrow stairs into a great echoing hall. The judge sat at the far end of that hall. Though his podium was only a table, he wore his black robes and clutched his gavel. At his right were his secretary and the court clerk, at his left were members of the hospital staff, each equipped with the files of the patients. In the front sat a lawyer representing the attorney general of New York State.

The doctors and nurses, the lawyers and their staffs all looked neat and spruce, a striking contrast to the heavily sedated prisoners in their gray pajamas. Under the relentless, ruthless questioning of the attorney from New York State, the prisoners grew nervous and confused. They gave halting answers, or in their eagerness they talked too fast to be intelligible. Or they wept, thus demonstrating, of course, that they were unfit to plead. The interrogating attorney seemed to take a special delight in confusing them. His attitude never failed to infuriate me.

Then the staff psychiatrist would take the stand. His testimony, spiced with psychiatric terms, sounded extremely impressive. It was far easier to doubt the Victor Rosarios of this prison world, especially when they made the same ridiculous statement each time. Furthermore, everyone knew that psychotics always claimed they had been framed. Clearly, the man lacked insight, just as his keepers claimed.

"Motion denied," said each judge laconically. "Next case, please."

Director W. C. Johnston was the last to testify at the trial. He concurred with his staff as to Rosario's "impaired judgment" and professed to see nothing extraordinary in his drastic change of opinion after he was confronted with my affidavit. On the stand, he denied that I had threatened to deluge the hospital with unfavorable publicity. The hospital records, however, show that Rosario was found to be "recovered" two days after my meeting with Johnston.

The trial ended. The judge reserved his decision. After deliberating for months, he finally awarded Rosario sixteen thousand dollars for malpractice of the doctors during his final year at Matteawan. For the three previous years he received no compensation because in the habeas corpus proceedings he had been found to be insane. Though sympathetic to Rosario, the trial judge had to abide by the earlier rulings.

The State appealed. The case had opened the way for similar suits. The higher courts (Appellate Division and Court of Appeals) reversed the decision, stating in essence that while Rosario's sufferings were unfortunate, the acts of the doctors were "errors in judgment" rather than malpractice. Rosario received nothing.

Victor Rosario still works hard and saves his money. He is sending both children to college. "They will not be like their father—so dumb, so ignorant," he told me. "They will never be in such a terrible position as I was."

"Victor," I replied, "if you'd been dumb and ignorant, you'd still be at Matteawan."

5 | Anatomy of a Rape

SHORTLY AFTER I CLOSED THE FILE on the Rosario case, Zapata and I also closed the door on our Twenty-third Street office and moved—up in the world but down in location—to 277 Broadway, across from City Hall. The move was at my instigation, and making it was not easy; it was, in fact, tantamount to a tug-of-war.

"Everyone knows where we are, and this is a central location," argued Zapata.

"A central and lousy location," I retorted. "They'll find us downtown. We're doing well, and we have to impress people with that fact. We're not going to do it in this loft. The suite I have in mind is all paneled; it has five large offices, a spacious reception room, and a separate conference room and library. It will have class, and you will have the largest, grandest room of them all. Think of it, Nelson, visualize yourself in a paneled, windowed office: six windows, wall-to-wall carpeting, a crystal chandelier."

My argument, and the layout itself, won him over. The move was expensive; it cost about ten thousand dollars to set up the suite. But we needed it for our image, and once we were established, Zapata was as thrilled as I. Another advantage was that the new office was closer to all the subways, an important consideration with demands for our services coming from all parts of the city.

That was when I indulged in my first really good car—a big blue Pontiac convertible. My kids were thrilled, but Morris called it "a status symbol on wheels."

"Maybe," I allowed, "but it gets me where I need to go in record time."

Record time was what I was making in those days. All the courts opened at 9:30 A.M., and there were mornings when we had court cases in Manhattan, the Bronx, Queens, and Brooklyn. Judges did not like to be kept waiting, nor did clients. I needed a good machine for all that running around, and I had it in my convertible. I also needed a reliable machine in myself, and I had that, too. I thrived on being busy and on being wanted. I will say, however, that at that period 75 percent of our clients came to see Zapata and 25 percent to see me—that is, on their initial calls. Once they had stepped into our office, we divided them up and they stayed with the one who originally interviewed them.

But there was one man—Eddie Martinez—who had come to see Zapata and, immediately on learning that I was in the office, told our secretary he wanted to see me. She telephoned me, and since I happened to be free, I said, "Sure, send him in."

Standing in the doorway, he was really something. He resembled one of those Charles Atlas ads but with clothes on, and his clothes emphasized a body that was as muscular as any I had ever seen. His muscles looked as if they might burst through his jacket. He was also exceptionally handsome, with dark eyes, a straight nose, and a full, sensuous mouth. One side of his face looked as if a cat had recently clawed it—but the marks took nothing away from his good looks. Though he was fair-skinned, his hair was midnight-black and wavy. He could have been a movie star. I couldn't quite believe his muscles—I tried to tell myself it was padding.

While all this manly beauty was registering and reregistering on me and I was thinking that he was even a more beautiful Atlas type than Morris, Martinez said, "I wanted to see Mr. Zapata at first, but when I learned he had a good lady lawyer here, I knew you'd be better for me." He spoke in a soft, mellifluous voice just slightly tinged with a Spanish accent. I could not fault his English, but his words surprised me.

"Why'd you want a lady lawyer?" I asked.

"Because I have a bad problem." He groaned and looked extremely disturbed. "They say I raped my wife's sister."

I have a way of using the punch line right at the beginning, and I shot it at him: "Did you?"

"*No!*" he said loudly. "But I am so ashamed, so embarrassed. Her husband's family came to beat me up, to kill me. I had to hide. And my wife"—his lips trembled—"she left me, went back to Puerto Rico with the kids."

One half of my mind was listening to his story, but the other half was still wondering about those muscles. I couldn't help myself, I had to know. I walked around my desk, and as if only to comfort him, I said, "Hey, don't get so upset, take it easy," and patted his shoulder and ran my hand down his arm. He was not padded. "What kind of work do you do?" I asked. "You appear very powerful."

"Beautician," he answered. "At least I am nearly through with the course. I almost finished enough hours to take the test for the state license. I work in a beauty parlor on weekends."

He had really thrown me a curve. I said, "Come on, don't kid me. You don't get a strong, thick neck like yours setting hair. You look more like a wrestler or a weight lifter."

His eyes widened. "How did you know?" he asked.

"Easy," I answered. "My brother was on the wrestling team in college, and I had a friend who was the heavyweight wrestling champion of the world in the Olympics. I used to be crazy about wrestling." I tried to keep a retrospective grin from curling my lips as I remembered the time that Olympic champion got me down on his bed and attempted a few unorthodox holds which only my well-placed knee aborted. In spite of my new client's protestations of innocence, maybe I was a little wary of him—had he, too, tried some of those holds on his sister-in-law?

"I also wrestle," he said. With surprising modesty he told me that he was the wrestling champion of Puerto Rico. He had had hundreds of matches. "Here," he continued, "I work sometimes as a longshoreman, but I want to quit all that. I am much more interested in being a beautician. I love to do women's hair."

"That must make it very nice for your wife," I said.

His face clouded. "My wife." He sighed, shaking his head. "We were getting along okay. She was glad I was taking this course. She didn't want me to wrestle anymore. She wanted me to have a regular job with a regular salary. She helped me save the money for the course."

"Before or after your sister-in-law accused you of rape?"

"Before!" he shouted. "I don't understand it. I come home and there's this note from my wife saying she has gone to Puerto Rico with the baby. And now, since Maria—that's her sister—says I raped her, my wife has written that she never wants to see me again. She and her mother accuse me of being an animal for breaking into Maria's apartment and doing all those terrible things."

"What terrible things, exactly?"

He didn't answer. The muscles in his neck were taut, and his fists were clenched. He stared down at the table, breathing hard.

Gently I repeated, "What terrible things are you accused of doing? Look, you came to me because you preferred a lady lawyer, you said. Now maybe you've got to forget I'm a woman and concentrate on my being your lawyer. If I'm to defend you, I've got to know the whole story."

He continued to breathe hard. "Maybe you won't want to defend me."

"I have a feeling about you. I don't think you did anything wrong. Your distress is too real. And believe me, I know what you must be feeling. An accusation like this is devastating. It strips you naked in public; you feel everybody must be looking at you and wondering if you did it. Relax. I know that's easier for me to say than for you to do, but if you are innocent, then let's dig our way out of this pit together."

He looked at me dubiously, and his tenseness did not diminish.

"Where was this so-called rape supposed to have taken place?" I asked.

"In Maria's apartment. She told the cops I came through a window and raped her."

"Where were you arrested?"

"My apartment. I live only one block away from her. I went to her house to look for Lucy and my kid. Lucy's my wife."

"How long have you been married?"

"Three years. I was twenty-two when we got married."

"How'd you meet your wife?"

"She and her sister Maria lived in the same house as my friend Alfredo. One day when I visit him, I see the two girls."

"Were they pretty?"

"Yes, they were both nice, real nice. Maria is a year older than Lucy. She liked me at first. When she saw me in her building that day, she said, *'Ay, qué pollo.'* "

I could see Maria's point. He was some chicken, all right. "So what happened then?"

"Well, she asked me to their apartment, and we got acquainted, the three of us, and pretty soon we all started going to the movies and to dances."

"The three of you?"

"Yes, but I began to like Lucy better than Maria. Maria was too pushy. Lucy was gentle. Pretty soon I fall in love with her. When we got married, Maria wasn't nice to me anymore. She started to get very nasty—not in front of people, but if we were ever alone, she'd make dirty cracks."

"What did she say?"

"She said I was no good. I chased around with other women; I was no good for Lucy. She said I was only out for one thing—you know, what women got."

"Um," I said. "Continue."

"Anyhow, I came home this Saturday after working in the beauty parlor, and I find this note on the kitchen table. It's from Lucy." He looked at me with misery in his eyes. "I worked so hard for her and for our baby, Belinda. I love them both. And then I get this note—" He broke off, took out his wallet, and extracted a battered piece of paper. "This is it—can you read Spanish?"

"I can read it," I said, looking at it. "It says she left you because you ran around with other women. She was jealous."

"It's not true!" he protested. "I worked very hard. I go to beauty school and work all weekend. I went straight home after work—where would I have time to go out with other women?"

"Oh, it can be done—between shampoos, even. Where there's a will. . . . Did your wife know of any specific incident?"

"Never!" he exclaimed. "Except in the note, she never complained to me about other women. When I used to be on the road for wrestling matches, she didn't like that, especially after the baby was born. That's why she was so glad when I decided to become a beautician."

"You ought to do well in that line," I told him. "Women clients always prefer to have a man work on them. My sister's a beautician, and she says the men get fantastic tips."

He nodded. "I already have a good following. I like to do special hairdos, and I hope, also, to become a hair-coloring specialist."

"You've got yourself a customer. Tell you what—when all this mess is over, you can work on my hair for a year, for free. How's that for a fee?"

He came over to me and ran his hand through my hair. "You have strong, thick hair. It's a nice color. I like blond hair. It's a deal." For the first time that afternoon, he smiled. "I have faith in you. I think you will help me."

"I am sure I can. Now, let's get down to cases. I take it after you got Lucy's note, you went over to see Maria, yes?"

"Right away," he said.

"When was that—about what time?"

"About five."

"She was alone?"

"That's right. Her husband's a waiter in a midtown restaurant. He gets home about eight thirty every evening."

"Was she reluctant to let you in?"

"No!" he exclaimed. "She was very friendly, too friendly. When I showed her Lucy's note, what do you suppose she says to me?"

"I couldn't guess," I answered dryly.

"She says, 'Forget about Lucy, Eddie, she doesn't love you anymore. Look, I knew you first, I'll take good care of you. You can live with José and me. You know I always liked you. . . .' And then she puts her hand on my shoulder and moves real close to me."

Martinez's response had not been flattering. Instead of yielding to the temptation she was obviously offering, he, catching sight of a hair dryer he had lent her, pushed her aside and picked it up.

"What are you doing with my hair dryer?" she said.

"It's my hair dryer," he corrected. "I need it for my work. I'm going now."

"You're not getting that back," she yelled. "You're no good. Lucy was right to leave you. You're fooling around with all those women at the beauty parlor. I know what's going on in that fancy beauty parlor of yours with all those Jewish bitches!"

"I'm getting out of here, and I am taking my hair dryer with me," he told her firmly.

"Oh, no, you don't," she screamed. She lunged at him and dug her long fingernails into his face, inflicting several deep, ugly scratches, one of which bled profusely. *"Gran hijo de una puta* [big son of a whore], get out, get out!"

Clutching the hair dryer, he ran into the hall and down the steps. He was upset and unhappy as he returned home and applied some medicine to his bleeding cheek. Not long afterward, the bell rang and he opened the door to two policemen.

"I am Detective Bronson," said one of them. "You are Eddie Martinez?"

"Yes."

"You are under arrest."

"For what?"

"You were in the apartment of Maria Torres this afternoon?"

"Yes."

"Who scratched your face?"

"She did, but why are you arresting me?"

"For rape and burglary."

"Why? I didn't rob her. It was my hair dryer."

"Just come with me. I said rape, not rob."

The detective put handcuffs on Eddie. As he was led away, he was aware of the neighbors watching. He felt dreadful. However, at least the two men who arrested him were not of the ilk who had assisted Carmen Ortiz. They did not rough him up. On the contrary, they were even courteous to him. As Martinez told me about this exemplary behavior, I was not surprised. I had found that in certain types of rape cases, mainly those involving members of a family or friends, the police are not always convinced of a suspect's guilt. They are aware that there might be extenuating circumstances. Maybe Eddie's despair touched them, too. Once behind bars, he actually tried to commit suicide, but, convinced of the folly of this action, he had a friend bail him out.

"For the sake of my wife and my little girl, I must fight this thing," he told me. "Maybe if I am exonerated, they will come home."

"I am sure they will," I said. Inwardly, I was disturbed over his scratches. To a jury, that wounded cheek might have the impact of a mark of Cain, for when twelve upright men and women are trying a sex case, they instinctively tend to be prejudiced against the defendant. Men viewing an alleged rapist think of their wives, daughters, sisters, or girl friends in similar situations; women identify with the attacked. In Eddie's case, the jury might be convinced that the scratches had been inflicted as Maria Torres sought to defend her honor. However, there would be no sense in telling him that. I said, "I must speak to your wife."

"You can't," he moaned. "I have told you—she is in Puerto Rico. She hates me for what I am supposed to have done to Maria."

"You go home and calm down," I said soothingly. "I am going to write to her. I think she'll come if I tell her how important it is."

He was dubious but he left, and I dictated a letter to his wife, telling her it was imperative that I see her. My letter ended: "For your own and your child's sake as well as that of your husband, I urge you to return to New York to confer with me. If you fail to do so, you may regret it the rest of your life."

As I had expected, she returned immediately. Eddie picked her up at the airport and brought her straight to my office. She proved to be a very pretty young woman of twenty-one. Though they had been married three years and she was the mother of an eighteen-month-old child, she still seemed shy and totally unsophisticated. It was evident, too, that she distrusted her husband. She barely looked at him. Telling him to wait outside, I took her into my office. "Sit down and tell me about yourself, Lucy," I said gently.

In common with her husband, she spoke good if accented English. She explained that she had been born in Puerto Rico but raised in Brooklyn, where she had completed three years of high school. She had been only seventeen when she married Eddie Martinez. He had been her first, her only lover, and her home had been her whole world. Her lips trembled, and she blinked away tears.

"Where did you get the money to go to Puerto Rico?" I asked curiously. "I thought you and Eddie were pouring all your savings into the beauty course."

"My sister gave me the money for the trip. She was always very sympathetic to me—it was she who told me how Eddie was fooling around with other women at the beauty parlor. Oh, I was so hurt. I cried and cried—and Maria said I shouldn't cry, I should leave him. I didn't want to go—but Maria—"

"You mean you left your husband because your sister told you to?" As she nodded solemnly, I continued, "Had you yourself ever heard anything about your husband's having love affairs?"

"No, I didn't hear anything, but Maria did."

"Why were you so quick to believe her?" I asked.

"She was always much smarter about men than me," Lucy said simply.

"I thought you wanted Eddie to be a beautician."

"I did."

"Well, you must have known he'd be in contact with other women. Did he ever give you any reason to mistrust him?"

Slowly, slowly, my prodding questions were beginning to make an impression on her. She looked at me dubiously. "No, he didn't, but look what happened to poor Maria. I could never live with him after this." She sighed.

"Lucy, he says he didn't hurt your sister at all. He didn't climb through her bedroom window. He went there after he found you were gone. He thought she might know why you left him. He says she opened the door when he rang her bell. It was only five in the afternoon. Would anybody in their right mind climb through a window in broad daylight? It doesn't make sense, Lucy."

I could see that light was beginning to dawn. *"Dios mío,* do you think Maria planned this?" she said.

"Look, Lucy, why did you leave so suddenly? Who helped you pack? Who gave you the money? Who took you to the airport? Why was Maria so helpful, Lucy? Think about it! Didn't you both meet Eddie at the same time? Didn't she like him as much as you did, before he decided to marry you? Didn't she suddenly change her opinion after that? She was trying to separate you."

"Ave Maria, she must have wanted him for herself!" Lucy exclaimed.

"Yes, Lucy, I think that's true. If Eddie's telling the truth, you must help him. Go back to him. Give him a chance. He loves you. He's always worked so hard for you, and he misses the baby."

Tears rolled down her cheeks. "Oh, I will go back, I will!" she cried. "I understand now."

"May I bring him into the office now?"

"Yes, please, thank you."

I buzzed my secretary. "Have Mr. Martinez come in," I said into the intercom.

Eddie walked in slowly, hesitantly. He looked at Lucy like a whipped dog. I really felt sorry for him.

I said quickly, "Lucy wants to help. We've both come to the conclusion that Maria was jealous because you married Lucy—she wanted to break up your home, and she wanted to see you suffer as much as possible. That's why she made up this ridiculous story about the rape."

Eddie looked at Lucy. She was still crying. "I will come back," she told him. "Belinda and me, we will come home."

He put his arms around her. It was a beautiful tableau, but

I had to interject a word of warning. "All we need to do now, kids, is convince the jury that right is on our side."

Judge John R. Starkey tried the case. A handsome Irishman in his mid-sixties, he had a ruddy complexion and a mane of snow-white hair. I had looked into that countenance on many occasions. In the days when I was a fledgling lawyer, he had been one of the five judges in County Court. We had also met outside the courts at political dinners and meetings of the Bar Association. With a drink in his hand and a gleam in his eye, he had never failed to regale me with a new, slightly off-color joke. I was a good audience. I love a good sexy joke, even when it's very pointedly directed at me. When the Martinez case came up, the judge, meeting me in the hall outside the courtroom, said insinuatingly, "How're you getting paid by that handsome young client of yours, Sara?"

I looked at him blandly. "Not with money, Judge," I said, pretending to tell him what he wanted to know.

The D.A. was John Kerman, whom I also encountered in the hall outside the courtroom. He was flanked by Maria Torres and her husband, José. I looked at her with some dismay. Slender and fragile of figure, she was very beautiful. I could envision her on the witness stand; in my mind's eye, I could see her weeping as she told her sad story. Undoubtedly, "beauty in distress" would make quite an impression on the jury, especially on its male members. She had already made an impression on her husband. Though considerable time had passed since the alleged assault, José Torres's eyes were fiery, and more than once he muttered, "I still want to kill that bastard."

When he saw me with Eddie and Lucy, he turned threatening. Glaring at Eddie, he said, "We will get even with you later."

Lucy clutched Eddie's arm. "Please, José," she begged in

frightened tones, "wait for the trial. We will all find out the truth then."

"Why did you go back to that animal?" José demanded furiously.

Lucy put up her chin defiantly. "He is my husband."

I stepped between them. "Let's go into the courtroom," I said to my client.

Maria was the first witness. A murmur ran through the courtroom as she stepped to the stand. As I had expected, her beauty was all in her favor. People were disposed to feel sorry for her. She appeared demure and composed, but there was an angry glitter in her eyes as she looked at Eddie, seated at the counsel table. Of course, if she had been, as she claimed, raped, she had every right to be angry. As she testified, her anger was replaced by tears. They ran down her cheeks, and at times she sobbed so bitterly that her answers to the D.A.'s questions were unintelligible.

As I listened to Kerman's direct examination, I began to feel very apprehensive. I wondered if Eddie might have deceived me. I glanced at him, but I could not catch his eye. He was staring straight ahead, his hands tightly clenched before him on the table.

Maria, meanwhile, was growing more and more upset. Her distress evidently touched Judge Starkey, for he asked a court officer to bring her some water. "Do you wish a recess?" he asked her soothingly.

"No." Maria gulped back a sob. "I—I want to finish with this." With a wealth of corroborative detail, she continued with her story.

I thought the D.A. would never turn to me with the words "Your witness," but finally he ended his examination.

I did not question Maria immediately. Instead, I asked for a recess to read the statements made by the witness to other authorities before she took the stand at our trial. Often, over the passage of time, a witness will change a story or contradict a statement made immediately or soon after the occurrence. Maria, however, had not deviated from her original charge. If she was lying, it could be brought out only by cross-examination.

When the trial resumed and I rose to question her, Maria's attitude changed. She did not throw me any of the melting looks she had directed at District Attorney Kerman. She looked at me belligerently, as if daring me to challenge her veracity. I did not. I spoke quietly, gently, asking her where she had met Eddie and when. I took her over much of the ground I had covered with Lucy and Eddie—their earlier friendship, the movies, the dances they had all attended.

"He treated you with respect in those days?" I asked.

Maria had become more relaxed. "Oh, yes," she assented. "He was okay in those days. He never did anything wrong. He was very respectful before he marry my sister."

"Maria, the day this thing happened, you were home, isn't that right?" I asked, still gently.

"Yes."

"Your husband had gone to work?"

"Yes."

"Did you see your sister, Lucy, earlier that day?"

"Yes."

"When and where?"

Maria tensed, looking at me warily. "At—her home," she said hesitantly, and I knew she had sensed the direction of my thrust.

"What were you doing there?"

Maria stared at her hands and did not answer me. I raised my voice. "Weren't you helping her pack?"

Maria rolled her big dark eyes at the judge and then toward the jury box as if wanting help from them, help or protection. It was the wrong reaction. I'd only asked an apparently harmless question.

I raised my voice a little. "Look at me, Maria," I commanded. Indignation and alarm warred in the glance she threw at me. "Isn't it a fact, Maria, that you connived to break up your younger sister's marriage? You helped her pack after her husband, Eddie, left for work; you told her to write the note; you paid the passage to Puerto Rico for her —you even took her to the airport!"

"Yes," yelled Maria furiously, her face contorted with hatred. "He is no good for anyone. He fooled around with those women. He is an animal. He is rotten, no good." She added further accusations which she delivered in a voice grown raw with rage. Finally, she gasped, "Can I—have a drink of—of water, Your Honor? I—I am too upset to continue."

The trial was recessed until the following day. At my side Eddie whispered, "I never gave her any cause for such insults."

I looked at that handsome face and that muscular body. He had given her plenty of cause; I only hoped I could get the jury to agree that it was her jealousy and not his actions that had brought us all into court.

That evening, I had a chance to relax and indulge in my favorite pastime, dancing. Morris and I and a number of other lawyers and judges attended a newspaper reporters' ball at the Astor Hotel. It was a splendid affair at which many pop singers and comedians performed. The orchestra was playing a rumba and I was jiggling away with my husband when Judge Starkey wriggled by.

He gave me an ominous grin. "He's guilty, Sara," he whispered. "I'll give him twenty-five years. She's convinced the jury."

Before I could answer he had gone. "Oh, Morris," I moaned, "I'm sure he's innocent. If I lose, I'll never forgive myself."

"Oh, come on, cookie," Morris said reassuringly. "The way

you told me that story, he's going to get off. Of course, I never know whether you've told me everything. You get carried away sometimes, you know, and sometimes you plain lie. To yourself, I mean."

"Maybe I do sometimes," I allowed, "but not this time. He's innocent."

But would I be able to prove that to a jury? Judge Starkey's words had really upset me. I had the feeling he wasn't kidding. When I am in the middle of a trial where I am really heart and soul on the side of my client, when I am as convinced of his innocence as I was in this case, I can't sleep. All during the course of the trial, I lie awake. Eddie's case was no exception, and when we got home from the dance, though I was exhausted, sleep did not come to me. Instead, I tossed and turned all night, mentally reviewing every word uttered during the day's proceedings, and in my mind's eye seeing beautiful, tearful Maria sobbing on the witness stand with the eyes of a sympathetic jury fastened on her. Superimposed on that picture was one of Eddie clutching the prison bars and protesting his innocence. Finally, I got out of bed and sat in the living room formulating questions and points I meant to bring up in the summation.

The following morning when I arrived in court, I found it packed with spectators. People love to sit in on a sex case. Even though I had had very little sleep the night before, I did not feel tired. Once I have stepped over the threshold of the courtroom, my batteries are recharged. Maria mounted to the witness chair. She looked at me defiantly. Obviously, she, too, had a set of batteries in good working condition.

Stepping toward the chair, I faced her. "Maria," I said quietly, "the day this happened, you stated on direct examination you were in bed taking a nap around five in the afternoon?"

"Yes. I heard a noise, and this guy"—she pointed a finger at Eddie—"came through the window."

As she paused, I prompted, "Go on, tell this jury what happened." Don't leave out a single fabricated detail, I added silently.

"He sat on the top of my chest. I screamed. He punched me in the mouth. He told me to keep quiet or he would kill me. Then he put his private part in my mouth. After a while, he turned his head and put his head between my legs and stuck his tongue in my vagina. . . ." She was speaking more quickly. The words literally poured out of her. "He tied up my mouth with a cloth. I gave that cloth to the policeman who came to my house after I reported the rape. It shows the blood on it from my mouth. And then he got off me. He tied my hands in front of me with a rope. My wrists got all swollen when I tried to get the rope off later. The doctor saw my mouth and wrists. He knows I was beaten." Her chest was heaving, and she was close to hysteria as she continued, "And then he got off my chest and he came into me and he finished inside me." Looking at Eddie, she spat, *"Gran hijo de una puta!"*

The jury was stunned. Eddie sat like a man turned to stone. I, however, was positive that it was fantasy time. Maria, the woman scorned, was telling it like she wanted it to be, not as it had been. The gymnastics she had now vividly and meticulously described would have been impossible to perform, even for a wrestler. I set out to prove that point. Inch by inch, I took her back over the alleged crime, from the moment Eddie supposedly leaped from a nearby garage roof to the ledge in front of a neighbor's window and then swung through her own bedroom window, capping this bit of Tarzanry by first planting his fist in her mouth, and then his penis.

Angrily and more positively than ever, she answered my questions, repeating step by step the previous recitation. He had sat across her chest, and while still straddling her, he had put his face between her legs. It was this same story, she averred, that she had told the detective at the precinct, the doctor who had examined her at the hospital, the police officer who had visited her apartment and who had taken as evidence her ripped panties, the bed sheet, the rope used to tie her wrists, and the bloodied cloth that had bound her mouth.

I had conducted a painstaking and very slow cross-examination thus far. I wanted the jury to hear her words. I also wanted a recess. I had to conduct a simple experiment at home. Looking at the clock, I saw at last that it was 4:45 P.M.—late enough. "Your Honor, I will need at least two more hours with this witness," I lied. "I am tired, and I am sure the witness is also. May we recess until tomorrow?"

"Okay, we'll agree to that," Starkey told the jury.

I literally raced home. Much to my relief, Morris had already arrived; his car was parked in front of the house. Bouncing through the door, I yelled, "Hey, Morris, come here. I need your help."

He came into the hall. "What can I do?"

"Come here," I beckoned, going into the den. "I want to try something." Lying down on my red-carpeted floor, I said, "Sit on me, honey."

Morris did a double take. "You kidding? So early in the day?"

"Come on." I giggled. "This is strictly in the cause of justice. I've got a witness with a real wild imagination. Sit on my chest, but be careful—right over my bosom and face me."

Morris laughed but obliged. He was getting heavier than I had realized. "Like this?"

"Like that," I panted. "Now turn and without moving your body, try to put your head between my legs." Morris is athletic, but even he has his limits. "Okay, you're excused.

But you wait until tomorrow—I am going to have something to tell that judge."

That night I slept a lot better.

I could hardly wait until the trial resumed. As soon as the witness returned to the stand, I asked to approach the bench with the D.A. "Judge," I whispered, "I went home last night and experimented with my husband and—"

"I know," the learned judge interrupted. "It can't be done. I, too, like to experiment."

"Could we have a demonstration here in the courtroom, just in case the jurors aren't that adventurous?" I urged.

"Well, Sara, who are you going to use as the female? You?" Judge Starkey inquired.

"Judge, I'm the lawyer. We'll use court officers," I said, barely able to control a giggle.

"Go ahead," said the judge.

"Hey, wait a moment," the D.A. protested. "Your Honor, I don't like this idea."

"Well, I do," the judge said. "You've got the green light, Sara."

Stepping back, all business, I repeated my request in proper legal jargon, asking two fat court officers to assist. There were a lot of guffaws as the courtroom buffs anticipated the explicit sex scene.

One of the court officers ambled forward, looking a little red in the face, at least that part of his face that wasn't shaded by a long handlebar moustache. "Hey, Sara, what do I do?"

"You get up on the prosecution table"—I indicated the D.A.'s side of the room—"and lie down, flat on your back. You're going to be Maria."

His flush mounted right up to a receding hairline. "Hey, Sara," he mumbled, but he obliged. He made a good Maria, except that his stomach was bigger.

The other court officer played Maria's version of Eddie; he

was almost as heavy as the first, and when he straddled him across the chest, the whole courtroom shook with suppressed laughter.

Under my urging, Maria told the officer on top how to sit. "You move higher," she said. "Put your legs here—there, that's how it was."

Then, at Maria's further instructions, he twisted his body to put his head between the other's legs. Both grunted and groaned with effort, and then gave up.

Everybody in the courtroom was laughing, everybody except Maria. Her thoughts were very easy to read. She knew she had made a serious error. However, embarrassment did not still her tongue. Quickly she explained that she had gotten the anatomy of her rape all wrong. She changed her testimony, and then she was excused.

Next, Kerman questioned the officer who had investigated her apartment after the alleged rape. He told the court that he had gone to the apartment after Maria's release from Kings County Hospital. He had observed no injuries on her, but he did produce for the prosecution the bloodstained white cloth with which Eddie had allegedly bound Maria's mouth. He knew nothing of the whereabouts of her torn panties or the rope which had been used to bind her wrists. I wondered if these pieces of evidence had ever existed.

Detective O'Hara, one of the arresting officers, recalled that when he and Bronson had arrived at the Martinez apartment, he had seen a fresh, livid scratch mark on Eddie's cheek. "He admitted being in her apartment but said he hadn't robbed her—that it was his own hair dryer. I realized he misunderstood me. When I explained that she was accusing him of a burglary and a rape, not a robbery, he seemed dumbfounded."

I shot a glance at the jury. I had chosen as my foreman a retired police captain, and at that moment I knew my instincts had been good. He was an intelligent, fair-minded man, and he knew a lot about false rape accusations. He had a measuring look in his eye.

Detective O'Hara also admitted that it would take an exceptional athlete to jump from the roof of the garage next to Maria's house to her window. On the basis of her confused testimony and O'Hara's remarks, I convinced Judge Starkey to make a visit to her apartment. He obliged by ordering a bus for the next day.

It was like a picnic. We all went: judge, jury, court reporters, prosecutor, defense counsel, Eddie Martinez, Maria, and, of course, the two court officers. When we arrived at the apartment, it was clean and neat, with newly painted white walls —courtesy of the landlord, who had hired a special crew to paint it overnight.

The jury peered out of the window toward the nearby roof, and so did the judge and the D.A. An intruder would certainly have risked his life to leap through the window in the manner so graphically described by Maria, but the feat could have been accomplished by an agile, muscular man— a wrestler, for instance. Was lovely Maria worth that attempt, or had she invited Eddie into the apartment?

After we returned to the court, the district attorney rested his case. "I have no further questions," he said.

"What do you mean, you bastard?" I whispered angrily. "Don't tell me you're not calling the doctor who examined Maria!"

"He can't add anything," the D.A. whispered back, looking at me wide-eyed.

I was not deceived by his show of innocence. I smelled a rat, several rats. I had to get in touch with that doctor; his name was Schwartz. I called Kings County Hospital but failed to reach him. I needed more time, and the judge gave me until the following day to bring him to court.

After a series of frantic telephone calls, my office finally located Schwartz. He was performing an operation, and I literally had him pulled out of the operating room. "You must come and testify for me," I said. "My client could get twenty-five years if you don't."

He promised to be there the following afternoon, and I assured him he would be put on the stand immediately if I found his testimony would serve our cause. "Be sure and bring the record of Maria Torres's examination." Just to be on the safe side, I said it twice.

Once I had the doctor's cooperation, I felt better. Though until I met him I couldn't be sure what he might have to say, I had the feeling that he could not attest to the validity of a rape that had never taken place.

Back at the courtroom, I put my defense witnesses on the stand. Shy little Lucy was the first. She had been nervous about testifying until I told her that if she spoke the truth, no one could shake her, and the truth is what she told. It flowed serenely from her lips as she described her happy home life with Eddie, and Maria's sly campaign to wreck it.

"Always she say he is unfaithful to me," she explained. "She told me I should leave him. Every day she would tell me new stories about how he was unfaithful to me. She was my older sister. I believed her. I let her persuade me to go back to my parents with my little girl. I let her buy me the plane tickets. Then she come over and help me pack and take me to the airport. She say I should never, never return to him." She looked at her husband. "But I loved him. Oh, I was so happy to see him again—and I knew in my heart he had never touched Maria."

Eddie, seated next to me at the defense table, watched her intently. "Poor Lucy," he said to me. "I'm so sorry she must go through this. Her family doesn't talk to her anymore."

"Wait until after the trial," I hissed. "It'll be Maria who'll be getting the silent treatment."

Eddie was my next witness. I had just put him on the stand when one of the court officers, the rapee, told me that the doctor had arrived. I hesitated in my questioning of Eddie.

"Come on, Mrs. Halbert," the judge said. "Let's get on with it."

I explained that the doctor had arrived and asked him for a five-minute recess to speak with him in the hall. "I may want to put him on the stand," I said.

The judge obliged and I led Dr. Schwartz into the hall outside the courtroom. "Thanks, Doctor," I said. "I am so grateful that you came. I want you to answer some questions before I decide whether or not to call you as my witness." I put the questions to him, and his answers stunned me.

Leading him back into the courtroom, I asked the judge if I might put him on the stand in place of Eddie Martinez. As the judge gave me permission, another murmur ran around the courtroom. I could practically feel the vibrations that were coursing through the jury box.

"Just a few questions, Doctor," I began. "When you examined Maria Torres on the day in question, did you find spermatozoa in her vagina?"

"No."

"How long does male sperm live after an ejaculation?"

"Twenty-four to forty-eight hours."

"One more question, Doctor. Did she have any bruises on her mouth and wrists?"

"No bruises anywhere. If there were, or if she had pointed them out to me, they would have been entered in the medical record."

"Thank you, Doctor."

There was no cross-examination, and the D.A. avoided my searching glance. I could certainly see why he had not wanted to summon the doctor.

Then I recalled Eddie Martinez. He was not eloquent, but his account of his meeting with Maria rang true. The defense rested, and my summation would come the following day.

That night, sleep eluded me completely. Had I omitted anything? Had the jury gotten the full picture? I took out my Bible. Often I find inspiration in it. The basic problems of life have not changed in the thousands of years since it was composed. I remembered the story of Joseph in Egypt, and I reread that passage. It did inspire me. I knew just what I would tell the jury. Papa would certainly approve of his little Sara.

I arrived in court early the following morning. There were not many people in the courtroom, and as I was standing near the exhibits in evidence, I saw the cloth that had allegedly been tied over Maria's bleeding mouth. Picking it up, I examined it closely. Certainly it was blood-marked, but in such an odd manner—with four long, parallel stains. I also noted that it had three lengthwise creases. I folded it up along the creases and saw that the long marks of blood lay one on top of the other, showing that they were the result of a single staining that had soaked through the cloth. I stared at the folded cloth and had a revelation!

"Oh, my God," I muttered under my breath. "How did I miss that?"

A little while later, the judge entered and the court was in session. I began my summation. I was truly psyched up, oblivious of the regular court buffs and the other spectators who filled the courtroom. Like a prizefighter, I was all tension, ready to pounce on my captive jurors. I built up the story, acting out Maria's feelings, her frustration over Eddie's choosing her younger sister, her feelings of rejection, her dreams, her growing hatred against the man who had failed to return her love, her eventual accusation of rape, an accusation which she must have repeated to herself day after day until the date of the trial, a trial she must have known could end in a twenty-five-year prison term for him.

I got to the cloth—the cloth I had found on the table.

I produced it.

"I have folded this cloth along the lines of the obvious creases. Look at the stain of dark blood. Look at it!" I commanded the jury as I held it like a sanitary napkin so that all of them could see that long, long stain that went practically the length of the cloth. "You don't have to be a woman to know what this really was. If it had been tied around her head, across her bleeding lip or mouth, there would have been blood only in the center part of the cloth. There is no way it could look like this—and furthermore, this cloth, this napkin, is too short to encircle her head. Use your God-given common sense!"

I paused, letting my words sink in, and I saw response in the eyes of the jury, and I knew they understood me. I picked up the Bible.

"Ladies and gentlemen," I said. "This is a story as old as the Bible. Maria coveted her sister's husband, just as Potiphar's wife coveted the handsome overseer in her husband's household." Picking up the Bible, I turned to the passage in Genesis that described the episode and read it aloud. "Ladies and gentlemen," I continued, "just as Potiphar's wife tore the mantle from Joseph as he fled from her advances and shouted 'Rape!' holding up the mantle, so Maria is crying 'Rape!' and pointing to the scar on Eddie's cheek as proof that she fought off her assailant."

Though the D.A. showed real imagination in his defense of Maria, Eddie Martinez was acquitted in less than an hour. Coming to the defense table, he threw his arms around me and kissed me.

Judge Starkey winked at me. "Part of your fee, Sara?" he drawled.

"Yup, Judge," I said.

I was happy. Eddie was happy. Lucy was ecstatic. Maria, however, stalked furiously out of the courtroom. Her progress was aided by her husband, who gave her a shove that nearly felled her.

A few minutes later, I was surrounded by twelve indignant jurors. Angrily, one of them demanded, "Why don't they go after real criminals instead of persecuting a hard-working man like Eddie Martinez?"

Though it was extremely unfortunate that Eddie Martinez had to go through the pain and humiliation of that false accusation and its resulting legal entanglement, he was fortunate that his case was tried before the women's liberation movement—for what I consider well-meaning but misguided reasons—forced through a legislative amendment to the New York State Penal Law that did away with the requirement of corroboration in rape cases.

As the law stands now, a man can be convicted on the mere accusation by the alleged victim of a sexual assault. No corroboration is necessary. Many laymen believe corroboration means that there must be a witness who actually saw the sexual assault take place. This is not true. Corroboration can involve a scratch on the face such as the one sustained by Eddie Martinez, a scream heard, torn garments, broken furniture, physical injuries to the woman's body or sexual organs. The law used to require evidence independent of a mere accusation.

I debated against the new amendment on several radio and television panel shows. On New York's Public Broadcasting Service, Channel 13, I had the opportunity to argue against an attorney from the Appeals Bureau in the office of New York County District Attorney Frank Hogan who helped draft the legislative amendment on sexual assault. Though the attorney was a fine legal scholar, he seemed totally unaware of the emotions that can seethe through a courtroom when a defendant is being tried on a charge of sexual assault. "After all," he stated, "rape is just another form of physical assault, so why should we require more evidence in rape than any other assault?"

My opponent's statements angered me. In my reply, I used much the same arguments I had employed during the Martinez trial. "Have you ever seen a juror recoil in anger merely because of the nature of the accusation?" I demanded. "Do you sincerely believe that a sexual assault is really the same as any other physical assault? How would you feel if someone touched your wife's breast? It's just a touching, but you are angry. You are ready to *beat* the fresh s.o.b. who dared to put a hand on your wife or your sister, your mother, your daughter. You feel you must protect the women in your life. When you face a person accused of a sex crime, you feel the victim might have been one of them. And then again, on the other hand, how would you feel if you were accused of touching the private parts of a young girl? As a defendant, would you feel that this is just an ordinary simple assault, or a degrading accusation which makes you ashamed to lift your head?"

During my debate on TV, my own experiences in defending men accused of rape made me identify strongly with their plight. So often a defendant is innocent of the crime of which he stands accused. I am not saying that all women who cry "Rape!" are as vindictive as Maria Torres. More often than not, they have been sexually assaulted, but many times they are uncertain as to who assaulted them, and they can easily accuse the wrong person. In New York not long ago, a number of women all identified a young man as their assailant, only to change their collective mind when his double was found. In another recent case, a Queens County assistant district attorney was a victim of mistaken identity.

However, when such people appear in a courtroom to answer the accusation of an alleged female victim, they are at a distinct disadvantage; her word can be accepted as gospel truth, and the jury may be out to avenge her honor. Certainly, I am not on the side of the rapist. I am only saying that the emotions aroused by the plight of the rape victim often blind jurors, especially when they hear her cry out, "That is the man!"

In my estimation, we lawyers are not trampling on the rights of outraged womanhood when we demand corroboration; we are merely seeking justice for all.

⑥ | Jungle Habitat

BY MY TENTH YEAR of practice, I was always busy. We'd been getting more and more cases, really building up our Hispanic clientele. "It's all that dancing, Sara," one of my colleagues, with a sense of humor and maybe just a little sense of jealousy, told me. "You and Zapata going to all those big Puerto Rican parties. What does Morris say when you swing and sway to those Latin rhythms?"

"He says, *¡Olé!*" I would quip. I was used to those comments, to the inference that I was working with handsome Manuel Nelson Zapata because he was a man and I was a vulnerable woman who might just be having a little hanky-panky on my big leather office couch—after hours, of course. These suggestions always crop up when a woman goes into partnership with a man. People simply refuse to believe that it is for business reasons. In my case it was, and I didn't give a damn what they thought. It had been á good idea going in with Nelson. Yes, even after ten years, I could still say that the double harness was working well and I was getting around a lot.

Circulating never hurt me at all. Then there was all the publicity we were getting. Nelson and I shared a lot of headlines in *El Diario*—he was always being written up in that paper—and I figured in a lot of stories in *The New York Times,* the *Post,* and the *Daily News* as well. We were working from morning until night; we never made it home until the evening was half over.

That was the only difficult part for me. Morris was always complaining that he never saw me; he also said it was hard on his digestion. Meals really presented a problem, and had ever since I had started practicing law, because Morris felt that as a family we should eat together. When Judy and Jackie were younger and still living with us, Morris had always insisted that they wait until I came home to have dinner. Consequently, dinner could be at six but often was at nine. This was a lot easier to square with the kids than with Morris. We did a lot of arguing in those years, and we were still arguing, even though the kids, with Judy married and Jackie away at college, were no longer involved. The only way I could get around Morris was the way I got around the kids. I told them bedtime stories about what happened to Mama in court, with the emphasis on the funny side of the law. These tactics could work with Morris, too, though the content was different. He got the "For Adults Only" portion, and in order to justify my late hours, I had to stress the serious side of my work. Morris had to understand that practicing law was more than a business with me, it was a mission. Most of the time he agreed with me, but occasionally we did not see eye to eye over a case, and generally these were murder cases assigned to me by the court.

Morris did not really like me to take those court-assigned cases. "You have a big work load, Sara," he would protest. "You're too busy to take these extras. Your health will suffer."

"I don't take that many," I would reply. "I know I used to accept from two to five a day, which added up to hundreds a year, but now I only do it as a special favor to some judge. Unless I'm already in the middle of a trial, I don't feel right about refusing, Morris. Those people need me."

I admit it wasn't always easy for me to take those cases. I did not receive any fee for my services, and the trials could go on for weeks at a time. One trial lasted three months. That really hurt me because I was carrying my share of a huge office rent and also had to pay other lawyers to handle my clients. But I felt a moral obligation toward those indigent clients. There was no Legal Aid Society to fight for the poor then, and it was very difficult for them to get competent legal representation. Competent, I might add, is synonymous with hardworking. It wasn't just standing up in court and representing a person. It required making investigations and interviewing witnesses. This could prove costly; it could also be dangerous. In working for the poor, you needed to go into ghettos, where, for the destitute, crime was often a way of life, and any stranger fair prey. Kids born in these areas had three strikes against them before they uttered their first yell. That was really brought home to me when I told a judge of Kings County courthouse in Brooklyn that I would be glad to do what was called "a service to the court." This was one of those free cases and one that Morris certainly did not want me to take—the story was a horrible one—but even though I shared his compunctions, I could not refuse.

The man I was asked to represent was named Arlo Brown, and he was black. He had been in jail a year on charges Charles Dickens would have understood; this man was akin to Fagin in *Oliver Twist*. He allegedly rented out his gun to young kids for robberies, his payment being a certain percentage of the take.

A year earlier, he had made such a deal with Jackie Tobin and Jimmy Boyd, aged, respectively, fifteen and sixteen. Armed with Brown's revolver, they had gone out looking for a victim and found him on Eastern Parkway in the person of Irving Schwartzman, a salesman on his way home from a hard day's work at a clothing store.

"Hey, mister," one of the kids had said, "can I borrow a dime?"

Schwartzman had looked at them dubiously. "I'll see if I have one."

While he was fumbling in his pockets, Jimmy Boyd had produced his gun, held it to the man's temple, and pulled the trigger. The bullet had shot both Schwartzman's eyes from their sockets. The boys had run, leaving him for dead. But Schwartzman hadn't died; his mental faculties were unimpaired, and he had been able to furnish an accurate description of the last sight he would ever see in this world —those two boys.

The kids had been picked up, and it was then that Arlo Brown had come into the picture. "He gave us the gun," accused Jackie Tobin.

Before I went to interview Brown, I knew he was crippled, but when he was brought into the waiting room at the jail, I had a shock. He looked half-dead. His skin was gray, his dull eyes were set in a skeletal face, and he was bone-thin. He supported himself on crutches, hanging limply between the wooden sticks, his legs trailing uselessly behind him. His voice was as thin as his body, a croaking whisper.

"I never gave them no gun," he wheezed. "Had it around my house, and they found it. They used to come 'n' take it 'n' put it back, wouldn't even tell me where. Sometimes, if they was lucky, they gave me a little somethin'. I never knew how they got it, though. Didn't ask questions."

That was his story, and that was all he ever told me, but since he admitted taking a cut, I had the idea the boys had told the truth; he might not have planned the holdups, but probably he had loaned them his gun, and not for a game of cops and robbers. Still, since I was his lawyer and not his judge, I needed to use his defense. But before I could introduce it in court, it had to be proved. I decided to investigate his apartment and ascertain if a gun could be secreted there and remain undiscovered by the tenant.

Investigation in this case would not be easy. The building was in East New York, which was not a location through which I could stroll at my ease. I needed an escort, and

Frank Zapata, one of my partner's brothers, was elected. Frank is blond, blue-eyed, fair-skinned, a hefty-looking character who resembles a German butcher—there is nothing Hispanic about him. However, he knows his way around ghetto areas, and he has a strong right arm. I needed that arm in an area that looked as if it had recently been visited by a squadron of bombers.

Battered buildings with boarded windows faced broken, refuse-strewn streets. Thin, angry-looking kids congregated on corners. Some of them invaded the streets to play stickball, but mostly games are not their bag. Life is hard and brutal here; either you make it, or you go under. The apartment house where Arlo Brown lived was one of the worst in that neighborhood of candidates for the wrecker's ball. Its dark, ill-smelling halls were cold and dank. When we went inside, I had the feeling we were being watched, but we couldn't see anyone through the gloom.

Arlo's apartment was on the third floor. I had expected it to be empty, but when I opened the door, I found the living room inhabited. A girl of twelve or thirteen was sitting on an old kitchen chair, surrounded by ten other children ranging in age from about two to seven. They were dressed in filthy rags, which, considering the neighborhood, was not surprising. What was surprising was their silence. They were all playing, jumping up and down, gesticulating to one another, but not saying a word.

"Are they deaf and dumb?" I asked the girl, who was obviously their baby-sitter.

"Nope." She shrugged. "They talk."

"But why aren't they saying anything?" I demanded.

"Because I gotta take care of 'em. Parents left 'em here. 'N' I say if I gotta take care of 'em, they gotta be quiet. If they're not quiet, I tell 'em, I throw 'em outa the window."

"But why do you have to take care of them? Some of them ought to be in school."

She shrugged again. "Dunno. Parents don' send 'em to school."

"Do they stay here all day?"

"All day until their parents come 'n' get 'em."

"You ought to be in school," I said.

"Me?" She laughed. "Nobody want me in school. I just come out of the nuthouse, see. 'Sides, I got my own kid to watch." She made a vague gesture at the group, indicating, perhaps, one of the youngest children. Then she looked at me suspiciously. "Why you here, lady?"

"I'm a lawyer. I work for Mr. Brown, who rents this apartment. You suppose you could show me around?"

"Okay, I show you."

Leaving Frank with the kids, I followed her through some four rooms, all leading off a long, dark hall. It was a terrible hole; it looked as if it had never been cleaned. Dustballs on top of dustballs rolled across the floor and congregated in the corners, mingling with plaster that had flaked off the walls. Cobwebs clung to the ceilings, and a large population of cockroaches did not confine their activities to the kitchen. There were also mice scurrying around. I suppose a gun could have been hidden under the filthy square of linoleum in the bathroom or maybe under the cracked tub that was so old it stood on four feet. A thin trickle of water continually dripped from a single faucet, and I had the feeling that it was the only water that ever found its way into that tub. The air was heavy with the smell of urine. There was ample evidence that some of the kids didn't relieve themselves only at the toilet.

Once, walking into a place like that might have made me sick, but in my ten years as a lawyer, I had taken many similar tours through ghetto apartments. This was one of the worst, but it was not the dirt or the mice or the cockroaches that got to me—it was those kids being cared for by a mentally defective baby-sitter who had threatened them into silence. It wasn't natural for children to be so silent. It wasn't natural for ten active children to be cooped up in a fetid apartment when they should have been in school. How would they grow up? What kind of a future would they face? I had the answer to that in Jackie Tobin and Jimmy Boyd.

Even with my investigations on his behalf, my defense of Brown would be weak, but it was all I had. I couldn't let him take the stand. He had a record, and, ironically enough, he had something in common with poor Mr. Schwartzman in that a bullet had turned him into a useless cripple. Ordinarily he would have taken a plea, but because of Schwartzman's injury, practically any judge would have given him twenty-five-to-life. He didn't want to take a plea, and so there was a trial. The codefendant was Jimmy Boyd, who at sixteen was old enough to be arraigned in the Supreme Court; Jackie Tobin was being tried in Family Court. The judge who would be presiding over us was my old nemesis, Samuel Leibowitz, but I was no longer afraid of him. Time had changed things for both of us.

In early 1957, when I was just starting out, Leibowitz, in his sixties, was in his judicial prime; ten years later, he was on his way out. Each year, he had a stay of execution, as it were, and his judgeship would be renewed for another term. At seventy-three, he had about two more years before he would be forced to retire. Consequently, like many another old lion, some of his teeth were drawn, and no longer was the courtroom strewn with the unconscious forms of mangled lawyers. If he waxed too vitriolic, the counsels could retaliate by asking for his removal. With the fearsome specter of inactivity facing him, his growl had become a low mutter, and with me, he positively dripped honey, to the point that if I entered a courtroom where he was presiding, he would actually pause mid-trial, fix his eyes on me, and intone, "Drop everything, drop everything. You see that young woman over there, she's one of the best!"

I'd say, "Gee, Judge, you don't have to stop the trial," but he always made a big deal of it. I had the feeling that he didn't want me to say any more nasty things about him, but by that time I didn't feel nasty. I had actually developed a certain affection for him. I'd learned a lot from him. I was never intimidated by any other judge, for nobody could be worse than Leibowitz—he had been my trial by fire. He had also taught me some very good legal tricks, like giving a demonstration. There was no one better at that than Leibowitz. If there were some point of the defense he did not think the jury understood, he would recruit the court officers and have them play the scene as it was supposed to have happened. That way, he often brought out things the defense didn't want brought out. I learned how I could sometimes use those demonstrations to benefit my side of the story.

Leibowitz and I were really on good terms at last. Occasionally we'd meet in the hall, and once when I was with my friend Marie Lambert, who became head of the prestigious New York Trial Lawyers Association, he said, "Look at you both, two of a kind, that's what you are—two of a kind."

"Oh, come on, Judge," I snarled, copying his intonation, "you know you made a man of me."

"God forbid!" he replied with a wink.

Consequently, when I tried this case before Leibowitz it was different from what it had been a decade before, as far as I was concerned. But Jimmy Boyd had a young lawyer defending him, and Leibowitz, maybe just to keep his hand in, really put him through the wringer. In fact, there were times when he became so vituperative that he himself would growl to the court reporter, "Don't put that on the record," to which my irate colleague would respond, "Oh, no, you don't, Judge. I want that all on the record, everything you've just said to me!"

"Um." The judge would cock an eye at him and then at

the court reporter, and the foul language would not go on the record. Nobody would dare do that today, but ten years ago Leibowitz got away with a lot.

The trial of Arlo Brown lasted about three weeks, and I did my damnedest for him. I fought as vigorously as I could because unless you are vigorously defending your client, you are not doing your job. It was not an easy situation for me. The injured man was in court every day; his family brought him. Before the assault, Schwartzman had used most of his salary to put his son through medical school, an effort requiring great sacrifice on his part and that of his wife. Now the money had stopped, and the boy had been forced to give up his studies. It was the son who now led his father to the stand so that he could describe the attack that had blinded him.

That family really grew to hate me. They could not understand how anybody could defend this animal who had been actually responsible for inflicting that terrible injury. I could feel their animosity washing over me in waves as I sat at the defense table. I said as much to Leibowitz. I felt bad about Schwartzman myself. Here he was, not much past forty, with his whole life shattered.

I also did a lot of thinking about the sixteen-year-old who had done the shooting. He had been completely impassive during the trial, not a shred of emotion on his face. While the jury was out deliberating, I had a discussion with Jimmy Boyd. I said, "Don't you feel sorry for that man? He's totally blinded, and you did it."

He turned his blank face and cold eyes on me. "I don't feel nothin'," he said.

"You don't feel at all sorry?" I persisted.

"Like I said, lady," he replied, "I don't feel nothin'."

"What do your parents—" I began, and then I stopped. "Come to think of it, I've never seen your parents in the courtroom."

"Hell, lady, I don't know if my parents are alive or dead," he said. "I don't know my father. My mother—she's been gone for years."

"You never hear from her?"

"Nope."

"Who do you live with?"

He shrugged. "Sometimes with friends, sometimes on the street."

"On the street!" I exclaimed. "How can you live on the street? Where do you sleep?"

"Hallways—sometimes in the alley, when it's warmer. Sometimes I hole up with a friend."

"How do you eat?"

"Garbage cans."

"How long have you been living this way?"

"Since I was twelve."

It was a horror story, but he didn't seem horrified; in four years, he had stopped feeling anything. His philosophy was simple: he had certain basic needs—he needed to eat and to sleep. If he got tired of the alleyways, the hallways, and the garbage cans, he couldn't go to a friendly neighborhood social worker; they didn't penetrate into his section of the jungle. If he wanted better food and a place to sleep, he had to forage for it like any other wild animal, and in a jungle it's dog-eat-dog and the strongest wins. Armed with a revolver, he was the strongest.

It took me a while, but I think I finally got through to Jimmy Boyd. In asking him to tell me about himself, perhaps I gave him some shred of the identity he had never possessed. He might have been one of those silent children in Brown's apartment, or one of the abused, battered kids who somehow escape ending up in the morgue, but he might as well have ended in the morgue for all the chance he had to make anything of his life.

"Jimmy," I said after our talk, "don't you really feel sorry about blinding that poor man?"

He looked at me. "Guess so," he mumbled. "Guess maybe I do."

It was only a faint glimmer that I saw—or imagined I saw—in those eyes, but if I had made him think, it was something.

However, he would do his thinking in jail, because the jury brought in a verdict of guilty for both Boyd and Brown. I have an idea that Brown died in jail. Jimmy Boyd, however, got a short sentence because of his age. I don't know what sort of a sentence his friend Jackie Tobin, who had done the most talking about the gun and where they got it, was given in Family Court.

After the trial was over, I could still feel the hot eyes of Schwartzman's family drilling holes in me. It was then that Leibowitz became my defense counsel. "You see that woman?" he said to them. "She took that case for free—she did all the investigation on her own. She didn't get five cents out of it. She didn't choose to defend Arlo Brown. She was doing a service to the court."

That made them understand, but there were others who did not understand—there always are, and among my colleagues, too. One of them, a civil lawyer who had watched the trial, said to me, "Don't you think you do a disservice to society when you defend savages like that Brown?"

I looked at him incredulously. "I certainly never expected to hear a lawyer ask me a question like that," I said. "These people have to be defended by a competent lawyer if our present system of justice is to work. A trial is an adversary proceeding. If a D.A. presents all his rehearsed witnesses and the other side has nothing, it's not an adversary proceeding; the defendants take a fast slide into the sewer—every defendant, guilty or innocent. Would you like to see the innocent suffer with the guilty?"

I guess I convinced him, but that was one trial which stayed in my memory; it stayed there because of Jimmy Boyd and his cohort Jackie, because of all the other Jimmys and Jackies I had seen in that crumbling tenement—a building which, I found out later, wasn't even supposed to be occupied; it had been condemned, but there was no one to keep the squatters out.

When the cops found out I had been there, they were appalled. "My God, Sara," they chorused, "half the crimes in that neighborhood start in that very building!"

Why shouldn't they, when the very surroundings show that nobody gives a goddamn for anybody in that district?

The memory also stayed with me because of poor blinded Irving Schwartzman. He wasn't aware of it, but we met practically every day. Though he couldn't go back to his old job, he refused to become inactive. He started to operate a newsstand, selling his papers to me and a lot of others in the very building where his case had been tried.

7 | Fall Guy for a Drug Lord

EVERY SUCCESSFUL ORGANIZATION has its imitators, and the Mafia is no exception. One of its counterparts is located in Harlem and has branches all over the country. Since it is a younger operation, it is not quite as sophisticated as its model. Its leaders have not gone legitimate on a big scale; for the most part they are hoods rather than dons. I had always known that the Black Mafia existed, but I learned much more about it after I took the case of Jackie Lauder. Jackie's first name should have been Patsy, because that is what he was—a patsy for Larry Peck, a small-scale godfather who was the so-called Mr. Big of the drug racket. I first heard about Jackie on a spring day in 1972, when Mary Lauder, his wife, came to see me. A small woman, trim in a nurse's uniform, she settled on my couch and got right to the point of her visit. "My husband's in bad trouble," she told me. "If you can help him, I'll be able to pay you. Not all at once; I'm a nurse's aide now, but I'm studying to become a registered nurse and I'm nearly through with my course."

"Never mind that," I said. "Tell me about your husband's trouble."

"Jackie—his name's Jackie—he's in jail. Some guys up there with him said as how you might be able to help him."

"Why's he in jail?" I demanded.

She sighed. "He's involved in the Howard murder case," she told me, adding quickly, "He didn't have anything to do with it. He's completely innocent."

"Oh." I repressed a shudder. The Howard case had hit the

papers over a year before, but I remembered the ghastly details. Lonny Howard, a narcotics distributor, had been the target of a pair of hit men. They had invaded his apartment, riddled him with bullets, and as an extra precaution killed both his wife and his twenty-year-old daughter. Ironically enough, Howard had survived to tell the tale that had put his assailants behind bars within a week of the shooting.

"What had your Jackie to do with that?" I asked.

Her eyes filled with tears. "They say he was the finger man, but he wasn't. He didn't know what those killers were going to do. That's what he told me, and I know he was telling the truth."

That afternoon, I heard a lot about Jackie Lauder, small-time gambler, alcoholic, and errand boy for Larry Peck, the man who had ordered the Howard killing. As his wife started her story, I had been wondering why such a well-spoken, intelligent woman was involved with a man of Lauder's ilk. I did not wonder long. Jackie Lauder, it seemed, had not always been hanging on the frayed fringes of the drug trade, nor had he always been a gambler and a drunkard. He had started gambling to augment a pitifully insufficient income and, in common with many alcoholics, he drank to forget that the high ambitions of his youth had come to nothing.

During the early 1940s, Jackie Lauder had managed to enroll at the University of Chicago, no mean accomplishment for a young black man. He wanted to become a writer and was majoring in literature. He had completed two years of his course when World War II broke out and he enlisted in the Navy. Obviously, he was officer material, but the Navy officials saw only his black skin and he was assigned to kitchen duty, on which he remained for the duration of the war.

By the time he was demobilized, Lauder was disillusioned and depressed. During his stint in the service, he had married and was the father of a little girl. His wife, a shrewish, demanding woman, nagged him to make more money, and since it was impossible for him to return to school, he utilized his Navy training and became a cook in a Brooklyn hospital. His paycheck was still not large enough to satisfy his wife, so he supplemented his income by betting on the horses. Eventually he began to lay bets for other employees and soon became known as the hospital bookie.

His moonlighting brought him to the attention of the police, and he was arrested numerous times. Generally he served short sentences, but once he remained behind bars for nine months. He began to drink heavily, and his wife divorced him. He was well on the way to becoming an alcoholic when he met Mary Smith, the young nurse's aide who became his second wife.

Despite his depression and his alcoholism, Mary had seen his potential, and shortly after their marriage he yielded to her urging and opened a candy store in Harlem. It did not prosper. The cops, seeking profits and mindful of his former record, kept arresting him on phony gambling charges. Though he complained to the police authorities and even to the mayor's office, no one seemed able to believe that a "known gambler" could be speaking the truth. Finally Lauder gave up his store and took a selling job in a fish-tank store owned by Larry Peck, whom he had met while he was working as a bookie.

Though Peck had been a big-time gambler when Jackie first knew him, he had subsequently gone into the far more profitable occupation of dealing in wholesale narcotics. With Peck in this enterprise was Lonny Howard, his former first lieutenant and now one of his distributors. Howard had his headquarters in the Bronx, where he ran two mills for the packaging of heroin.

Peck later closed the fish-tank store and gave Jackie a job managing one of his other legitimate enterprises, an auto service station in Harlem. Occasionally Jackie was recruited to run errands for Peck, carrying harmless-looking little brown-paper bags from one place to another. Howard was one of those who received them; Peck would send him kilos of heroin on consignment.

One day, Howard was arrested at his mill and taken to jail. Frightened, he sent Peck a request to arrange for his release, but his plea was ignored. A day or so later, however, Howard was released, and on a suspiciously low amount of bail. Fearing that Peck would conclude he had "ratted," Howard went to visit the gangster at his palatial Westchester home to reassure him. Peck received Howard coldly and simply told him he wanted the money for the last consignment of heroin. Promising to collect it as soon as possible, Howard left.

Jackie's involvement began shortly afterward. Two men started hanging around the service station. One hailed from Philadelphia and was known as "Yellowfinger." He was well-dressed and seemed to have lots of money, but he never discussed his business and Jackie had no idea what sort of racket he was in. His companion, however, was well-known and heartily feared by Jackie and many other people. Nearly seven feet tall and very burly, he was named Bert Fowler but he answered to the nickname of "Harry-O." He made no secret of his occupation—he was an enforcer. His activities, as described later at Jackie's trial, included administering terrible beatings to extort the money owed his clients. The beatings were only a sideline; his main business was narcotics, from which he made over two hundred thousand dollars a year.

One afternoon when Jackie was tending the gas pumps, Harry-O and Yellowfinger met with Peck in the service station office. Jackie overheard a snatch of their conversation: "That guy's got to go." "Yeah, he's got to go." After that meeting, Harry-O and Yellowfinger left the neighborhood, and Jackie forgot about them.

One evening about two weeks later, Larry Peck came over to Jackie, who was at the pump. "I haven't heard from Lonny since he got out of jail," he said. "He owes me money. I don't get any satisfaction talking to him on the phone. I want you to go over and put a little pressure on him. Also, you could ask him if he needs any more manita. I got another shipment." (Manita is a composing agent for narcotics.)

Jackie called Howard and arranged to see him at midnight. After he closed the service station that night, he stopped off at a bar for a few shots of booze. There he caught sight of Harry-O in the mirror. He went over to him and asked, "Where've you been?"

"Me 'n' Yellowfinger been out of town," Harry-O replied. "Deal down south. Got back yesterday."

Jackie had a few more minutes of conversation with him and then, mindful of his appointment, said, "I gotta go. Later." "Later" is a slang expression meaning "Be seeing you," but those who overheard and repeated the conversation for the benefit of the court did not translate the term, and the D.A. attached a much more sinister significance to it. He insisted that Jackie meant "I'll see you later tonight." And indeed he did see Harry-O, for when he arrived at Howard's building, a fashionable high-rise on Riverside Drive, Harry-O and Yellowfinger were loitering in the driveway. Waving to them, he went toward the door. If he had been sober, he might have wondered why they were there, but the six shots of whiskey he had tossed off had dulled his reason.

The door to the building was locked, but Howard, who was expecting Jackie, buzzed him in. He emerged into a huge lobby, protected by closed-circuit television and a doorman, who was sitting in a little office near the elevators. Jackie, feeling friendly toward everybody, waved to him, too, and got into the elevator. There was another passenger in it, a white man. Later, when the doorman testified that Jackie had entered the building not alone but in the company of Yellowfinger and Harry-O, the white passenger who could have denied this could not be found.

Jackie's meeting with Howard was amicable. He gave him Peck's messages and had a drink with him. His host then walked him to the door. As Jackie opened it, he saw Harry-O and Yellowfinger crouching in the hall, their guns aimed at the doorway. He froze in terror, and they, leaping to their feet, thrust him roughly aside and ran into the apartment. Scared into sobriety, Jackie fled. Without waiting for the elevator, he dashed down the stairs to the street and then went into hiding. As he later explained to Mary, "I was afraid they were going to kill me, too."

He disappeared for two days, during which time Mary reported him to the police as missing. When he returned, at his wife's urging he called the police, asking if they wanted to see him in connection with the murders. He knew that Howard must have told the police that he had been in the apartment just before the killers had arrived. The cops asked if he wanted to make a statement implicating Peck, but Jackie was afraid. "Okay, okay," he was told. "You're not needed. Howard identified the killers."

A week later, Harry-O and Yellowfinger were picked up in Philadelphia and brought back to New York. Neither man would take a plea, but while they were in jail awaiting trial, Harry-O decided to turn state's evidence. Only Yellowfinger went on trial, and Harry-O testified against him, describing what had happened in the Howard apartment. His story shocked the whole courtroom. Yellowfinger was convicted, but before he was sent to prison, he received a message through the jail grapevine. "Act crazy and get committed to Bellevue. Once you're there, we'll get you out."

Yellowfinger wasted no time in obeying, and his crazy act fooled the psychiatrists at Bellevue, who committed him to the hospital psychiatric ward. Unfortunately, his rescue did not conform to specifications. Shortly after his incarceration, the New York papers headlined the deaths of three patients who had accidentally been given overdoses of narcotics. One of those patients was Yellowfinger.

I happened to have a client who was in Bellevue at the time Yellowfinger was there. The client, John Williams, had come down from Matteawan for the psychiatric observation he needed in order to stand trial. He had been in the bed next to Yellowfinger and had seen the heroin administered.

The D.A. had spoken to Williams in the hope of getting a statement implicating Peck. Williams refused to speak unless his lawyer was present, so the D.A. asked me to come to the jail where he was awaiting trial. When I arrived, however, Williams turned stubborn and refused to talk. Evidently he, too, was afraid of Peck. With the death of Yellowfinger, the chances of snaring the narcotics czar were considerably lessened. The one possibility left was Jackie Lauder. True, he was a very small cog in that large machine, but he was still a part of it. The D.A. issued his orders, and Lauder was arrested.

"He's innocent," Mary Lauder declared as she concluded her story. "He hasn't been near Peck since the murders. He was warned to stay away from the service station. He's been trying to work as a gypsy cabdriver, but he's so scared, Mrs. Halbert—he's so scared of Peck. He thinks they're out to get him, like they got Yellowfinger. But he doesn't know that much about them. He didn't have anything to do with those murders. Peck told him to go talk to Howard, and he went —he always used to run errands for Peck, and this was only another errand. Oh, Mrs. Halbert, do you think you can help him?"

Instinctively I felt that Jackie was important to the D.A. only as bait that the prosecution hoped to use to land the shark, Larry Peck.

"It is possible he may be innocent," I said cautiously. "Anyhow, I'll go and see him and let you know."

Jackie Lauder was imprisoned in the Tombs, a grim Manhattan jail which, after holding generations of the condemned, was itself later condemned. In 1972, however, it was in full operation. When Jackie was brought into the little cubicle where I waited, I received a shock. He looked so familiar that I was sure I knew him, but a second later I realized that he had a strong resemblance to one of Doré's drawings of Mephistopheles. There were the peaked eyebrows, hair growing from a sharp point on his forehead, big, popping eyes, an aquiline nose, and, to complete the likeness, a pointed beard. However, he was a very small devil, no more than five-two in height, and very dark. He gave me an impish smile which revealed a wide gap between his two front teeth.

Though I emerged from my conference with Jackie less convinced of his innocence than his wife had been, he still interested me. He was certainly not the type of criminal I was accustomed to meeting. He was obviously intelligent. He spoke well, and his candor made me want to befriend him. Furthermore, in spite of his long record of gambling arrests, I was almost positive that he was not the sort of man who would coldly and deliberately plan a murder.

However, it was going to be difficult to extricate him from his present troubles, for when he was picked up by the police, he was drunk and he had made an "admission" of sorts. Though he had denied having anything to do with the killings, he had repeated the words he had overheard in the service station during Peck's conference with Yellowfinger and Harry-O: "That guy's got to go." Under further questioning, he had also admitted that he had seen the two gangsters in the driveway of Howard's building. The police contended that he must have known why they were there.

Judge John Murtagh presided at Jackie's trial, which finally took place about eighteen months after the murders. The jury was composed of seven whites and five blacks.

Lonny Howard, a handsome man and obviously well educated, made a very impressive witness. It is not often that
the victim of a hit man survives to talk, but Howard was able
to give a most compelling description of the night's events.
He recalled how Jackie had come to see him and how, as
Jackie was leaving the apartment, the other two men had
rushed in, guns aimed at him.

"I screamed," he remembered. "Then I asked, 'Did Larry
Peck send you here to kill me?' They said they had come to
get the money I owed him. They wanted all of it."

Howard had protested he did not have that much money
around his apartment. They had not believed him. While
one trained a gun on him, the other had searched the room
and come up with three thousand dollars. Then, ripping the
telephone cords from the walls, they had trussed him up in
a way that would have caused him to strangle had he moved
his legs or arms. Going into the back bedrooms, they had
brought out his wife and his daughter, who had arrived from
the South with her baby boy that very day. Both women had
been terrified. Eva, Howard's wife, had gasped, "What do
you want?"

"Be quiet," she had been cautioned, "and nothing will
happen."

Picking Howard up, the two men had carried him into his
bedroom and laid him across the bed. After tying up his wife
and daughter, they had made Eva lie beside Howard and
pressed the young girl down near her.

Howard, who had been lying face down, heard two shots.
Screaming a second time, he had managed to roll off and
under the bed, where Harry-O had pumped bullets at him.
One went through his leg, one pierced his shoulder, and the
third sped through his eyebrow.

Harry-O's testimony later told what happened next. After
they believed Howard to be dead, Yellowfinger had demanded that Harry-O give him his gun. "I didn't," he told

the court. "I was scared he meant to kill me on the spot. So when I wouldn't hand it over, he said, 'Let's go through the other rooms.' We found Howard's grandson asleep in his crib. Yellowfinger pulls out his gun and aims it at that crib, and I said, 'Not the baby, don't kill him. He's fast asleep 'n' he's too small to bear witness, anyhow.' So he didn't do it. Then we went out of the apartment 'n' we met Jackie Lauder downstairs 'n' he says, 'Everythin' all right?' an' we says, 'Sure,' an' we separated."

After the murderers had gone, Howard had managed to extricate himself from his bonds and crawl out from under the bed. Though he was bleeding profusely, he had inched himself up on the bed to where the two women still lay. He had looked at the limp body of his wife, thinking she must have fainted, until upon closer examination he saw the blood and brains oozing from a terrible wound on her head. He had steeled himself to look at his daughter and found that she, too, had been shot in the head at close range. "I held her in my arms," he told the jury in a broken voice. Pausing, he turned to stare directly at Jackie with blazing, hate-filled eyes.

"Do you want a glass of water?" Judge Murtagh asked.

Howard shook his head, and in a broken voice he continued. "After I laid her back on the bed, I crawled out of the room. They told me I left a long trail of blood on the rug behind me. I managed to get to my next-door neighbor, who happens to be a correction officer. He called the police. I could talk a little when they came, and then I blacked out."

It was a horrifying story, and even though it was damaging to my client's case, I was as moved as the jurors. But my emotions did not prevent me from seeing that Howard's testimony had been cleverly molded by the D.A. He still hoped to put pressure on Jackie and scare him into implicating Peck. The whole trial was about Peck, but such was the power he wielded over his domain and his people that all the witnesses twisted their testimony to entangle Jackie.

The prosecution painted the picture of a fictional master criminal, and lowly Jackie was put into that particular frame.

"I knew he was nervous when he came to my apartment that night. I was suspicious about Jackie, the way he behaved when we had drinks," testified Howard under the D.A.'s interrogation.

"How come you didn't say anything about your suspicions and Jackie's nervousness for more than a year?" I asked Howard during my cross-examination. I was really angry. Everyone had known where Jackie was during the past eighteen months. He had communicated with the cops at the beginning. He had been in Gambler's Court when Yellowfinger went on trial, yet until Yellowfinger was murdered, no one had shown the slightest interest in Jackie.

I posed the questions at the trial, but nobody had any answers. Both Howard and Harry-O insisted that Jackie had planned the job. In fact, Harry-O testified that before going to Howard's apartment, Jackie had visited his home. "To give me instructions," he explained blandly. "He also gave me a gun and told me and Yellowfinger to follow him in our car to Howard's place. He rang the buzzer and had Howard identify him via closed-circuit TV, then we all went in and up in the elevator with him."

His lies infuriated me. I was positive that Larry Peck was behind Harry-O's efforts to make Jackie Lauder appear as the man who had plotted the killings. Later, I questioned Harry-O's wife and grown daughter, asking if they had seen Jackie in their apartment.

"Oh, no," they both insisted. "I went to my room at nine P.M.," said his wife. "I knew he was expecting someone. I always go to bed when he's expecting people."

"How is it Jackie gave you a gun?" I asked Harry-O. "You had your own gun."

"I never would've used my gun for that sort of thing," he answered glibly.

"What happened to the gun Jackie gave you?"

"Me 'n' Yellowfinger dumped both our guns in a garbage can after we finished in Howard's apartment. And then Yellowfinger 'n' me, we went to White Plains to Larry Peck's house to collect our money. Lauder didn't come. But it wasn't Peck who gave us our instructions, it was Jackie did that."

Harry-O, enforcer, was one of the most evil men I have ever cross-examined. Though he was a rich man, a big man according to gangland standards, he avoided pointing in the direction of Peck. Evidently, he, like everyone else, was afraid of the gangster, and so it was to Jackie Lauder that his finger pointed. It is particularly ironic to me that Harry-O, by making a deal with the D.A. and turning state's evidence, got off with a short sentence. At this writing, that cold-blooded killer is free.

Without Jackie's statements that he had seen the killers near Howard's building and had heard the conversation in the service station, there would have been no possibility of a conviction; but these statements, along with Harry-O's fabricated testimony and Howard's horror-permeated recital, dimmed his chances considerably. The authorities needed a scapegoat, and as I concluded my defense and planned my summation, I was very worried about the outcome.

I had compared Larry Peck's organization to a vast machine of which Jackie Lauder was a small cog, and I could still use that analogy, only now it seemed to me as if the cog were going to be crushed by that machine. In spite of all the evidence against him, I was sure Jackie had never planned those murders. Part of my feeling was based on my belief that many of the prosecution's witnesses were lying, and part on my growing knowledge of Jackie himself. In jail, where there was no liquor to dull his mind or alter his character, the real Jackie had emerged. I knew that Jackie, and I believed in him. He had become my brother, and I was determined to fight for his freedom.

In my summation, to put the blame where it belonged, I intended to accuse the one man every witness had avoided implicating, the man Jackie had also refused to involve: Mr. Big, Larry Peck. I knew I was heading into the danger zone, but just defending Jackie was so dangerous that no one in my law firm would even come into the courtroom. My associates all told me I was crazy to tangle with Peck, but, crazy or not, I had to state what I believed to be the truth.

Finally, the moment came. "Ladies and gentlemen," I began, addressing the jury. "This is a story of an old-time black man, an errand boy. 'Here, nigger, deliver the narcotics.' That's what he was told. That's how he was treated. Jackie Lauder had been a gambler. There is no question about it. He was a drunk, no question about that. He was a black man who had given up on life."

I told the jury about his background, his university accomplishments, his cruel experience in the Navy, the pressure that had been put on him once he was demobilized. I described how he had drifted into the small-time gambling rackets and how he had met Mr. Big. I scoffed at the accusations other witnesses had leveled at him. He had had nothing to do with any of the big narcotics operations, I insisted. "Does Jackie Lauder have a Cadillac and a beautiful highrise apartment like Lonny Howard? No, he lives in a cheap little walk-up, and he drives a battered old Chevy. This is no big-league gang lord. He isn't in on the planning end of these deals."

Then I really let myself go.

"Ladies and gentlemen, there is an evil spirit hovering over this trial, an angel of death, a macabre chess player. He was the one who said, 'He shall live, and he shall die.' He's the one who called all the shots, and, ladies and gentlemen, he still walks the streets. *He still walks the streets!*"

When I finished my summation, there wasn't a sound in the courtroom and I was totally wrung out. The jurors deliberated for hours. When they finally filed into the courtroom, they had not been able to reach a verdict, and you could tell from the looks that passed back and forth that they were still at loggerheads. A mistrial was declared, and the jury was dismissed.

Judge Murtagh came to me and gave me a compliment that still thrills me. "Mrs. Halbert, I want you to know that you delivered one of the finest summations I have ever heard."

The case had received a lot of press coverage, and the producer and reporter from the Channel 13 television program "The Fifty-first State" had attended every day of the trial and had been present when the disgruntled jury had come into the hall, separating into antagonistic little clusters on either side of the door. It was easy to see that it had been a case of black against white, except that two whites had eventually agreed with the blacks about Jackie Lauder's innocence.

Two days after the conclusion of the trial, Channel 13 devoted a three-hour "Fifty-first State" special to it. There were interviews with Jackie and me, and with a number of jury members, each faction explaining its position on the subject of Lauder. The blacks agreed with me that Lauder was the fall guy for Larry Peck. They were convinced that he was unaware of Peck's plans. They knew that living in the ghetto meant that you were, out of necessity to survive, often blind and deaf to your environment. The whites on the jury, except for the two who agreed with the blacks, insisted that Lauder had known exactly what he was doing and that he had fingered Howard.

The producer of the television show wanted me to repeat my passionate summation and describe Mr. Big, whom, with my help, they had managed to photograph coming out of another courthouse. As he was emerging from the building, I was hiding behind a stone pillar. I pointed him out to the

TV cameraman, and they caught him glaring angrily into the camera. He really looked furious, and I was sure that he was well aware that I had provided the identification. Though I was reluctant to repeat the words of my summation on national television, my anger over Jackie's plight helped me to ignore the dangers inherent in my verbal "fingering" of Peck. Again I described Mr. Big, the macabre chess player, the angel of death, and this time I named Larry Peck.

However, I think the star of the show was Jackie Lauder himself, who spoke beautifully and proved that he had, indeed, the potential to be much more than an errand boy for a gang leader.

A few days after my television appearance, I went into court to hear F. Lee Bailey try a case before Judge Murtagh. The trial took place in the same courtroom where I had defended Jackie Lauder. Bailey's client was William Phillips, the rogue cop who had become famous during the Knapp Commission hearings on police corruption in New York City and who was now accused of killing a pimp and his whore. While I was sitting there, in came Larry Peck's lawyer, whose office was located across the street from mine. During a recess, he walked up to me. "Holy smoke, Sara, what kind of a crazy thing did you do on television?" he demanded.

"What do you mean?" I retorted. "I only told the truth. Everybody was talking about your client during the trial, even if they didn't mention his name. His participation was certainly no secret."

"You have to be crazy," he exclaimed. "The day after the show, he was in my office. 'That bitch,' he said. 'She's going to find out what it means to tangle with me.' He's a dangerous man, Sara. I had a hell of a time persuading him not to go after you."

For weeks after that conversation, I was afraid to put my foot down on the gas pedal for fear my car would blow up.

One day I was standing in the garage waiting for the attendant to bring it out to me. With me was one of the young associate lawyers who had refused to watch me defend Jackie Lauder. "So I'm chicken-livered," he had said. "So I want to live a little longer, Sara."

While we waited in the garage, I noticed a tall, well-dressed black man wearing one of those broad-brimmed pimp hats. He also had big, obscuring dark glasses flat against his face. I recognized Larry Peck, and so did my friend, the fainthearted lawyer. He plucked feverishly at my sleeve, whispering, "Sara, we're getting out of here. C'mon, we're getting out!"

I didn't budge. "You get out," I advised. "If I run, he's going to think I'm scared, and then I'll really have a problem."

Turning on my high heels, I clicked my way up to him and planted myself squarely in front of him. "Mr. Peck?"

He stared down at me. "You're making a mistake, lady," he muttered.

"Oh, come on, I know you're Mr. Peck. You know I know you, and you know me."

"You're making a mistake," he repeated.

"Wouldn't you like to help poor Jackie Lauder?" I demanded.

"Leave me alone," he commanded fiercely. At that point, the attendant brought up his car, a shiny new Cadillac. Leaping into it, he whizzed out of the garage.

"Wasn't that Peck?" I asked the attendant.

"You're damned right," I was told. "He parks his car here all the time."

Three months later, at a trial in the Bronx, I saw Larry Peck again. He had been arrested on a narcotics charge. I walked up to him and said, again, "Mr. Peck, don't you want to help Jackie?"

This time he didn't make any pretense about not knowing

me. "Look, Mrs. Halbert, leave me alone. I got my own problems," he rasped. "Jackie got into trouble because he talked too much. Enough said. Meanwhile, I got my own problems."

"Okay, okay," I responded. "But if you ever change your mind, give me a call."

He has never changed his mind, and Jackie Lauder really needs help. A second jury, handpicked by the district attorney, and all white, saw only the horror of poor, wounded Lonny Howard bending over his dead wife and daughter. Those two horrible murders needed to be avenged, and Jackie Lauder, the alleged finger man, went to jail while Harry-O, the real killer, walks the streets a free man.

Jackie's fifteen-years-to-life sentence is tantamount to life, since he is over fifty and has a long way to go before he is even eligible for parole. However, in losing his freedom, he has found himself and has realized some of that potential he lost down a bottle. He has become the prison librarian, and he carries on an extensive correspondence with women who saw the Channel 13 television show. He is not only a philosopher; he acts as a counselor as well, and his wisdom saved one young woman from suicide. Mary, his devoted wife, now a registered nurse, visits him every week.

I wish I could say that I know Jackie will eventually get his freedom. I can only say that I am going to try to reopen the case. This time, I hope that the verdict will be in his favor.

8 | Incest

ONE OF THE MOST SENSATIONAL and controversial cases I have ever handled involved Francisco (Frank) Ortega, a Puerto Rican man accused of raping and impregnating his fifteen-year-old daughter. When he came to my office, he had already been convicted and had served nine months of a ten-year sentence. However, the case had been taken to an appeals lawyer, who was able to prove that the presiding judge had not been impartial and had exerted undue influence on the minds of the jurors. A new trial had been scheduled by the Court of Appeals.

Frank Ortega's large dark eyes were filled with melancholy, and there were deep lines around his mouth, making him appear older than his thirty-five years. Yet, when I looked at him, I could see no hint of shame or guilt in his demeanor. Almost the first thing he said to me, as he sank down in the chair near my desk, was, "I do not see how she could say such a thing, such a crazy thing, about me; and that judge—he believe her. The way he look at me. The things he say!"

"Never mind the judge," I told him. "Let me hear the circumstances leading up to that accusation."

Slowly, under my careful questioning, the story emerged. He and his first wife, Olivia, had married very young. "We grew up in the same little village in Puerto Rico. We think we are crazy in love, and we were not, either of us, even twenty when our daughter Silva was born. By that time, we knew we were not suited. We fight all the time, and finally Olivia leave me and go home to her mother. I went to the

States, to New Jersey, and after a while Olivia, she get married again and go to live in Florida. The baby stay with the grandmother."

"Couldn't you have taken her with you?" I asked.

He shook his head. "There was no money. Then, when I get a job, I get married again, and soon there is a baby son."

"Did you ever visit your daughter?"

He shook his head. "I could not afford to go back, but Olivia, she visited her. She go back and forth from Florida a lot, but I don't hear much about Silva until suddenly Olivia's mother writes me and tells me she is having big trouble with her."

"What sort of trouble?" I asked.

"She is running around with a man who is too old for her and married besides. She won't pay no attention when her grandmother scolds her. So her grandmother thinks I should come and take her back to New Jersey. I can afford to go, so I do."

"How is it your ex-wife didn't take her to Florida?"

"She is sick and can't go," he explained. "So I go to Puerto Rico and see Silva."

"That's the first time you'd seen her since she was a baby?"

He nodded. "The first time."

"Was she glad to see you?"

He gave me a puzzled glance. "She was very glad. She was excited and laughed a lot. Even when I told her she must come back to the States with me, she was not sad."

As I listened to him, I could well understand Silva's point of view. The arrival of Frank Ortega was something new and exciting in her life, and since she had never had a father-daughter relationship with him and since she was, as her grandmother insisted, man-crazy, she might easily have seen him as a man and not as a father. Under those circumstances, how would she have reacted to his wife, her stepmother? Even at the beginning, it was a situation filled with conflict. The more we spoke, the more I was positive I was right.

"What happened when she came to New Jersey?" I asked.

"We put her in school and arrange for her to have English lessons." He sighed. "That was part of the trouble. She don't like school. She didn't know any English, and it is hard for her to learn it. She came home sulky and cross and cried a lot. She said the other kids laughed at her because she don't speak good."

"Did she start having dates in school?"

"No," he said. "She told me the boys laughed at her."

"Is Silva a pretty girl?"

He shrugged. "She is maybe a little chubby."

"I see," I said. I was beginning to see a lot more. It must have been very difficult for Silva Ortega to accustom herself to a new community where there were not many Puerto Ricans, where she had difficulty in school, and, above all, where she did not even have the consolation of her married lover. Her father was busy at his job every day, and at home there was his second wife and his eight-year-old son. Silva must have felt very lonely indeed.

"Did you have much trouble with her while she was staying with you? Did you ever quarrel?"

He shook his head. "No, we get along fine. I didn't know anything was the matter until suddenly she disappear, and even after that, she wrote me such a nice letter from Puerto Rico."

"She went back to Puerto Rico? How did she manage that?"

He frowned. "My ex-wife came and wanted to see her. I will not have that woman in my house, so I make arrangements that they meet at a neighbor's. Silva didn't come home."

"Did she go off with her mother?"

"Her mother gave her money to go home. Silva told Olivia she was not happy with me. But the first I hear of all this is when Silva say it in court. The letter she wrote me after she ran away, it was very loving."

"What did she say?"

"She said she missed me, but she was very unhappy in the States and wanted to be back in Puerto Rico. She ask me to forgive her for running away like that and making me worry. I was really very worried when she didn't come home. I didn't know what had happened to her. I called everywhere, and I go to the police and report her as missing. I was so glad to get that letter." He sighed and fell into a moody silence.

"Was that letter introduced as evidence at your other trial?"

"No. I told the lawyer about it, but he don't think it is important."

"I think it's very important," I said. "I want you to bring it to me. Now, when did you first hear about this accusation?"

"When Olivia brought my daughter to the factory."

"When was that?"

"Oh, about six, seven months after Silva run away. She send up word to me where I am on the job that she is downstairs and want to see me. So I meet her in a private room. I am very surprised that she should come like this to my place of business, but I learn later that my ex-wife, Olivia, brought her there and said, 'You go up and see your father.' Olivia stayed downstairs."

"What happened when she came upstairs?"

"Well, when she come into the room, the first thing I see is this big belly. I am furious. I say, 'Who did this thing to you, Silva?'

"She says, 'You did it, Papa.'" He paused, his eyes filled with a reminiscent fire. "Can you imagine?"

"What did you say?"

"I said, 'You crazy? How come you tell me such a crazy thing?' "

"And what did she say?"

"She don't say nothing. She bursts into tears and runs out of the room, and I run out, too, and go down to Mr. Harvey, my boss. I say, 'My daughter is here, and she say a crazy thing to me. She says I make her pregnant.' Then I go find Olivia, and she is furious.

"She point her finger at me, and she yell, 'Look what you have done to your own little daughter. You are an evil man.'

" 'It's not true!' I yell back.

" 'I think it is,' she tells me. 'When I saw her in Puerto Rico and I ask her who give her this big belly, the first thing she says to me is, "Papa did it." She was unhappy with you—she tell me that. That's why I give her the money to run away. I am telling the police about you, and you will go to jail for a long time. I hope you rot.' "

Ortega's eyes clouded. "Soon after, they come, the police, to the factory, and they put handcuffs on me and take me away to jail. Mr. Harvey and my wife, Maria, they get me out on bail, and then there is the trial and I am given a ten-year sentence. You know the rest. How can I be in such trouble? Why does nobody believe that I didn't ever do such an awful thing?"

I believed him. He did not seem the type of man who needed to get his kicks by raping his own daughter, and, furthermore, his actions had not been those of a guilty man. A guilty man would not have demanded, "Who did this thing to you?" Certainly, he would not have confronted his employer with the news of his daughter's terrible accusation.

I said, "Look, Frank, I believe you didn't do it."

His whole face lighted. "You are? You believe me?"

"I believe you," I said. "However, the fact remains that

your daughter was pregnant. Somebody did it. Who do you suppose it was?"

He looked at me blankly. "I don't know."

"What about the man in Puerto Rico, the married man?"

He stared at me. "Maybe it could've been him. I am so upset I never think about who did it."

"And neither did your defense counsel, obviously," I said tartly. "Was he possibly of the opinion that you might have been guilty?"

"I don't know. He never say very much to me."

I could almost guess what must have happened. Confronted with a pregnant teenager and her outraged mother, the lawyer might have been disposed to believe that Frank Ortega had, indeed, raped his own daughter. Surely a young girl would not have dared to level such a horrendous accusation at her father unless she were speaking the truth. That is what the judge must have thought. Ortega could not have been a good witness in his own behalf. He was not articulate, nor were his thought processes rapid. He could not perceive obvious conclusions. Blinded by his distress, possibly he had thought that his denial was enough. By the time we had finished our conversation, I found myself itching to get that girl on the stand.

However, I had to wait, and, in the interim, I spoke with many people who knew Ortega. First on my list was Maria, his wife, a short, plain woman with intense dark eyes that radiated the conviction that her husband was innocent. "I would as soon doubt my God as doubt my husband," she told me. "He did not do this terrible thing. He is a good man, and he was good to her. It was not easy for him to bring her here, we are not rich people, but her grandmother said she must go away from Puerto Rico, so he did it, and I encouraged him to have her come."

"Did you get along with her?" I asked.

"Oh, yes." She nodded. "Always." She looked at me in a

puzzled way. "I was amazed when I found out she had been unhappy. Always with us she was very nice, and she did not act unhappy. Of course, she did not do well in school, but that was not our fault. We were shocked when she ran off —and then to come back and say such an ugly thing! My husband is not guilty, Mrs. Halbert. It is the girl who is guilty, and may God have mercy on her soul, for she is a liar."

It was impossible not to believe Maria Ortega. Though she was Frank's wife and therefore not an impartial witness, she was also deeply religious and it would have been a breach of her faith to lie. Ortega was also very religious and had been a deacon in the local Baptist church. The minister of that church also believed him innocent and had supplied some of the bail money; the congregation had taken up a collection to help pay the appeals lawyer. During that second trial, they held daily prayer meetings for Frank's exoneration.

Equally positive of Ortega's innocence was his boss, Frank Harvey, who had also helped pay for his bail. Harvey gave me a very graphic description of the day Silva Ortega came to see her father. "You should've seen his face," he told me. "He came rushing into my office. He was dead white, and he was furious, outraged. He couldn't believe it, and neither could I. He was a real nut about religion. He never would've pulled such a stunt. He was a damned good worker, too. Steady. You could depend on him. He could really turn it out. That's how come I made him foreman. You ought to talk to Mrs. Higgins, our bookkeeper. She likes Frank a lot. She can't understand why so many people believed that girl."

"Would she be willing to be a character witness?" I asked.

"Sure thing, and I will, too. I want to help that poor guy."

By the time I had spoken to these people, I was more than ever convinced that Frank Ortega was completely innocent of the crime of which he stood accused. However, my partner, Nelson Zapata, did not share my convictions. He had flown down to Puerto Rico to interview Silva Ortega, now the mother of a plump baby boy.

"When I asked her if her father had raped her, she burst into tears and ran out of the room," Zapata told me. "She would not speak to me anymore." His own eyes were glistening with tears. "Poor little girl," he said.

"Poor little girl," I mocked. "You've never been able to resist a woman's tears. Let someone cry on your shoulder and you are won over. Did it ever occur to you that she might have been crying because she sent her own father, an innocent man, to prison?"

"Why don't you talk to her, Sara?" Nelson retorted, frowning at me. At that time he frowned at me a lot in the course of a working day. With each case I tried, the seams of our partnership opened a little wider.

I am sure that one more thread fell out when I said, "I don't need to talk to her, Nelson. I believe him. I believe all the people who are ready to testify for him, including a whole church congregation. When I speak to little Miss Silva Ortega, it will be when I have her on the witness stand."

Though I was entirely convinced of Ortega's innocence, I was worried about the process of jury selection. I had the feeling that my brother Dave spoke for a great majority of the general public when he said disgustedly, "How can you defend such an animal?" If I had been able to select the jurors, I would have felt better, but in New Jersey the judge did the selecting. However, I did prevail on him to let me ask each of the final twelve one question: "Please look at me and search your heart. Do you feel resentment or anger or do you have a sense of guilt by association merely because of the nature of this accusation? Please let me know if you feel that kind of anger."

Twelve jurors had assured the judge that they would be fair and impartial. After my question, four of them asked to be excused. As I had anticipated, it was going to be difficult to defend a man accused of forcing himself on his young daughter, a child who was a newcomer to his house, a stranger completely dependent on him.

The star witness for the prosecution, Silva Ortega, finally faced me in the courtroom, and I knew I had one very definite advantage: I had a fund of feminine knowledge that a male lawyer would lack, and I knew just how I would use it.

There was a stir in the courtroom when Silva Ortega climbed onto the witness stand. Though she was close to seventeen and a mother, she wore the skirt and sweater, the flat shoes and bobby socks of a high-school girl, and she did look very young. Otherwise there was nothing remarkable about her appearance, nor was she in the least pretty. Plump and pale, with a flat face and small eyes, she resembled neither parent. Once seated in the witness chair, she stared at me apprehensively. I spoke to her gently as I asked her age. She seemed to relax a little as she furnished that information but tensed again as I continued questioning her in Spanish with the use of a court interpreter.

"Silva, how did you happen to come back to the States after you ran home to Puerto Rico?"

"My mother made me come," she mumbled.

"Why?"

"Well, she came to visit me some six months after I returned to Puerto Rico, and she saw my big belly and she asked me how it happened." She paused, blinking at me.

"And what did you say?"

"I told her I didn't know why I had this big belly. Mama took me to a doctor, and he said I was pregnant. When my mother got angry, I told her, 'Papa did it.' "

"And your mother made you come back to the States?"

"That's right," the girl said. "I didn't want to come, but she didn't ask me any more questions, she just pulled me out of the house, and the next thing I knew, we were on a plane and we came back."

"So you came back and you went to the factory, and then what happened?"

"Mama made me go upstairs and see him."

"Did she go with you?"

"No, she stayed downstairs and had me go alone."

"And what happened then?"

"Well, he saw me and he said, 'What's this, who did this to you?' and I said, 'You did it, Papa." And he said, 'What's the matter, are you crazy?' "

I felt considerable satisfaction. She had repeated the same words that Ortega had used in describing the incident when he first retained me.

"What did you do after that?" I asked.

"Nothing," she said. "I started to cry, and I ran out of the room."

I was even more pleased. Certainly, if she had been telling the truth to Ortega, she would have had a different reaction; she would have been angry and accusing. But she had not denounced her father. In her own words, she had wept and run out. Now, as she faced me, I could see she was becoming very agitated. However, I did not press her. I changed my line of questioning. "Silva, how old were you when you had that big belly?"

"Fifteen," she muttered.

"How long had you been menstruating?"

There was a flicker of surprise in her eyes as she answered, "Since I was eleven, maybe."

"How often do you get your menstrual periods?"

Her surprise increased. "Every twenty-eight to thirty days."

"Well, when you didn't have your period, you must have known what that meant."

She hesitated. "I—I didn't know."

"You didn't know?" I repeated. "Didn't you think you might be pregnant?"

"Well, I—" Tears appeared in her eyes. "I wasn't sure."

"Silva," I said patiently, "your father did certain things to you, wasn't that right?"

"That—that's right." She sobbed.

I sensed a weakening in her, and I raised my voice slightly as I continued. "Wouldn't you have thought that the reason you were not menstruating was because your father had done these things to you? Isn't that right?"

"Y—yes." She wept.

I changed the pattern of questioning a second time. "Now, Silva, you didn't know your father until you met him when you were fifteen?"

"No." She gulped. "I didn't know him."

"Now, let's go back to exactly what happened. You said you were unhappy at home. Did your father ever mistreat you?"

"N—no." Tears ran down her cheeks.

"Until the day he hurt you, of course."

"That's right."

"Was your stepmother there?"

She hesitated and then said, "No, she had gone out."

"Where did she go?"

"She—she went to—to the laundromat," Silva said nervously.

"Did she take your little brother?"

"Yes, she took him."

"Did she take all the laundry to the laundromat?"

"Yes, she took it all."

"That was why she was going to the laundromat. She took all the dirty linen," I pursued.

"Yes, all of it," Silva said.

"Now, you were all alone with your father, isn't that right?"

"Yes."

"Did he take you into the bedroom at some point?"

"Yes," Silva said eagerly. "Yes, he pulled me into the bedroom."

"Did he say what he wanted?"

She paused. "Well, yes, yes, he say something like that. Yes."

"Did he push you onto the bed?" I asked. She nodded, but before she could speak, I continued, "And you said, 'Please, Daddy'? You must have realized something bad was going to happen to you, isn't that true?"

"Yes." She nodded again.

"He pushed you onto the bed, you said? Was there a cover on the bed?"

"No, there was no cover, only sheet."

"Your stepmother had put fresh linen on the bed? Isn't that what she did, Silva?"

"Yes," she gasped. "That's right. That's what she did."

"When he did this to you, he took his pants off and you were struggling and he made you spread your legs and you were crying, 'Daddy, don't do this!' He took his pants off and exposed himself—he got on top of you and he put his private part into you?"

Silva was breathing hard. "Yes, yes, that's how it happened."

"Did it hurt, Silva?" I said softly.

"Oh, yes, it hurt so," she moaned.

"He forced himself onto you and it hurt so and he made you cry and he made you bleed?"

"Oh, yes," Silva responded. "I was bleeding all over, and it hurt so!"

"You really bled a lot," I pursued. "The blood went all over the sheet and he did this terrible thing to you and you were crying and you were bleeding." I had reached the high peak of excitement. Then I softened my tone and said gently, "There must have been blood on the sheet."

"Oh, yes, there was," she asserted.

"What did you do? Your stepmother had just taken the laundry away."

"I—I took the sheet off the bed and I—I washed it."

"You did? But the blood went on the mattress, didn't it? What did you do with the mattress?"

"I—I got Clorox and I—I poured it all over the mattress," she declared.

"That's a strong smell, isn't it? And what did you do with the sheet?"

"I—I washed the sheet and—and I hung it in the bathroom."

"Well, didn't your stepmother come in and say, 'Why is this sheet hanging in the bathroom?'"

Silva looked at me blankly. I continued, "And didn't she go into her room and ask, 'What is this smell on the bed?'" Darting a glance at the women on the jury, I saw them all nodding. I could practically smell the Clorox myself, the Clorox I used to dump in the huge family washes I did when I was younger, but I wanted the men on the jury to smell it, too. Turning to the judge, I asked for a recess.

"Court adjourned," he agreed, "until tomorrow morning."

The following morning, Silva was back on the stand and I was facing her, Clorox bottle in hand. I held it toward her. "You said you poured Clorox on the mattress, Silva?"

"Yes, I did."

"Out of a bottle like this, you poured it?" I stressed.

"Yes, I did," she agreed.

"Do me a favor, Silva," I said, thrusting the bottle at her. "Smell this."

She took a long whiff and coughed violently. "Oh, I—I made a mistake," she gasped. "I—I didn't p-pour it, I—uh—d-dabbed it."

"Did you? Well, let me pass this bottle around the jury. I want the men to smell it."

The bottle was duly passed around, and I saw surprise mirrored on the faces of men who had never before come in contact with undiluted Clorox, the bleach that countless women add to the water when washing sheets. It was obvious that straight Clorox could not have been on the sheets and mattress without everyone in the house being aware of it and asking questions. And why would Silva Ortega have been so eager to destroy the bloody evidence of her father's criminal act, anyway? Well, it was possible to argue that pain and shame had kept her silent, so I left it to the jury members to raise that question and answer it as their logic dictated.

Turning away from the jury box, I went on with my interrogation of Silva Ortega, but my attitude had changed. I was no longer trying to be either kind or gentle. She had already proved herself a liar, and she knew it. She was obviously befuddled, and the time had come to pounce. "Silva, why did your father take you to live with him in the first place?"

"Because my grandmother, she wanted me to—to live there," she stammered.

"Why did she want you to live with him? Isn't it because you had boyfriends she couldn't stop you seeing? Isn't it because she couldn't control you that she sent you here?"

"No, no," Silva shouted angrily.

"And isn't it a fact that when you found yourself pregnant, you wanted to protect the boyfriend who got you in that condition, and so you accused your father?"

"No, no, no," she wailed, beginning to hiccup hysterically.

"Let's go back to that scene in the factory. When you had that confrontation with your father and he asked, 'Who did this to you?' why didn't you say, 'Daddy, you know you raped me?' Why didn't you say that, Silva? Wasn't that the logical thing to say?" She had no answers for me; she was still hiccuping. " 'How can you deny it, Daddy?' Why didn't you say that, Silva? 'You know you raped me, Daddy!' But you didn't say that, did you, Silva? You just ran out of the room without saying anything."

Silva was so shattered she could hardly get down from the chair, and I, glancing at the jurors, saw expressions of disbelief on their faces. I could also see that the district attorney was very nervous. He asked for a conference with the judge. "I want to bring the baby into court," he told us. "That kid looks like Ortega."

I glared at him. "So it looks like Ortega," I repeated. "So haven't you ever heard of a kid resembling its grandfather?"

Frank's employer and his bookkeeper took the stand. Both testified as to his fine character. They mentioned that he was a responsible worker and a very religious man. The minister and several members of the congregation confirmed that testimony. Finally it was time to put Frank on the stand. Before I did, I had a conference with him. Because he was a slow thinker, I was careful to tell him, "You are going to have to convince the jury that you never could have done such an awful thing. There's a lot going for you now, Frank. The jurors' confidence has been shaken and some of them might be in your corner, but we can't be sure. It's up to you to convince them that you are innocent. And you'll need to be damned convincing. If they think there's the slightest possibility that you might have done it, you'll get convicted again. Do you understand me?"

"I understand you," he said. "But can they not see that I am telling the truth?"

"They didn't see it before, Frank, and you told the truth that first time, too. There must be no room for doubt. Now, I am going into everything she said, and when I ask about her testimony, you must answer truthfully from the bottom of your heart. When I ask you if you knocked her down and raped her, I want you to stand up and say, 'No, I am not that kind of an animal!' Do you understand that, Frank? Will you remember to say it?"

"I will remember," he promised.

Knowing his passive nature and gentle disposition, I was still a little worried when I finally faced him. Looking up at him, I said, "You heard your daughter's testimony, Frank?"

"I heard it."

"You heard her say that you dragged her into the bedroom. You heard that, didn't you, Frank?"

He was beginning to breathe hard. "Yes, I heard it."

"You heard her say that you made her spread her legs, that you got on top of her—" My voice was getting louder and louder, and from the look in his eyes, I could see that he was becoming angrier and angrier. "She said you knocked her down and put your private part into her. Did you do it, Frank? Did you?"

He leaped to his feet. "No, no, no! What do you think I am? An animal?" he cried in a voice so full of pain that I was dumbfounded. Here were my own words but uttered with such a scream of agony that I could scarcely recognize them. He had screamed as if he were screaming out his whole life, and for me that crescendo of anguish was too much. My throat constricted, and it was impossible for me to utter another word. In a croaking whisper, I asked for a glass of water, and when it was brought to me, I turned away from the jury and drank it slowly, blinking back my tears. There was absolute silence in the courtroom. No one even moved. It was as though we had all been momentarily turned to stone. When I was able to speak again, I said, "I have no further questions. Your witness, Mr. D.A." The D.A. cross-examined Frank vigorously, but when he came down from the stand, I felt that everyone had shared some of his misery and that everyone wanted him to be freed.

———————

That night, I didn't sleep. I didn't sleep for the next three nights; instead, I walked the floor, framing and pondering my summation. I was dead tired when I finally entered the courtroom to give it, yet the moment I stood before the jury box, all my personal feelings fled. I concentrated on the words that I had to say, the words that might free an innocent man.

I reconstructed Silva Ortega's story, and as my climax I read her letter to her father. It was not the letter of an outraged young girl. She had no denunciations to hurl at him; she had only apologies. "I'm sorry, Daddy," she had written. "Please forgive me." Would a ravished teenager have written such a letter? Would she have written any letter? Wouldn't she have told her mother what had happened, the mother who had been so quick to send her back to Puerto Rico? Wouldn't she have told her grandmother? By the time I finished my summation, I had the distinct impression that the jurors believed, as I did, that whoever had fathered the illegitimate baby, it was not Silva Ortega's father.

Still, as the district attorney gave his final speech, I had some doubts. He spoke well, and there was a certain logic in what he said—false logic, of course, but would the jurors know?

Tensely, I waited for them to finish their deliberation. It did not take long. Soon they were filing back into the jury box. The foreman rose. "We find the defendant, Francisco Ortega, not guilty."

I had scored a victory, but in my mind the biggest victory was the way I had scored it as a woman. Only a woman would have thought to mention Silva's menstrual periods, and only a woman could have led her down that Clorox-scented path to her doom. For Frank Ortega's sake, for the sake of his wife and his little son, I was damned glad that I had had the opportunity to be that woman.

9 | The Voodoo Baby Murder

IN MY YEARS AS A LAWYER, I have had many cases involving the "battered-child syndrome"—infants and young children admitted to hospitals with injuries which have been purposely inflicted, often by one or the other parent. Far too many of these children do not survive even the first year of their existence and are, in effect, brutally murdered.

When such a case is tried, the sympathy of the jury is always with the helpless child. It is difficult for a judge or jury to believe that there can ever be mitigating circumstances. The facts are too shocking, too disgusting, too horrible. Even the court-assigned lawyer defending the accused parent shares the stigma. I know, because a few years ago I stood before an angry jury and an outraged judge to plead for sympathy, leniency, and understanding of a woman named Floria Segura, on trial for the brutal murder of her daughter, Peggy. The child's bruised body had been covered with cigarette and hot grease burns. The autopsy had revealed that she had been so badly beaten that her liver had been literally torn apart.

Our firm was brought into the case by Jaime Segura, Floria's older brother, who came to us shortly after her arrest explaining that he and his family believed her to be innocent. We named a fee, and he left to discuss it at home. A few weeks later, visibly distressed, he returned to tell us that his family was too poor to raise the money.

Meanwhile, Zapata had visited the girl in jail and had taken down her version of what had happened to Peggy. She was, she had told him tearfully, innocent of her child's death.

"I loved my baby," she had said, sobbing. "How could I hurt her?"

Zapata had told me that he found her manner moving and her story plausible. In his notes he had written: "This woman is no killer, and not an insane killer either. She is cogent, reasonable, and rational, and she is profoundly affected by her daughter's death."

Though Zapata and I often had differences of opinion, I usually respected his character evaluations. But I also knew he could easily be swayed by weeping women, so his contention that this woman was no killer failed to impress me. His other notes did. They contained an account of her life history, a sordid tale of betrayal by parents and lovers alike.

Particularly interesting was a suggestion that witchcraft might have been involved in the child's murder. From other Puerto Rican clients, I have learned something about the type of witchcraft in question, and I regard it as a curse on the community. Far too many superstitious Puerto Ricans are terrorized by it, and it is found throughout North and South America and in many Caribbean islands.

It is called *brujería,* and it contains elements of Haitian voodoo and African spiritualism. It is an offshoot of another so-called faith known as *espiritismo,* but it is not nearly so benevolent. *Espiritismo* followers believe in an invisible world filled with the spirits of the dead who are in purgatory working toward divine acceptance and who exert good or evil influences on the living. Its practitioners are dedicated to healing the troubled and afflicted by calling on these spirits and on the Catholic saints. Those who follow *brujería,* however, add devils to the spirits they worship. In *brujería* a curse, spat out in revenge or anger, will supposedly command, confuse, or kill. The exorcising of such curses and of devils is a sacrament of this faith, and in the storefronts or lofts called *centros espíritos* that line the streets of Hispanic ghettos, exorcism ceremonies are frequently carried out by a medium, who also acts as president of the congregation. All the panoply of voodoo can be found in these places— votive candles, ritual dances, animal sacrifices. *Brujería* is also a flourishing business, for nearly all its followers practice some form of it at home, and neighborhood *botánicas* are virtually witch supermarkets, filled with such wares as herbs, roots, perfumes, bats' blood, snake oil, even grave- yard dust, to be distilled into potions which supposedly en- sure good health, bless important undertakings, eliminate rivals, and neutralize curses.

If Floria Segura had been beguiled by that perilous faith, she might, in one sense, be innocent of murder; if there was such a possibility, I wanted to handle her case. In helping her, I might strike a blow at the cult. Too often, judges and district attorneys had insisted that people under its sway should be judged insane. They are not, any more than Holy Rollers, Jehovah's Witnesses, and members of other far-out Christian sects are.

I went to see the presiding judge and explained that our firm had been approached by Jaime Segura. "Since the court must appoint a lawyer for her defense, can't it be me?" I asked. He agreed, and I went to visit Floria in the women's division of the prison on Riker's Island.

The room reserved for the interviewing of prisoners there was drab, unadorned, and so small that its walls seemed as encroaching and as intimidating as the bars outside. The atmosphere limited confidences and stilled conversation. But I hoped for very full communication with Floria Segura. I was not entirely convinced of her innocence. If I came away with any feeling that she was guilty, as a mother who adored her own two children I would have difficulty in de- fending her.

Floria Segura was a small young woman, stoop-shouldered and slightly plump. She wore an ill-fitting dark dress, a faded blue cardigan, and flat shoes. Dragging her feet, she sat down listlessly in a chair and stared at me out of slightly protruding brown eyes, wide-set in an olive-skinned face framed by black, neatly combed hair. She might have been pretty if despair had not dulled her eyes and stiffened her mouth. Her gaze slid away from mine to linger on the tightly clasped hands in her lap. She said nothing.

As I looked at her, my doubts as to the accuracy of Zapata's statements began to evaporate. In spite of the charges against her, she seemed pathetically vulnerable. In her large eyes, I saw the mute anguish of the trapped animal.

I was glad I had mastered Spanish; I needed to speak to her in her own language. Leaning forward, I said gently, "Floria, I am Sara Halbert, your lawyer."

It was very difficult to draw her out. Though it had been a full six months since her arrest, she seemed in shock. At our first meeting she hardly spoke; she only nodded. Finally, she responded to one of my questions—in English, which we spoke thereafter. It took many more meetings before I had her trust and, piece by piece, her story. I was certain it was the truth.

Floria Segura, the seventh of eleven children in Puerto Rico, had been six when her family moved to New York. Shortly after their arrival her father died, and her mother, forced to care for her many children, became more a strict disciplinarian than a loving parent. Floria, a timid, withdrawn little girl, seethed with repressed anger against her mother. Deeply in need of understanding and affection, she found none in her home. Her brother Jaime, thirteen years her senior, was the only one who cared for her, but he did not live with the family. At eleven, the desperately unhappy child found the equivalent of love with a man twice her age and ran away with him to Puerto Rico.

Her infuriated mother traced her through relatives and followed her to Puerto Rico, where she placed her in a strict

Catholic home for wayward girls. Floria remained in the institution for two years. Then she could bear the isolation no longer, and again she fled. She lived like any stray, foraging for food in the fields and stealing it whenever possible. Many men sexually abused the little girl, but only one, Angel Felipe Rodriguez, offered her a home. He was old enough to be her father, but he was the first man who had wanted her to share his life. Docilely, she went to live in his dirt-floored shack.

Before her fifteenth birthday, she became the mother of a baby girl, Ida, whom she loved desperately. By this time her lover had taken to smoking marijuana and drinking to excess. When he was drunk, he beat Floria. Fearing for the safety of herself and her child, she ran away a third time.

Destitute and frightened, she managed to get word to her brother Jaime. He flew to Puerto Rico, saw her, and made arrangements to bring her and the baby to live with him in the Brooklyn apartment he shared with another brother. He also helped her to get a job cutting thread in a garment factory for forty-three dollars a week. During her off hours she played with little Ida. By the time she was sixteen, however, she had become very restless. Possessed of a primitive, sensuous nature, she craved male companionship. One Sunday morning at church, she met Hernando Vallejo.

Vallejo was a quiet, nice-looking man with a gentle manner. He had a low-paying job in a shoe factory. Two weeks after their first meeting, Floria moved in with him. It was an off-and-on arrangement that lasted some five years and brought the couple a daughter named Peggy, born when Floria was about nineteen. By then she was growing restless again. Though Hernando was kind to her, he was also stingy, and their quarrels over money had resulted in her leaving him more than once, taking the children with her. She supported them by factory jobs, increasing her salary each time. For one eight-month period, she worked in a lamp factory earning sixty-six dollars a week, the most she had ever made. Finally, in March 1973, she made a complete break with Vallejo and, taking the children, moved into a fifth-floor walk-up on South Street. She got welfare support by explaining that her husband had deserted her.

She did not remain alone long. During one of her separations from Vallejo, she had met Ray Morales, the manager of a *centro espírito* on Bedford Avenue, a few blocks from her house. At this point they became lovers, and, soon afterward, Peggy's troubles began. Floria, however, was amazingly unaware of the causes.

"One morning," she told me, "I had to go talk to the people at school about Ida. Ray, he baby-sit Peggy for me. When I come back, he say to me, 'Look, Peggy is sick.' I look, and I see her face all puffy and red. 'What happen?' I ask. 'Did she fall or something?' He shake his head. 'I don't know what happen, but maybe we better get her to a doctor.'"

They took her to the emergency ward of Cumberland Hospital, where Morales called himself Luis Vallejo and professed to be the child's father. Through my investigations, I learned that when Floria was out of the room, he told the authorities that she had beaten the baby, attempting to absolve himself of any complicity in what was clearly a case of child abuse.

Both parents, nevertheless, were accused of abuse and neglect when the case was reported to Family Court. The baby was kept in the hospital ward for observation and treatment. Floria was bewildered by what she considered to be an unjust accusation and fearful that her daughter would be taken from her. Morales suggested that she abduct the child, which she did, and the hospital authorities simply dropped the matter.

The Family Court had also determined that Morales should stay away in the future from Floria and the two children. "I don't know why," Floria said. "He didn't do nothing wrong."

I was beginning to think that Ray Morales had done quite a bit that was wrong, but I merely said, "Did he still visit you?"

"Oh, yes," she replied. "He was very nice, very good to me. He make me very happy. I don't see why he shouldn't come."

An intelligent, observant mother would have realized that little Peggy's injuries had occurred while Morales was baby-sitting, but Floria was incapable of deductive reasoning. She acted impulsively and out of animal needs. She needed Ray Morales—he was a good lover. She did not see beyond that. Home from the hospital, Peggy cried incessantly, day and night, and Morales suggested that the baby might be possessed by devils. Floria, a lapsed Catholic, did not believe in *brujería,* but at his urging, and, I believe, only to placate him, consented to have Peggy's "demons" exorcised at a ceremony in his *centro espírito.*

Her description of the ceremony chilled me. "The room was hot, very hot, and it smelled of perfume and incense. The air, it was very heavy. Ida and me, we could hardly breathe."

"You took Ida, too?"

"Hadn't nobody to leave her with," Floria explained. "Ray was at the *centro.* Ida was scared. We were both scared. There were these people in long black capes and big animal masks, very big, very ugly. Ray told me they were witches. I don't want to give Peggy to them, but he say they scare out the devils."

"What did they do with the baby?" I asked.

"They put her on a big, long table. Ray say it is an altar. It is covered with a dirty old black cloth, and there are big, tall black candles on it. They take off Peggy's clothes and rub oil all over her body. She don't like it. She scream and yell, but Ray tell me that is because she is possessed and her devils are afraid. I say maybe she is scared, but he tell me I don't know nothing about devils." She shuddered again.

"They, these people, they seem like devils to me. They jump and yell and scream around Peggy and ever so often they throw water on her—Ray says it is holy water—and—and then they grab her up and they're chanting all sorts of words I never hear before and then they start throwing her back and forth like she is a ball, and all of a sudden I see big black dolls, they come out of the darkness and they are thrown, too, and Peggy's eyes are big, big, they look like they are coming out of her head and she is screaming so loud and I know she is scared out of her mind. I can't stand it no more. I run in and I grab her away from them. Ray laugh at me and try to grab her back, but I don't let him. I take Ida's hand and all of us we run and run and run until we get home. I never want to go back there." Tears filled her eyes. "I wouldn't have gone, neither, only—" She paused, shaking her head.

"You did go?" I asked.

"Well, Ray, he told me the devils weren't out of her because I didn't let them finish. So she is still yelling a lot at home and I thought I—I would see if—if maybe he was right. But it didn't do no good."

On a hot Friday in July, Floria left her two children with Morales when she went to the welfare office. Her landlord had raised her rent, and she hoped welfare would increase its payments to her. She could not afford a baby-sitter, and she did not dare let the children stay alone while she made the long trip to the welfare office, at the other end of Brooklyn. When she arrived at the office, they took her name, noted the time she had arrived, and gave her a number. Hours later, after lunch, they finally called her. When she told the clerk about the rent raise, he asked for the landlord's official notice. She had not received it. The clerk told her he could do nothing without the paper and advised her to speak to her landlord and come back again. Her all-day wait had been in vain.

Tired and dispirited, she started home. She did not arrive until close to four. When she came into the apartment, she found Peggy, Ida, and Morales on the couch. He was brushing Peggy's hair, but the baby looked very ill. "Like dying," she later testified.

" 'What happen to Peggy?' I ask. He don't answer me. He say something peculiar. He say, 'You try to come in here earlier this afternoon?' "

"I say, 'No, I come now. I been in the welfare office all day. They don't give me money. They say I need paper."

He ignored her explanation. "Somebody try to open the door three times, and I told Ida to see who was there and she say 'Nobody.' "

"I tell him again, 'I come now.' And I take the baby from him and hold her. She look terrible, and she throw up all over me. I want to take her to the hospital, but Ray won't let me do it. He remind me about Family Court, and he say better not take her. I say, 'Look how sick she is,' but he don't pay no attention. He say he has to go. I tell him, 'But she is so sick, please stay and help me take her to the hospital.' He tell me if I take her to hospital, they keep her and not give her back to me no more. Then he go, real quick."

"What did you do?" I prompted as she fell silent.

"I change her diapers—she is all wet—and then I put her in crib, but she don't look good to me. An' something has happen to her forehead. It is swelling up and turning purple. I don't know what to do. I still want to take her to hospital, but I am afraid, and then Hernando comes because it is Friday and he has money for me." (Peggy's father visited every Friday after work to see the baby and bring Floria money.) "He look at her and want to know why is her head all swollen. And then he show me something I haven't seen. On her stomach under her blouse there are big bruises. I tell him I don't know how they come."

Vallejo asked Floria if she had taken the child to the hospital. Remembering Morales's warnings, she assured him that they had just returned. He asked her to prepare a *malta* for the child, a punch made of beaten egg and malt. She went into the kitchen to make it, but she was too upset to do anything except stand there wondering what had happened to the baby. Hernando angrily made the *malta,* but when he tried to feed it to the baby, she threw up again. His anger and his concern increased. He and Floria had an argument, and she ordered him out of the house.

"I call you later," he told her, "and the baby better be well."

"What did you do then?" I asked her.

"I don't know what to do. I am so scared about Peggy. I keep going to look at her, and she lie so quiet. I don't know if she's just quiet or if she is sleeping. Finally, I decide she must be asleep, and I draw the blinds and go into the other room. Then Hernando call me and ask how is she? I tell him I think she is better because she is sleeping. But after I hang up, I tell Ida to go look at her, and she comes running back saying she looks funny. I go into the bedroom, and she looks so pale and her skin is so cold and her whole body and her face—they are swollen and black and blue. And she lies so still, so still, and she don't seem to breathe at all."

Tears ran down Floria's cheeks as she talked. I put my arms around her and soothed her.

"Don't cry," I told her gently. "I am sorry I have to make you go through it again, but it's necessary."

Floria could not give me a clear account of what had happened; I had to piece it together. From what I could gather, she decided to take Peggy to the hospital even if it meant losing her. However, she needed help. She ran to the *centro* to find Morales. He was there sweeping the floor, and his brother Efraim was with him. She told Morales about the baby, begging him to help her, but he would not pay any attention. He told her to go away, he was busy; but she insisted, and, probably because she was screaming and he was afraid of a scene, he finally agreed to accompany her back to the apartment. His brother went with them.

"They come to the bedroom," Floria said. "They look down at Peggy and—and Ray says, he says"—she began to cry again—"he says she's dead. I can't believe it. I—I pick her up and—and—hold her and she is so cold, so cold. And I talk gentle to her and I try to wake her up but her eyes are closed and they don't open and she is so cold. . . ."

At Morales's suggestion, Floria called the police. Also at his suggestion, she told them that Peggy had fallen from the crib. Maybe that was what had happened, she did not know. Even though the child had sustained similar injuries the last time Morales had baby-sat for her, Floria still did not connect the two incidents.

The police officers arrived a few minutes after Floria's call. They were joined by a patrolman and two detectives. The men examined the child and curtly demanded to know what had happened to her. Morales did the explaining.

"He tell them she fell from the bed, and the floor hit her and also a bedpost," Floria said. "Then they tell us they will be back after they have spoken to the medical examiner, and they go away again. One man, he stay with us until they come to take Peggy to the morgue."

"What happened after that?" I asked.

"Well, Ray is very nice to me. He take me and Ida and we go to his parents' house and we put Ida to bed and then we sit up and talk the rest of the night. He ask me about Hernando, if he come to give me money. I tell him we had a fight and I also say I wish I'd taken Peggy to the hospital because if I had she might be still alive. But Ray, he tell me it was the spirits done it to her. He say they come three times and knock on the door. He says he heard them knock, and he says that Peggy is free of the devils now and just to make sure he is going to light candles to banish any other spirits in my apartment when we go back. He goes and lights candles and prays over each of them and he says that way me and Ida will be safe. But I don't care about the spirits. I want him to call the police and find out what happened to the baby. Maybe they know what kill her."

"You didn't think it was the spirits?" I asked.

She shook her head. "I don't believe in spirits. Ray, he does, but I don't."

That morning, Morales called the police and was told to bring Floria to the station. When they arrived, they were told that the detective who wanted to question them would not be on duty until four that afternoon. They spent some of the intervening time walking around the neighborhood; eventually, they went into a coffee shop for lunch. Floria noticed that Ida shrank away from Morales and would not sit near him.

At length, they returned to the police station and waited for the detective, who arrived promptly at four. Detective Walter Crosby was one of the men who had come to the house. Crosby, after questioning Morales and Floria for a long time, arrested the young woman for murder, and when she was unable to raise the high bail she was sent to the Riker's Island House of Detention for Women.

The dates for the preliminary hearings and the trial were finally set for October 1974, more than a year after the baby's death. In preparation for the trial, I had tried to speak with as many people connected with the tragedy as I could find. One of the first persons I had tried to contact was Floria's former common-law husband, Hernando Vallejo, but I could not locate him, nor could the investigator we sent out. However, I had a feeling I knew why he was proving so elusive. Ray Morales had, of his own accord, come to see me at my office and had told me that Vallejo had confessed that he had killed the child. Zapata had Morales sign a statement to that effect.

I knew, however, that Morales would be appearing as a witness for the prosecution, and I asked him why he had come to our office. "It is only to explain what happen that night. Do not worry. I say nothing to injure Floria. She is innocent and I love her," Morales assured us.

He had said much the same thing in a letter to the girl. Dated the prior January, it had begun, "My unforgettable love," and read in part:

> I met your husband who came to insult me with many bad words. I asked him what did he want from me and he answered nothing. He told me that what he had to do, he had already done to the most innocent one, who had no fault, he had to revenge himself that way since he could not do it to you directly, but the best way to make you suffer was to eliminate his image or portrait, his daughter, although it would make him suffer as well, but he had to do it. Even though he may go to jail and be sentenced for many years, still he was satisfied that he had you incarcerated also.

Floria had given me all the long, effusive letters written to her by Morales, and when she handed this one to me, she said, "You see, it is Hernando who has done this terrible thing."

Even though Vallejo had not arrived at her apartment until *after* Peggy was ill, she believed Morales, and since I had been unable to question her ex-husband, I was inclined to believe Morales, too. He had been very cooperative when he had spoken to us. In fact, I was depending on him to clear her at the preliminary hearing, as was Floria.

I had received a report from the district attorney's office containing the information that Floria had made an oral confession to Crosby stating that she had beaten her child to death. According to the detective, she had also admitted dangling her out of the window and pouring drops of hot oil on her. The spirits made her do it, she had said. However, when I confronted her with this statement, she went into hysterics, swearing she had made no such admission to Crosby.

The purpose of the preliminary hearing was to test the legal admissibility of the oral confession. I was hoping that with Morales's cooperation it would be thrown out of court. I knew how police could coerce witnesses, and I was sure that Crosby had asked the questions and that Floria, deep in shock, might not even have heard them. From my own experience with her, I knew she had a habit of silently rocking back and forth in grief. A cop looking for confirmation might have decided that any forward motion spelled acquiescence. She told me she had never said she had killed the baby—neither to the cops nor to the district attorney who had come to the precinct to question her. I felt, also, that when Hernando Vallejo was found, we would know who the real killer was.

Enid Cruz, my former secretary, then a first-year student at Brooklyn Law School, assisted me throughout the trial. It was her first "real" trial experience. We arrived at the court bright and early on October 23.

The first major witness was Ray Morales, who in a firm voice promised to tell the whole truth. The smile he wore embraced the whole court, but he also had a tender glance for Floria, seated between Enid and me at the defense table. My opponent, Assistant District Attorney Tom Davenport, stepped forward. I have never relished facing Davenport in court. It seems to me he has an avenging-angel complex and considers himself a Defender of Justice with a capital D and J. A tall, hefty man with a habit of talking out of the side of his mouth, he has intimidated a lot of witnesses. However, since Morales was his witness, he was very considerate of him. Slowly he took him back over the sequence of events on the night of the murder. I thought he would never get to what I considered the crucial question, but finally he got it out. "You talked with the defendant on that night, Mr. Morales?"

"Yes, I did," Morales answered.

"Did she tell you who killed the baby?"

"Yes, sir, she did." Morales looked him straight in the eye. "She told me she killed the kid."

I was stunned! His words reverberated through my head like a shot from a cannon. Beside me at the table, Floria, after one stricken look at the witness stand, started to weep. *"Dios mío, dios mío,* how he say this?"

Enid flung a protective arm over her heaving shoulders. I sat there frozen. Surely he knew I had all his letters to Floria and the signed statement regarding Hernando Vallejo's guilt which he had voluntarily given to Zapata. Then I recalled that a few days earlier, while visiting Floria in jail, he had asked her to return the "unforgettable love" letter and had been furious on learning that she had given all his correspondence to me. Now I knew why.

Morales was not content with a mere declaration of Floria's guilt. Glibly he described just what had been done to the baby. The court heard that Floria had struck her, thrown her against the wall and the bedpost, burned her with hot oil and cigarettes, placed her in an oven, and dangled her out of a window. He added that Floria thought it might have been the spirits who had killed the baby, but that he had soothed her, explaining, "It could not be the spirits who did this."

Listening to him, I was appalled less by the content than by the significance of his accusation. His description was so graphic that it was impossible to disbelieve it. By the time he had finished, I knew who had tortured that baby—it had not been Floria Segura, but her jealous lover, Ray Morales. However, Morales was not on trial. Floria was, and he had dealt her a most damaging blow. The only way I could hope to neutralize the harm he had done would be by the process of cross-examination.

Shortly after Morales had given his electrifying testimony, we had a recess. Much to my surprise, he approached me in the hall outside the courtroom, where Enid and I were talking with Floria's brother Jaime. Ignoring the furious looks that Jaime darted at him, Morales asked if he might see me privately. He added that he wanted to help Floria because he knew her to be innocent.

"Son of a bitch!" Enid whispered explosively. "First he buries her, and now he wants to help her!"

"Don't worry," I whispered back. "I can handle him."

Accompanied by Enid, I led him into a small conference room. I was determined at least to expose him as a liar. It was as Mama Lawyer that I faced him. I was gentle and understanding. If I longed to box his ears, he did not know it. I invited his confidences. He seemed despondent and remorseful, eager to extricate Floria from the predicament in which he himself had placed her.

"I want to help her," he repeated.

"By accusing her of murder?" I inquired. "You didn't help her much when you were on the stand."

"Let me tell you what happened," he said eagerly.

I took down his statement verbatim. In essence, he claimed that the police had forced him to say Floria had confessed to him; otherwise they would have arrested him. He described how, on the night of her arrest, they had kept him and Floria in separate rooms for many hours, with the detectives going back and forth between them, alternately interrogating the two of them. The police finally told him that Floria had said she had admitted killing Peggy to Morales. This is a common trick in police interrogations. Potential suspects are kept apart while they are questioned, and alleged statements by one are used to trap the other into damaging admissions.

Morales said he had become so frightened and nervous that he had told the police everything they wanted to hear, and when the assistant district attorney came to the precinct with his stenographer to take down the statement, he had repeated the lies because he was still afraid to tell the truth.

"You never saw Floria hurt her children?"

"Never."

"Then who did kill Peggy?" I asked.

"Hernando Vallejo," he said predictably.

With Enid as witness, I had Morales sign a statement. Thinking I had the case in the bag, I went back into the courtroom.

On my cross-examination, Morales admitted that he worked at the *centro*, that they practiced witchcraft, that he believed in spirits possessing people and making them "do things." I tried to show the court and jury that the spiritualistic beliefs attributed to Floria were actually Morales's own and that the confessions she had allegedly made were *his* confessions, stemming from those beliefs.

I badgered him repeatedly, trying to get him to admit that he had been in Floria's house watching both children on that fatal day. Furiously, I shouted, "Isn't it a fact that she left you in charge of the children when she went to welfare, and when she came home, the child was dying?"

He squirmed in his seat. "I would not be able to know that, because I was not there."

"And isn't it a fact, sir," I continued doggedly, "that you told her not to take the child to the hospital because of the previous report of injuries to the child, when you brought her to the Cumberland Hospital?"

Davenport leaped to his feet with an objection.

"Overruled," said the judge.

Morales had to answer. "No."

He was still lying to protect himself from a murder charge. I decided it was time to spring my first bombshell on the court. I asked Morales if he had spoken to Hernando Vallejo about this incident.

"Hernando," he responded, "told me he had killed his daughter."

The courtroom became very quiet. I glanced over at Tom Davenport. He had turned white. I couldn't blame him. Judge Barshay's eyes were bright with anger. Everyone, including the clerk and the court officers, strained forward. Enid's hand was on Floria's arm; Floria stared at Morales blankly. It was a propitious moment to toss my second bombshell.

"Did you tell me during recess that Floria never admitted killing the baby to you, but you only said it to the police because if you didn't, you'd be accused, and you would go to jail?"

"Yes."

"So she never told you that she killed the baby?"

"Never. The police force me to say she did."

"No further questions."

A shaken Davenport tried to rehabilitate this oscillating, lying witness. "Did Floria Segura tell you she threw her baby against the wall?" Davenport bellowed.

"Yes," Morales said.

"When did she tell you that? When?"

"The day of the death."

"Did you tell the police the truth?"

"At that time, no, because in other words I told them the truth according to what they asked me."

"Was it the truth that Floria Segura told you she had thrown the baby against the wall?"

"I told them that."

"Did Floria tell you that?" Davenport shouted.

"Yes."

"Then it was the truth you told the police, wasn't it?"

"Yes," Morales replied, "but I had been forced. The detective said to me that he got it out of her."

Davenport took out some grand jury minutes and quoted from them. Had Morales said this to the grand jury or that? Yes. Now he was changing his story again. No. Yes. No. Yes. It was dizzying.

"Tell us," Judge Barshay interrupted, "tell us those things she told you she did to the child."

Morales said, "She admitted she killed the kid."

Barshay threw his hands up in disgust. "Arrest this man for perjury," he ordered.

The court officers pulled Morales from the witness stand. Clapping handcuffs on his wrists, they led him off to be jailed at the Brooklyn House of Detention.

I had another shock when a Puerto Rican patrolman named Godofredo Perez said that at Detective Crosby's request he had spoken to Floria and in an oral confession to him she had stated that the spirits had ordered her to kill her daughter.

Barshay ruled that Floria's oral confessions to Morales and the two police officers, "having been voluntarily made," were admissible evidence at the trial to be weighed by the jury as questions of fact. This meant that it would be up to the jury to determine whether or not the confessions had been made and, if they had, whether they had been made voluntarily, before proceeding to the question of their truthfulness. He further ruled that the jury was not to be advised that Morales had been arrested for perjury.

If I got nothing else from that hearing, I got this: I was not yet finished with Morales.

I spent a great deal of time before, during, and after the hearing discussing with Judge Barshay and the D.A. as to whether I should have Floria plead insanity. Though he had been on the bench for many years, I believe the judge had never dealt with cases involving *espiritismo* or *brujería*. He was inclined to believe that the whole thing came under the heading of "mumbo jumbo" and that everybody involved with it was crazy. He suggested that I plead Floria not guilty by reason of insanity, or, since I insisted she was sane, guilty of manslaughter one (an inadvertent act of homicide in the heat of passion) or manslaughter two (homicide through a reckless act, without intent to kill). The sentence would be the same, as far as he was concerned.

As part of the plea-bargaining process, I discussed the latter plea with Floria. Leaving little Peggy with a man who had already injured her did come under the heading of extreme, if not criminal, negligence. However, each time I introduced the issue, she became hysterical. In common with many of the women accused of such crimes, she was unable to hear even a hint that she might have been partially responsible for Peggy's death, nor did the promise of a short sentence make any impression on her. "I love my baby. I never kill her. I never say I kill her. I will go to jail all my life but I will never say I kill my baby."

Since I was convinced of Floria's innocence, when the trial opened on Monday, October 29, our plea was still not guilty.

The jury selection was long and difficult. Many prospective jurors asked to be excused when they learned the nature of the case. Just from hearing the accusation, they knew they could not be unbiased. Finally we selected twelve jurors, eleven men and one woman, and two alternates, who swore they would be fair to both prosecution and defense.

The State's first witness was Dr. Dominick J. DiMaio, at that time deputy chief medical examiner for the Borough of Brooklyn, now chief medical examiner for the City of New York. I don't think I have ever been at a murder trial without encountering this remarkable, highly professional pathologist. At the time he appeared at the Segura trial, he had performed more than eighteen thousand autopsies.

Once I asked him what he felt when he conducted an autopsy. "You must see some pretty ghastly things," I said.

"I do," he answered, "but long ago I trained myself not to feel anything." However, his objectivity lessened when it came to children. "I get a knot in the pit of my stomach—no matter how used you are to death, how can you be completely dispassionate about the death of a child?"

Evidently the cruel death of little Peggy had aroused him. His medical testimony did not make pleasant listening.

After he had finished, Davenport asked, "Doctor, as an expert, based on these findings, could you reach a conclusion as to the cause of death?"

"Lacerations of the liver, contusions of the intestines, laceration of the mesentery with intraperitoneal hemorrhage, contusions of the body, abdominal wall, and scalp."

We broke for lunch, and I used the time to prepare an order to produce Morales from jail to testify for the defense. When the trial resumed, Davenport's next witness was Hernando Vallejo.

I had never seen him before. He was so different from Morales it was difficult to imagine how the same woman could have been attracted to both. Though both showed black lineage, Vallejo, the darker of the two, was taller and better built than the small, slight Morales, and there was something likable about him, an honesty and a sincerity completely lacking in the latter man, whom I found oily, obsequious, and devious.

Davenport used Vallejo's testimony to point out the sequence of events occurring on July 21. Vallejo related the conversation he had had with Floria regarding Peggy's bruises, and he revealed the lie she had told him about having taken the child to the hospital.

During my cross-examination, I asked him how well he knew Morales. He replied that he had seen him twice, at the police station and at the funeral home where the wake for Peggy had taken place. He later added that Morales had offered him money to pay for part of the funeral expenses. "I told him, 'No, thank you.'"

He had no way of knowing that his rival had accused him of murder. I said, "Mr. Vallejo, did you beat the baby that night?"

My question shocked him. "No!" he cried.

Davenport leaped to his feet seething with objections.

Maybe I was a little out of line when I asked that question, but I was sure Vallejo could not have hurt his little girl. My question was intended to implicate Morales.

Judge Barshay crisply reminded the jury that the question was not evidence; the answer was. "Under no circumstances may you draw the inference that he beat the baby. The answer is 'No.' That is the evidence from the witness stand. Just bear in mind that a person can be asked any question. 'Did you kill Cock Robin?' doesn't mean that he did. The answer is the evidence."

The technique I had used is called a "negative pregnant." I employ it when I want a jury to hear certain things that might not otherwise be introduced into the trial. The question leads the jurors to form certain desired impressions. When I do it the prosecutor usually gets mad, the judge scolds me, and I make a sad face and pretend I didn't know what I was doing. In this case I wasn't out to antagonize Hernando Vallejo. I wanted the jury to hear his reply so that they would exclude him as the possible killer. He had made an excellent impression on me, and I was sure the jury agreed.

Three police officers followed Vallejo to the witness stand. Patrolman Richard Martin, who was the first at the apartment that murder night, gave the court a brief, sequential report of his conversations with Floria and Morales. Detective Walter Crosby, in charge of the case, and Patrolman

Godofredo Perez, who claimed to have heard her confession in Spanish, echoed each other's testimony. With a flurry of "She stated to me's," they gave an account of Floria's alleged confessions. I didn't believe a word uttered by either.

The prosecution rested. It was my turn. I put Floria Segura on the stand. Throughout the nine months I had been visiting her at Riker's Island, she had worn the same scuffed flat shoes, drab print dress, and faded blue cardigan. For her court appearances, she wore a different dress each day, modest but attractive. It is a practice in jails for the prisoners awaiting trial to lend one another clothing when they are to appear in court. It is a morale booster, for a good appearance creates a better impression on the jury. The light flowered dress Floria wore on the day she testified matched a colorful ribbon she had tied, ponytail fashion, around her long, shining black hair. But she never abandoned her faded cardigan. She was always cold.

Before I got to the facts surrounding the crime, I had to establish Floria's mental capacity. This I did by asking, "How many brothers and sisters do you have?"

"I have seven brothers and four sisters."

"How much is seven and four?"

"I don't know."

"How far did you go in school?"

"Fourth grade."

"Did you ever learn to read and write?"

"No."

"How old were you when you quit school?"

"Eleven years old."

I brought her up to the time she had begun her affair with Morales, two months before Peggy's death. I asked her what kind of *centro* he managed.

"He said it was spirits."

"What kind of center do you call it?"

"For me, it's like working with the Devil."

"Did you ever go to the *centro?*"

"Yes, I went two times."

She did not know the address, only how to get there. She thought it might be somewhere on Bedford Avenue, but she was not sure.

I showed her a stuffed voodoo doll I had purchased at a *botánica* in Williamsburg. I asked if she had ever seen such a doll before.

"Yes."

"Did you see this at the *centro?*"

"Yes, they have that."

"What are they, at the *centro?*"

"They use it for killing people."

I stuck a pin into the doll's chest. "Something like this?"

"Yes."

I had her describe the exorcism ceremonies as she had described them to me. The jurors leaned forward to catch every word. They were hearing something out of a horror movie, something for late-night TV, but this was real.

"Where did you go on the day your child died?" I asked Floria.

"I went to welfare."

She told of her futile visit and her tragic homecoming. Subsequently, she described the interrogation at police headquarters. "You did it," Crosby had shouted repeatedly. "You killed your baby." She began to scream in the courtroom as she explained how she had answered, a bone-chilling sound that went right through me. "No, I did not," she had told Crosby. "You have no right to say that and tell me I did it. You don't know me."

I asked her, "Did you ever tell Detective Crosby or Patrolman Perez that you were possessed by spirits?"

"No."

"Do you believe in spirits possessing a person?"

"No."

"Did you tell them that the spirits told you to do these things?"

"No."

"Did you tell them that the spirits made you kill the baby?"

"No, I did not tell them that."

"Floria, did you ever beat the baby before that day?"

"No."

"Did you ever put the baby in an oven?"

"No."

"Did you ever hold that baby out of a window?"

"No."

"Were you ever possessed of spirits?"

"No."

"Did spirits ever tell you to kill the baby?"

"No."

"Did you ever tell Detective Crosby that now that you have killed the baby, your spirits are not hurting you anymore? That you are free of spirits?"

"No, that is not true."

"Did you ever throw the baby on the floor and step on it?"

"No."

"Did you ever smash the baby against the wall?"

"No."

"Did you ever punch that baby in the stomach?"

"No."

"Did you ever pour hot oil on that baby?"

"No, I never."

"Did you ever punch that baby or hurt that baby before it died?"

"No."

Through it all, she was reliving the nightmare of Peggy's death. I have never had a witness like her before or since. We were like two great waves, ebbing and crashing forward, whipping at each other and falling away. When I screamed, she screamed. When she wept, I had to bite my lip to restrain my own tears. The intensity each of us generated in the other crackled like lightning, jolting everybody in the courtroom. Some members of the jury were obviously shocked and on the verge of tears. Some looked white and shaken. I was exhausted. I had ended on a crescendo no one would soon forget.

"Your witness," I panted, and I sat down, drained.

Davenport would stalk her now. He picked up the voodoo doll I had produced earlier. Evidently bent on confusing her, he asked if it had been she who had brought it into court the previous day.

"No," she said.

"Is this the doll you saw at the witchcraft center?"

"No, I saw that doll yesterday."

He took her back to Peggy's admission to Cumberland Hospital. He asked if she had tried to find out who had beaten the baby the first time. Yes, she had. Had she left the baby with Morales before? Yes. Had she accused him of beating the baby? No.

"Then you believed—is that what you are telling us?—you believed Morales was the one who beat the child?"

"Yes."

"And yet you continued to leave the child with Morales? Is that what you are telling us?"

Davenport was trying to show that Floria's answers made no sense and therefore she must be lying.

"The father was visiting the baby regularly, is that right?"

"No."

"He didn't come to your house every week with the money?"

"Yes."

Whether he was aware of it or not, Davenport was actually demonstrating something that was vitally important to me as Floria's defense counsel: that her deductive powers were nil and that her capacity to understand even simple questions was very limited. They had to be rephrased over and over again. Her inability to comprehend, I suspected, had been the explanation of what had actually occurred at the precinct fifteen months earlier.

When an attorney, any attorney, begins his questions with "Isn't it a fact that . . . ?" watch out. He's ready for the kill, aiming straight for the jugular vein.

"Isn't it a fact that you took your baby to the center because you believed the baby was possessed of evil spirits?"

"No."

"Isn't it a fact that you complained to your boyfriend that the baby was crying all the time, never stopped crying, isn't that a fact?"

"Yes, I told that to him."

"And isn't it a fact you asked him if he knew anybody that could help you get rid of the spirits that this baby seemed to have?"

"No."

"Isn't it a fact that you would do anything to get out of this charge now, including lying?"

It was my turn to shout. I did, loud and clear. "Objection!"

Judge Barshay sustained me. Davenport took his seat. "I have no more questions," he told the court.

His cross-examination had surprised me. Not only was it unusually brief for him, but it had lacked his usual ferocity. Although we maintained a pleasant relationship outside, I had always hated his courtroom methods, his toughness, his steamrolling tactics, the way he mercilessly attacked my witnesses. Compared to his attitude toward some of my clients, his treatment of Floria was positively benign. Guilty or innocent, he could have ripped her apart. Perhaps he was afraid that her ability to open up completely, as she had with me, might damage or even destroy his case. Maybe he even felt sorry for her.

Morales spent only a few days in jail on the perjury charge and was released on bail. After the fiasco at the hearing,

Davenport did not want to call him, but I needed him in the courtroom. I wanted the jury to see him exposed as a liar.

I had discovered that he lived with his family in a ghetto project somewhere in East New York. I wanted to serve him with a subpoena, but I had been unable to find him. I had telephoned repeatedly, but no one had ever answered. Finally I located the project, and with another of Nelson's brothers, Felix Zapata, who often acted as my bodyguard, I drove there and parked in front of the building. After Felix got out of the car with the subpoena, I locked all the doors and windows and kept the motor running, just in case.

Felix had quite a saga to impart on his return. No sooner had he entered the project grounds than he was surrounded by a bunch of young punks out to rip him off. "All those gangster movies I've seen sure helped me," he said with a laugh. He put his hand inside his jacket, making it assume the shape of a hidden gun. Glaring at the boys, he said, "Listen, you mother-fuckers, one more move out of you and I'll blast the lot of you." The boys scattered. He went upstairs and pounded on Morales's door. Morales's mother opened it a crack. Felix kicked it in. He kicked so hard it fell off its jamb. Striding into the apartment, he found a quavering Morales, clad only in his underwear, huddled at the kitchen table. Felix thrust the subpoena at him. "Here, you mother-fucker"—his favorite term for friend and foe alike—"if you're not in court tomorrow morning, I'll blow your fucking head off."

The invitation proved irresistible. Morales and his entire family appeared in court the following morning. They had come to protect him from me. Since he had already been arrested for perjury and could be indicted on the same charge again, the court assigned a Legal Aid lawyer to advise him of his constitutional rights regarding self-incrimination. Laymen know this legal concept as "pleading the Fifth Amendment." The two closeted themselves in a private room, and afterward the attorney informed the court, off the record, that Morales had been warned he might incriminate himself but had still agreed to appear as witness for the defense.

When I got him on the witness stand, I asked him if he had taken care of the infant Peggy Vallejo while her mother went to the welfare office. He said no, he was at the witch-craft center at the time. He admitted it was a witchcraft center but, paradoxically, said they did not practice witch-craft.

"Do you believe in the Devil?" I asked.

"Yes," he said.

Picking up the voodoo doll, I casually strolled over to stand near Tom Davenport, seated at the prosecution table. Holding up the doll, I asked, "Did you ever have any dolls there that you used as part of your rituals, like this doll?"

I was rewarded by a stunned look from Morales. "Something like that," he answered reluctantly.

"And sometimes, if you wanted to put a curse on someone, did you put pins in a doll—like this?" With a grand flourish, I thrust a hatpin through the doll's heart.

Davenport, seated a few inches from me, whispered, "Oooh, my back." It nearly broke me up.

Simultaneously, Morales, visibly agitated, answered my question. "We used to do it, yes."

A moment before, he had denied practicing witchcraft at the *centro*. Now he was confirming that this ancient voodoo rite was part of the ritual. He went on to testify that the *centro* was open only two evenings a week, but by a strange coincidence, on the Friday of Peggy's demise, he had been there all day for the first time in he couldn't remember how long. In extracting this information, I had caught him in one lie; I was going to try for another. I asked him what he did with the baby when he took her to the *centro*.

"When we came out of the hospital, we took the baby

because from the beginning Floria thought it was spirits or something that did it. So we wait for the president to come in." It was the president, he explained, who would determine if Peggy were possessed.

"How does the president find out if the baby is possessed by spirits?"

"I don't know," Morales said.

"What did he do to find out whether the baby was possessed by spirits?"

Morales shrugged. "The president didn't show up."

"So how long did you stay with the baby at the center that first time?"

"We stood there from one to five o'clock waiting for him."

After that four-hour vigil, he said, they had returned to Floria's apartment. He contended that he had never taken Peggy back for an exorcism, that there had been no exorcism.

He insisted he had not seen the injured baby on July 21 until he came back from the *centro* with Floria.

"When you came to the house, did you see the baby?" I asked.

"Yes, I did."

"How did it look to you?"

In a low voice, Morales said, "The baby had bruises on her body and face."

"Was Ida there?" I asked.

"Yes." Morales then described how he had told Floria to call the police, stayed with Floria until the medical examiner had removed the body, taken Floria and Ida to his mother's apartment, returning to Floria's house the following morning, when, at eight thirty, he had called the police. Then, obeying their instructions, he had taken Floria and Ida to the precinct.

For the benefit of the jury, I helped him re-create the scene in the precinct house. He explained that Crosby had asked him if Floria had confessed to killing her child. "I didn't tell them nothing at the time," he said virtuously.

He went on to describe an interrogation lasting from "the morning to the nighttime," explaining how Crosby had gone back and forth between the two rooms until the arrival of the assistant district attorney. According to Morales, he and Floria were separated only by a partition and he was clearly able to hear her "crying, hollering to the police officers— saying she didn't do it." He added that she had changed her story later that night. "She said, you know, she hit the baby, because, you know, she had some kind of voice that told her."

I questioned him about his visits to Floria at Riker's Island. He confirmed seeing her every visiting day but denied he had ever mentioned the case. I wanted to bring in his letter as evidence that he was lying, but Davenport objected and Barshay sustained it.

"Mr. Morales," I said, "did Floria ever tell you that she killed the baby?"

His reply was inaudible.

The judge asked him to speak louder. His answer resounded through the courtroom. "Yes."

I clenched my fists. I wanted to blacken both his eyes. Again he was perjuring himself. Why? Was he frightened, stupid, or had he forgotten what had happened the last time he had lied in court? Possibly Judge Barshay's refusal to allow his letters to be used as evidence had given him the confidence to reverse his testimony again. I was not going to let him get away with it.

I seldom get angry at my own witnesses, but Morales was an exception to that rule. Sharply, I demanded, "Did you ever tell anybody she did *not* tell you she killed the baby?"

No matter what answer he gave, I was going to bring up his prior testimony. He didn't have the opportunity to reply. Davenport objected on the grounds that Morales was my witness.

I requested that he be made a hostile witness, but Barshay denied my request.

I confronted Morales again. Enunciating each word slowly and distinctly, I said, "Did—you—ever—tell—anybody—that—she—did—*not*—tell—you—she—killed—the—baby?"

Davenport's objection was overruled. I asked my question a third time.

"No," Morales mumbled.

This answer, too, had been inaudible. Barshay, turning to the jury, said loudly, "The answer is 'No.'"

Once again, I requested that Morales be declared hostile; once again, Barshay denied my motion but suggested I use prior testimony. I produced the minutes from the hearing. In a loud, clear voice I started reading them.

"'Did you tell me . . . that Floria never admitted killing the baby to you, but you only said it to the police because if you didn't, *you'd* be accused, and *you* would go to jail?'"

"'Yes.'" I read from the record.

"'So she never told you that she killed the baby?'"

"'Never. The police force me to say she did.'"

The judge interrupted my reading to ask Morales when and where Floria had told him she had killed Peggy.

"In the house, before."

"Before what?"

"In the house before we went to the police station."

"And then later you spoke to the police?"

"Right." He seesawed again.

I had proved my point. I had no more questions. Davenport declined to cross-examine. He didn't need to. Morales had reverted to his role as prosecution witness and under my examination had answered all the questions Davenport might have asked.

My next witness was eight-year-old Ida Rodriguez. Under the law, a child below the age of twelve may testify but may not be sworn unless he or she understands the quality of an oath and the consequence of telling a lie. Putting a youngster on the witness stand is, at best, a difficult and delicate task. A child as severely traumatized as Ida had been was particularly vulnerable. She still had not recovered from the shock of losing both her sister and her mother.

The day before I put her on the stand in front of the packed courtroom, I had taken her into a vacant courtroom. I wanted her to get the feel of the place. I put her on my lap on the witness stand, stroked her hair, told her funny stories, did everything I possibly could to relax her. Now, she was here and for one purpose only: to prove Morales had been in the apartment on July 21.

I was very careful with the child, a beauty, all dressed up in new patent-leather shoes, new dress, and matching bows on her fat pigtails. She reminded me of my Judy at that age.

Gently, I began. "Were you in the house when Peggy got sick?"

"Yes."

"Who else was in the house when she got sick?"

"Me and—" She hesitated.

"Was a man there or a lady?"

"A man."

"Was this the man?" I pointed to Morales.

"Yes."

"Is his name Ray?"

"Yes."

"Where was Mommy?"

"She was in welfare."

"Did you see Ray do something to Peggy?"

"No. He was brushing her hair."

"Did he tell you to do something?"

"Yes, clean the blood."

"Did he ever say anything to you about this?"

"Don't tell it to nobody."

I had no further questions. Davenport had none. He did

not wish to antagonize the jury by cross-examining her. The testimony was over. After our summations and the judge's charge, it would be left to the jury to sift through the inconsistencies; to work out the truth; to argue, for hours if necessary, to determine the facts as adduced by the evidence presented. My closing statement to the jury was one of the most emotional I have ever made.

"You have here a brainless person," I said in part. "A person that is like a blade of grass. The wind can blow her in any direction. If you think her tears were phony, that is your opinion. But I think you cannot resist the notion that everything that came from this woman was from the bottom of her heart. A heart she has. Moral character was never given to her. It does not spring forth from the infant by itself. It must be lovingly nurtured. Strength? She never had any. Morals? She doesn't know what the word is. Living as she did, she was a battered child from the beginning. Emotionally, she was dead. Morally, she was nonexistent."

I described her life up to her meeting with Morales. He was her boyfriend, I told the jury, whatever else he was. She still needed love—she needed sex.

"So Morales talked about witchcraft. Morales was left in charge of Peggy when she went to Ida's school, and when she came back, Peggy was hurt. Morales took her and the child to a hospital; Morales spoke to the people at the hospital; Morales urged her to take the child out of the hospital, told her that spirits were possessing her child, took her to the center, had the child thrown into the air. Morales was there when all these people were jumping around and the candles were lit and the oil and the water were sprinkled and the baby screamed and cried, and she took the baby away, and this stupid woman—forgive me for saying 'stupid woman'— this foolish woman, this woman who had no character, took the child back a second time.

"Was she foolish, was she careless? Perhaps. Was she following Morales's instructions, no matter what he said? And then, on that fateful day, she had to go to welfare because her rent was raised. She left Morales with Ida and the baby. When she came back, the baby appeared ill, and Morales said he does not know what happened. Morales said she fell. Morales didn't help Floria take care of the baby. Morales warned her, 'Don't you bring that child to the hospital again, because they will accuse us again.' "

I was all worked up. My cheeks were hot and flushed; my throat, as usual in these emotional moments, was dry, constricted. I had to take a drink of water. I went on with my summation. I told them about Hernando's visit and Floria's lie. "She was scared to go to the hospital because Morales had said, 'Don't go.' "

In conclusion, I said, "I am not going to say the baby committed suicide. As reasonable persons, with your experience, you are not going to say that the baby killed herself. But you are going to have to say to yourselves, before you find this woman guilty, that you are convinced beyond a reasonable doubt that Floria Segura committed this crime.

"That is the issue. That is what you have to decide, and I say, madam and gentlemen, you have no alternative, on the basis of what you have heard here, but to bring in a verdict of acquittal. Thank you." I practically tottered to my seat. I was emotionally and physically spent.

It was Davenport's turn. He was cold and unemotional, staying strictly with the evidence. Again, I was surprised.

Having dismissed the murder-two count as a matter of law, Judge Barshay instructed the jurors to consider one of four possible verdicts: manslaughter in the first degree; manslaughter in the second degree; assault in the first degree; not guilty. They went out at three thirty that afternoon.

The waiting was hard. It always is. Floria was removed by a court officer, and Enid Cruz and I spent the next few hours with brave smiles and crossed fingers. My court buffs joined us at the hamburger place across the street from the courthouse. This is a group of some ten to twenty retired men and women who regularly follow me from trial to trial. Often they wait with me through the night for the verdict to be brought in. They have become experts in spotting the guilty and the innocent. In the case of Floria Segura, their opinion was unanimous: innocent. They could not understand why Morales was not on trial. They were highly indignant when I explained that the police had taken the path of least resistance and accused the weaker of the two suspects.

The jury filed in at six thirty to request clarification on certain points; they also wanted definitions of manslaughter one and two. They returned at twelve thirty with more questions. When these were answered to their satisfaction, they filed out again. Twenty minutes later they returned, looking disturbed. They had reached a verdict: guilty of manslaughter in the second degree, "negligent or reckless homicide."

I was shattered. Enid wept. Floria sat there unmoved. The only time she had displayed any emotion was when she had testified. Now she was as cold as a stone—she might have been turned to stone. She did not even blink. She just stared.

Judge Barshay set a date for sentencing and informed the jury he would send the defendant for an examination at Kings County Hospital. Noting how crestfallen the jurors were, he added, "You can rest assured that my hands are not tied with this verdict. On November twenty-first, the day before Thanksgiving, she will come before me. God willing, I will do the right thing."

The jurors did a wonderful thing then. They came to me and told me what a difficult decision they had been forced to make. One after another, they came, thanking me and asking me to forgive them for finding Floria guilty. "I had no choice," one said. "We believed she never killed the kid, but she shouldn't have left her with Morales," another declared. A third insisted, "She was neglectful." Nearly everyone had something to say. We talked for a long time, but I noticed that one juror hung back despite the fact that it was getting very late. We left the courtroom together.

"Boy," he said, "you sure made a mistake when you picked me."

"What do you mean?" I asked.

"I mean I knew she was guilty the moment you opened your mouth when you impaneled us."

I was horrified. "Why didn't you excuse yourself? Why did you come on the jury?"

"Well," he said, "I didn't want to sit around downstairs and do nothing for two weeks. I liked the show you put on."

I went home, but not to bed. I couldn't sleep. I could only wait for morning to come so that I could talk to the judge. Meanwhile, I tried to understand what had happened. How could I have let this man get on the panel?

I have good instincts for picking juries, and, believe me, you need them in these cases. But there is no foolproof technique. The best of lawyers can make mistakes in jury selection. I had spent two days questioning about 150 or more prospective jurors. A lawyer has an unlimited variety of people from whom to choose. They are from all walks of life. They come and sit in a big room on the main floor of the courthouse, and when there is a trial, you sift through them to find people you think will be sympathetic to your client, or at least unbiased, and at the same time satisfactory to the prosecution. In New York State, it is the opposing lawyers, not the judge, who pick the jury. In a felony trial, both sides have to agree on a jury of twelve.

In Floria Segura's case, I had tried to select people who understood her situation. I did not want wealthy persons who think about the high taxes they pay to support her on welfare; I did not want motherly women who could not bear to think of a baby's brutal death (but then, who could?); I did not want law-and-order fanatics. But how does one know what these twelve people are really thinking? In this case, that of a poor baby beaten to death, but knowing nothing else about the facts, again and again the prospective jurors had looked at Floria with hate and asked to be excused. When, eventually, we had selected a jury, I was reasonably sure of the eleven men and one woman who were chosen. I thought I had established a rapport with them. But this man was a good liar. All night I castigated myself for not realizing he was lying.

Early the next morning, I drove to the Supreme Court building, found the door to Judge Barshay's chambers unlocked, went in, and dozed off on the big leather couch in his waiting room. He found me there later, and I explained what had happened.

"Was it juror number eight?" he asked.

"How did you know?" I exclaimed.

"Because when I was telling the jury not to discuss the case, he turned to another juror and muttered, 'I told you so.' I knew then that he was a bad apple in the barrel."

"I want to make a motion for a mistrial," I cried indignantly. "That man ought to be brought up on charges of perjury. He's committed a criminal offense."

Judge Barshay made me a cup of coffee. "Calm down," he said. "What purpose would it serve? I won't hurt Floria. She'll see a psychiatrist every week. Her little girl will be safe in a home, and she can see her. It won't be as bad as you think, Sara."

I left his chambers in a considerably better frame of mind. I had a feeling that Floria's time in jail was at an end, and I was right. Several jurors wrote Judge Barshay asking for mercy for Floria. He did not give her a further prison sentence but put her on probation, with the proviso that she see a psychiatric counselor regularly, as long as necessary.

To date, I have received three letters from the Segura family. The first was from Jaime, who thanked me profusely for my fight on behalf of his sister. He said he had more hope for her than he had ever had before, and he approved of the psychiatric treatment she was receiving.

The other two letters had been dictated by Floria. The first was sad. They had taken her little girl away from her and placed her in a Catholic foundling home. She missed her dreadfully. The next letter was much happier. She had decided that she, too, liked her treatment, and she had learned that she could visit Ida every week. She was full of hope for her future, and, on reading her letter, so was I.

10 | Cops and Robbers

I HAVE OFTEN BEEN INTERVIEWED on television about my cases, and sometimes I have nearly got into serious trouble. However, I have a client called Tommy Rios, by profession a cat burglar, and doing very well when out of jail, who never minds if I discuss his activities on TV or radio; he has done it himself and has spoken very frankly about himself and his activities. Thievery is his profession, and he's good at it. Furthermore, for him burglary is a game with rules. He never carries a gun, never breaks into private homes. His specialty is factories, where everything is insured against the sort of depredations carried on by Tommy and others of his calling. If I seem to be speaking rather fondly of him, let's face it, I am fond of him. He is my good bad boy. He has charm and honesty—yes, honesty, for he never pretends to be what he is not. In his world, the depressed ghetto purlieus of Williamsburg, Brooklyn, there is no "straight," there is only a desperate desire to rise above the terrible poverty, the overcrowded rooms, and the despair of being a second-class citizen. Some of Tommy's friends work as waiters, some are janitors. Tommy wants more out of life, and thievery makes this easy.

I first heard of Tommy Rios through a telephone call from his mother, who said indignantly, "My boy's in jail. They put him in with the homosexuals. He wants to get out of that division before he loses his virtue."

At that time, I was a relatively new lawyer and Tommy was a relatively new thief. He had been working in the field for only eight or nine years; he was nineteen.

The jail was in Comstock, New York, which is pretty far upstate. I made an appointment with the warden, and then, because I wanted to look my best, I got dressed up in my best cloth coat, a warm but short dress, high-heeled shoes. I had not reckoned with the weather or the location of Comstock.

When I got on the train, the conductor told me, "It's a whistle-stop. We usually pass it by, but I'll see we let you off." I had been on the train for about five hours, traveling through a vast white wilderness, when suddenly we halted. "Engine trouble," I muttered to myself.

"Comstock!" bawled the conductor.

I looked out of the window, aghast. I didn't even see a sign. All I saw was snow. However, I got out onto a small platform. As the train whizzed off, I saw nothing but a ramshackle station, totally deserted, and snow, snow, snow in all directions. Then I heard a dog barking in the distance. A dog meant civilization!

"Mush!" I said and started toward the sound. However, on walking off the platform, I sank up to my waist in snow. Never had I ever been colder or wetter. This was before the days of pantyhose, and wet, melting snow chilled my bare thighs and pressed itself into my bottom. Daunted but determined, I persevered, stumbling through the drifts, and eventually I blundered into some people who saw that I found a taxi to take me to the jail. I was wet, miserable, and in the mood to resent Tommy. However, when I met him, a small, slight young man with a devilish gleam in his dark eyes, I was unable to blame him for my ordeal. I liked him. He liked me. It was an instant rapport, and I was able to convince the warden to move him into the regular prison population. I also found out that he wasn't above turning informer if the occasion warranted it. If his penchant for confiding bits of news to the wrong people had become known in the jail, there would have been trouble. As the years passed and his record of arrests increased, I discovered that, indeed, Tommy often "cooperated" with the cops and the FBI.

When I first met Tommy, he was a do-it-yourself burglar. He sawed through the roofs of factories, leaping out and across those same roofs if pursued by the police. Later, he began to delegate his work and became a manager, watching the operation from a safe distance.

Though he resented being locked up with homosexuals, Tommy had no prejudice about using them in his business. One of them, a man called Cacho Compaz, had a real aptitude for climbing roofs, sawing off portions of them, and inserting himself inside. His nickname was "Sparrow." He was a little, twittery character with a high voice and a lisp, but one night he was not quick enough for four carloads of tipped-off cops, who arrived at the factory when it was allegedly being ripped off. Though Cacho was not in the factory, having heard that the cops were arriving, he was arrested, along with Tommy and a young woman, even though the latter two were reasonably, if not far, away from the scene of the crime.

Tommy called me, and Sparrow drew Tony Napoli, the chief of the Legal Aid Society, Brooklyn Division. The case got a lot of informal coverage since all the young Legal Aid lawyers were in and out of the courtroom snatching looks at their chief as he defended Sparrow.

On the day we were starting the trial, as Tony and I were crossing the street near Borough Hall, he said to me, "What the fuck's going to be the defense? Your client's got a record so long he'd trip on it if he took the stand, and mine's so twittery, he can't talk."

I said, "I don't know what the hell it's going to be. I'm going to say the cops did it."

He said, "Oh, boy, Sara, you invented chutzpah!" He shook his head, muttering, "Listen to her. She says the cops did it!"

Originally, three men had been arrested, but one of them had had a prior conviction in the Bronx and he didn't go on trial with Tommy. This gave me the idea he might have tipped off the Bronx Burglary Squad as to Tommy's doings, since in the opening statement it was mentioned that they had been following Tommy for the last six months.

Tommy was quite aware of their activities. The cops used panel trucks as covers, and one day, after leading one of those trucks to Manhattan and back and to Manhattan and back again, he stopped his car near the Williamsburg Bridge and hopped over to the truck behind him, saying, "Excuse me, could you tell me where the Williamsburg Bridge is?" thus informing the cop who was driving that his cover was blown.

When we started trying the case, I had one of these cops on the witness stand. I said, "Didn't Rios come up to you in your truck and ask you where the Williamsburg Bridge was? And didn't you answer, 'What the fuck, you're right in front of it'?"

"That's right, Counselor," agreed the cop.

This cop was also one of the detectives who had been tipped off about the burglary, and he described how, starting at midnight, they had parked in front of the factory building where the burglary was going to take place. About two in the morning, the cop said, they saw there were people on the roof sawing it open. "I was standing right in front of that building," he averred, "and I saw them with my own eyes."

"You were standing right in front of the building," I said, "and you saw people up on top of the roof?"

"That's right," he affirmed.

"How far back on the roof were they?" I asked.

"Oh, about twenty feet."

"How could you see them on the roof twenty feet back if you were standing in front of the building?" I asked.

I could see that he was getting nervous. At about that point, a recess was called, for which I was damned glad.

Taking Tony aside, I said, "I've a feeling that son of a bitch is lying. How can he stand in front of a building and see people on the roof?"

"I think he's lying, too, but try and prove it," Tony said.

"That's what I hope to do," I told him. Pointing to my head, I added, "Can't you see I'm wearing my Agatha Christie hat? Let's get out to that building and take a look at it."

"I'm with you," he agreed.

With Tony was Joe Bartlett, a young legal trainee who was tall, thin, and black, with an immense Afro. He was game to go, too. We drove out and stood in front of the building, but we had to get a perspective, so I said, "Let's get the owner of the building to open up."

We knocked on the door, and finally the owner came out. He looked at us in a startled manner. We were an ill-assorted threesome—a short, blond woman, a tall, skinny black guy, and a divinely handsome Italian who looks like an Irishman. "Who are you?" he said.

"Don't you know?" I answered. "We're the Mod Squad."

"Yeah?" he said. "Gee, I never thought I'd meet youse in person." He was extremely excited, and when I asked him to take us up to the roof, he was quick to oblige.

Once we had seen the location of the hole in the roof, we knew that the cop never could have sighted anyone up there. We went downstairs and looked around. Across the street there was a railroad fence with the subway track underneath. Even across the street, standing next to that fence, you couldn't see the top of the roof; only from the other side of that subway track could anyone see the roof. I took out my Polaroid camera and snapped some pictures. (That Polaroid camera, which Morris at my request gave me one birthday, has won me a lot of cases.)

Armed with those pictures, I got into court the next morning and resumed my cross-examination of the cop. Before I could show him my pictures, he said, "Counselor, I made a mistake yesterday. I wasn't standing in front of the building. I was behind the fence on the other side of the subway track."

I goggled at him. I knew then that he must have been following me the night before, and I remembered a green truck parked on a near corner. "Were you in that green truck?" I demanded.

"No, no, Counselor," he said. "I just happened to remember. After all, it took place a year ago, that robbery. You can't be perfect in every little detail."

"Well," I said, "you looked inside the building, didn't you?"

"Yes," he agreed.

"How could you look inside, Officer, when it was dark?"

"With the supersnooper," he answered, much to everybody's amusement.

"What's that?" I asked.

"It's got infrared lights—you can see in the dark," he explained.

"What did you see?"

"I saw Tommy Rios—he was sitting in the truck. They were preparing to load with the stolen stuff."

"There are two windows," I said, "one on either side of a big garage door. Which window did you look through? The right window or the left window?"

"I looked in the right window," he said, after a minute's pause.

"The right window," I repeated. "You're positive you looked into the window on the right?"

"Positive," he said.

"And you saw Tommy in the truck?"

"That's correct, Counselor."

"You're positive it was the right window?"

"I'm positive," he repeated.

After that, he got down from the stand, and a second cop took his place. He had also looked through the right window and seen Tommy Rios sitting in the truck while it was being loaded with stolen merchandise—children's underwear, mostly.

Shortly after the second cop had finished testifying, the court adjourned. As before, the three of us rushed back to the building for another round of investigations. We went to that right window and found it was all wrong for the cops' purposes. The right window faced into an office.

Armed with more pictures, I went back to court prepared to go cop trapping again, only to discover that my prey had eluded me again. "Oh, by the way, Counselor," he said, before I could open my mouth, "I made a mistake. I didn't look through the right window, I looked through the left window."

Obviously, he had followed me once more. I wasn't entirely defeated. I rallied to say, "But that left window was, as I remember, very dirty. How could you see anything through it?"

"I wiped it with my hand," he replied. "It was very dirty. My hand got all black."

At the end of that day's session, the three of us were back at the factory, and I found that the cop couldn't possibly have wiped that window clean with his hand, it was covered with barbed wire. I took a picture of the barbed wire.

The following day, I had him on the stand again. "Officer," I said in my most dulcet tones, "you say you wiped that window clean?"

"Yes, I wiped it all off, Counselor, from top to bottom, until it was clean enough for anybody to see through."

"And with your hand, you did it?"

"With my hand," he agreed confidently. He made a motion as if he were wiping a flat surface. "Like this."

"Didn't your poor hand bleed, Officer?"

"What do you mean, Counselor?" he asked in perplexed tones.

I showed him a picture of the window. "Is that the way the window looked?"

"Yes," he said.

"Here's a close-up of that same window, Officer. Do you see the barbed wire covering the windowpane?"

He flushed an ugly red and mumbled something I couldn't hear. I didn't need to hear it. I had him.

I was feeling rather pleased with myself when Tommy came up to me during a recess. "That was good what you did to that cop, but that second cop always confirms what he says. They—those jurors—maybe won't think two cops are lying. You want anything should happen to that second cop before he's called up to testify?"

I looked at him in utter amazement. "Something happening" usually means a broken leg or a broken head, one of those unfortunate accidents which generally involves a well-paid someone stumbling against someone else in a crowd. Tommy was not the type to use such gangster tactics. I said, "What do you mean?"

He said, "I could have things fixed."

I was getting nervous. "Fixed—how?"

"Well," he said, looking me squarely in the eye, "I have this voodoo thing—"

"Stop there," I shouted. "What do you mean, you have this voodoo thing? You don't believe in voodoo, Tommy?"

"Don't I?" he responded. "How do you think you've been winning all my cases, Sara?"

"B-but, Tommy," I stammered, "I thought it was because I'm a good lawyer."

"You're a good lawyer, Sara, but it doesn't hurt to have a few little things fixed."

"Okay, Tommy, believe what you want to believe, but it

would take a hell of a lot more than some mumbo jumbo to keep that cop off the stand tomorrow."

"Um," he mused, "we'll see."

The following morning, I was in court again, but the second cop didn't appear. The judge was furious. "Where is he?" he demanded.

"He called in sick, Your Honor," the D.A. said. "His back is out of commission."

"You tell him to get here tomorrow morning, back or no back," rasped the judge.

The following morning, the cop crawled in, half crippled. They had to help him up to the witness stand.

"Well," Tommy said to me, "what did I tell you?"

"Oh, come on," I said, "it was just a coincidence."

"Yeah?" he inquired. "You want something to happen to one of the jurors?"

"Oh, come on," I said again, "quit trying to convince me. I don't believe in that stuff. It was a coincidence, I tell you."

The next day, one of the jurors called in sick. We had a conference, the D.A. and I, and we used an alternate. I couldn't avoid Tommy's gleeful and triumphant glance. When I met him in the hall at the lunch break, I said, "Tommy, you've got to take me to see that place where all this witchcraft is happening."

"I'd be charmed." He grinned.

"I'm beginning to think you are," I replied.

That night, he drove me there in his car. It was one of those typical storefront *centros espíritos* that I had visited in the daytime when I was investigating the Segura case, and to my surprise and shock, on passing the man in charge of the place, I recognized Ray Morales. Our eyes locked, but I gave him no sign of recognition and he looked quickly away from me. However, when Tommy introduced me to the medium in charge, I said, "Didn't that man used to work in the *centro* where the baby was beaten to death?"

"That's the man," she agreed. "Ray Morales."

She was a strange little old woman with big, rather watery-looking eyes. She reminded me more of a witch than of a medium, and I had a few qualms as she motioned me to follow her into the depths of the *centro*. She led me to a dingy, dim area where there were lots of candles on tables and in wall sconces. Pictures of saints hung all around the room, and the place reeked of incense and other odors I could not identify. There was an altar covered with a black cloth smeared with wax drippings, and on the altar was a pack of limp, greasy playing cards. The medium picked them up and motioned me to sit at an adjacent table. As I obeyed, she sat down facing me. "You want me to tell your fortune?" she asked.

"So tell it." I shrugged. I was still in the nonbelieving stage, but I was willing to go along with her.

She handed me the cards, asking me to shuffle them. "Got any questions?" she asked.

The cards were so greasy, I hardly liked to touch them, but I obliged gingerly and gave them back.

"What about Tommy's case? How will it go?" I asked.

She cut the cards and studied them.

"You'll win the case, but you got problems. You, yourself, I mean. Your partner, he's a man and he's very jealous of you. And your husband, he has a big problem, too. He's just found out about it."

Well, I didn't know about the case—the outcome was still in the future—but I was having trouble with Zapata. I didn't see how she could have learned about him. As for my husband, Morris had just found out that he had glaucoma, and nobody except the two of us and the eye doctor knew about that. I gave her a contribution for the church and had Tommy drive me home.

"Well?" he said when he dropped me off at my house.

"Well, I'm not committing myself," I told him.

However, in a sense I had committed myself, for once he had told me about his witchcraft activities, Tommy started using charms openly. His girl friend, Dolores, who was also deeply into voodoo, came into court with a voodoo spray which she wanted to use on me to give me luck. I demurred, but when she insisted, I made her do it in the ladies' room; I knew that if the other lawyers or the court officers saw me, I would never live it down. I wasn't much for the spraying process, but one must keep a client happy, and I was fond of Tommy, so I went along with it.

Meanwhile, testimony was continuing in court. Tommy had told me in private that once he realized he was being observed by the cops, he had stopped the operation in mid-robbery, and while the truck was in the warehouse preparatory to being loaded, everybody started coming out of the building empty-handed. That didn't please the cops, who had been sitting around there for over four hours. They wanted something to show for their trouble, so they arrested everyone, including the informer. In order to make the arrest look authentic, the cops cleaned out the factory. All in all, they stashed twenty-three thousand dollars' worth of merchandise into the truck and took it all to the police precinct. They charged the thieves with making away with twenty-three thousand dollars' worth of goods, and the owner came down to have it vouchered.

I put him on the stand. He was a man with a thick Jewish accent and a habit of shrugging his shoulders philosophically —he needed to be philosophical.

I put him on the stand. "They stole twenty-three thousand dollars' worth of stuff?"

"That's right."

"Did you eventually get it back?"

"I got back some," he allowed.

"How much did you get back?"

A second shrug. "Maybe three thousand dollars' worth."

"But what happened to the other twenty thousand?" I cried.

With a third shrug, he said, "So the police've got it, maybe."

"Don't you know what happened to the rest?"

"So I don't know." He sighed.

Out of the corner of my eye, I saw the D.A. turning a pale purple and looking at his shoes. It was embarrassing for him. I felt even sorrier for him when, under my questioning, one of the cops said that they didn't have vouchers for the rest of the stuff and the voucher book was lost; as far as he knew, it was probably integrated in the property clerk's office—who could say?

During a subsequent recess, Tony walked up to me. "Hey, Sara, so you're really proving the cops did it, after all," he whispered with a wink.

"It looks that way." I laughed. We really had a ball with that trial, and the cops looked like a bunch of crooks. Neither my client nor Sparrow took the stand. They said nothing.

When summation time came, the courtroom was packed. It was a funny trial. Even my brother Schillie had come to kibitz, and I was in fine fettle when I stood up before the jury. It wasn't one of those cases where I could be outraged and fiery. I didn't have an innocent man to clear. As Tommy put it, "I am a t'ief," but he had been set up and framed by the cops, and I meant to get him off if I could. He had started to commit a crime, but a bigger one had resulted, and of that one he was innocent.

As I strolled out toward the jury box, my head was full of purple phrases, and I knew I was looking my best, dressed to the nines with all my gold jewelry gleaming. I started talking about lying cops, perjuring cops, crooked cops, and I was really wound up when all of a sudden I felt a marble in my mouth. I couldn't imagine what it could be. Suddenly, I had a flash; I had been at the dentist's that morning having a cap glued in, and the damned thing had become unstuck! I had to do something or I would swallow this very expensive tooth, and furthermore, I might even choke on it. I produced a cough—I coughed again and again, a regular paroxysm of coughs, and, gasping for breath, I said to the court, "Excuse me, excuse me, but I need a glass of water."

The judge ordered a court officer to give me a drink, and, taking it, I walked all the way back across the courtroom, and, turning away so that the members of the jury couldn't see me, I shoved the damned tooth back into position again, pushing it back with my thumb as I covered my mouth with my hand. Then, pressing my tongue against it so that it would stay in place, I went back to the jury. If I had let them see that large gap in my mouth, it would have spoiled my whole summation. I couldn't afford having anyone laugh, not then.

In a subdued tone of voice—I didn't dare open my mouth wide enough to yell—I continued with my summation. "The D.A. can't *prove* that my client had anything to do with it," I began. I discussed how he had been found empty-handed, no tools, no weapon. "Those cops lied about the roof and about the haul; they didn't find him at the scene of the crime. He was clean when he was found, but those cops weren't clean, his accusers weren't clean, ladies and gentlemen. So what have you got to go on, as far as my client is concerned? Nothing."

I walked out, and then Tony gave his summation and it was very impressive. After the D.A. had said his piece, we recessed to wait for the verdict.

Schillie joined me in the hall. "My God, Sara," he said in a low voice. "You know, when you got that cough, we were so wrapped up in your words, but that cough was a marvelous touch. We were so spellbound we could hardly wait for you to continue. I'm not only talking about me, I mean everybody. How did you happen to hit on that marvelous touch?"

"Hell, Schillie." I laughed. "That wasn't any touch. I was dying because a tooth fell out of my mouth." I flipped my tongue, and my cap fell out.

Schillie retrieved it for me. "Well, nobody noticed it," he said. "It was like you were inspired, Sara."

While we were waiting for the jury to come back, Tommy's girl friend joined us. "Gee," she said, "I wish he wouldn't always get into all this trouble. I want him to go straight. Maybe he will someday. You think so, Sara?"

"Maybe." I comforted her. Tommy had mentioned some such thing to me, but I was and am dubious. He likes good clothes, fancy restaurants, and all the other benefits of his profession. He won't want to give them up that easily.

"Sara," Dolores continued, "I am going to spray the court-room."

"Spray the courtroom?" I repeated. "But the jury is already out—it's too late for sprays."

"It's never too late," she said solemnly. Beckoning me to follow her, she slipped into the empty courtroom and went meticulously over the whole place with that voodoo oil spray. She left it smelling like a rose—so much so that when the judge came back to hear the verdict, he sneezed and whispered, "What in hell's that?"

"Smells like a whorehouse." I giggled, hoping he wouldn't notice that I, too, reeked of the stuff.

The jury returned, and the foreman announced that they had found the defendants, both of them, not guilty.

"So what do you think of witchcraft now, Sara?" a jubilant Tommy asked me.

"So I think you've got a good lawyer." I stuck my tongue out at him and laughed.

Postscripts

As READERS OF SUCH MASTERLY NOVELISTS as Dickens and Thackeray know, it is gratifying to see how all loose ends are tied in the final pages; we learn at last what happened to every character in the novel's large cast. Real life is not so orderly, of course, but it happens that in the time it has taken for this book to be written, there have been further developments in the incomplete stories of the clients I mentioned in the opening pages. Most, though not all, have been fully resolved, and it is satisfying to be able to bring those stories up to date here.

The trial of the little karate expert, Beulah Williams, was just about to begin when the district attorney decided that her statement to the police regarding **her own peril at** the time her would-be attacker menaced her put her in the class of victim rather than perpetrator, and the case was summarily dismissed, as it should have been months before.

Bill White, the man who suffered so much at the hands of the woman whose fall down the stairs brought him into court accused of murder, steadfastly refused to stand trial. His patient acceptance of his mistress's cruelty was the key to his problem: he could not defend himself—he was too timid, too afraid. He was equally afraid of the court and insisted on my letting him take a plea. Moved by his plight, the judge sentenced him from zero to three years, and, shortly after his incarceration, he was paroled, it being contended that he had already served a year in jail.

Joe Chandler was a different story. After repeated meetings with him, my initial belief in his innocence wavered. He had been accused of murdering a man in the course of an argument. He had, however, contended that he knew nothing about it and was down south at the time, and supposedly had witnesses to prove it. Still, I could see from his shifty glances and evasive attitude that he was not telling me the whole truth. Finally, I had it out with him. "Joe," I said coldly, "you're lying to me. Give it to me straight—you don't lie well." Suddenly a change came over him. He looked at me as if he wanted to get a heavy load off his mind. "I haven't slept since this happened. I was drunk. The man and his friends tried to rob me; I shot him." I had him cop a plea, and he is serving a short sentence.

Elaine Jackson, accused of murder because her boyfriend told the district attorney that she had confessed to him that she had beaten her baby to death, was out on bail awaiting trial when her ex-lover was brought into court for another child murder. In this case, the baby in question had been his own, and, as before, he contended the woman with whom he was living was the culprit. This time the district attorney did not believe him, and a jury subsequently decided he was the killer. Thereafter, the case against Elaine was dismissed by the district attorney, since there was no witness to prove her guilt. She had always protested her innocence to me. But someone beat that baby to death. If she is innocent, then her boyfriend must have killed her baby. It is sad indeed! Child abuse is a disease not easily cured in the ghetto.

Joseph James, the convicted killer of a correction officer, under sentence of death for murder, is in prison awaiting a decision on his appeal of his conviction. On June 6, 1977, the United States Supreme Court ruled that the conviction of a murderer accused of killing a policeman in the State of Louisiana could not be upheld because the law providing for a mandatory death penalty was not constitutional. Consequently, it is anticipated that Joseph James's life will be spared, since the New York law is strikingly similar. Furthermore, the governor of the State of New York has declared that he would commute the sentence of anyone condemned to death during his term of office because he is morally opposed to the death penalty.

I am immensely heartened by this turn of events for it means that James and others like him could have their sentences commuted to life imprisonment, which is punishment enough. I believe personally that none of us, whether judge or jury, has the moral right to determine who shall live and who shall die, and that by sanctioning legal murder, we become killers, too.

Death is neither an answer nor a solution to the problem of murder, and, as has been proved again and again, it is no deterrent to crime. The answer lies in correcting the social evils that lead to crime and in establishing an "evenhanded" justice which is impartially meted out to rich and poor alike. I am not such an idealist as to believe this can happen overnight.

The other day, as I walked up the wide stone steps of the Kings County courthouse, I had a sense of déjà vu. I was going to try a case against two men with a certain co-counsel named Manuel Nelson Zapata. I had been court-assigned to one defendant, and Nelson had been privately retained by the other. Inherent in that particular situation was a certain awkwardness. I had not worked with him for a couple of years—not since the day we had reached the first real agreement we had enjoyed for a long time: we had agreed to disagree.

A law partnership is a little like a marriage. Once you have passed the honeymoon stage, the moonlight and roses are gone and you begin to have a much clearer vision of your situation. Sometimes you don't like what you see. In the beginning, I had been content to take a back seat, to do a lot of legwork and a lot of investigation, while letting my supportive male partner take most of the credit. I was grateful to have a male partner, and I thought it would be only a matter of time before I stood on an equal footing with him. Sure enough, there came a time when I was handling as many clients as he, and was equally busy. Yet somehow he could never read those equal signs; he still talked and acted as if I were his little shadow. The proverbial camelback-breaker came when, after dismissing one of our associate lawyers for his improper handling of a negligence case, he blithely announced that henceforth I would handle all the paperwork and all the negligence cases. I was livid. "I am a trial lawyer, not a clerk," I retorted. "I won't do it!"

"No?" he countered in solemn tones. "Then I suggest we dissolve the partnership."

The words had scarcely left his lips before I jumped in with a hearty, "Done. Let's!"

He was shocked. "I didn't mean it. Don't take me literally."

"It's time, Nelson. I want to do my own thing. I don't want to be your appendage anymore."

"B-but haven't I always treated you with respect?" he stuttered.

"No, you haven't," I answered coldly. "I'm finished, Nelson."

I won't say I wasn't feeling nervous when I moved out of our office and back to my Court Street digs in Brooklyn. In spite of my twenty years in law, I was still wondering if I, a woman lawyer, could make it on my own.

It seems odd to me now that I ever entertained such doubts. Directly after they were installed, my telephones started ringing, and they haven't stopped since. I am just as busy as I ever was—in an office I share with three male associates. In fact, just after Zapata and I split up, I found myself with a headline-making case involving one John Lindquist, a client who was convicted of murdering a woman on Fire Island, New York, and is now in Attica prison. I lost the postconviction appeal for a new trial, but I have uncovered new evidence and I will pursue the matter

further—because I believe in his innocence. The Joseph
James case was another A.Z. (After Zapata), and there have
been a great many others.

Now, at Kings County courthouse, I was a trifle uneasy at the
thought of working beside Zapata again. I knew that when
I met him in the courtroom, he would try to do his usual
number on me, subtly suggesting that though as co-counsels
we were equal in the eyes of the law, he possessed the larger
share of that equality. I had no intention of letting him get
away with it anymore, but how do you wage a battle against
intangibles? Well, I would soon find out, I thought, as I
stepped out on the fifth floor, where the courtroom was
located.

As I entered, I had a moment of seeing old ghosts: Leibowitz glowering at me from the bench, and Zapata as I had
first known him, a fiery, ambitious young Puerto Rican lawyer, sitting at the table next to me, my hand on his arm
holding him there by sheer force to keep him from leaping
over the barriers and attempting to strangle the judge. Then
I blinked and the ghosts vanished. Looking around me, I
smiled. It was definitely twenty years later, for seated on the
bench was a black judge; the court reporter was a woman;
and at the prosecution table was yet another woman, a
youngish lady from the D.A.'s office.

I took my seat at the defense table beside Zapata. His
manner was cool, and it grew even cooler when a correction
officer asked us if we were still partners. I felt Zapata wince
at my hearty negative.

Zapata did some more wincing during the course of the
trial—because the fight was between two women, myself
and the lady D.A. It was a battle royal. She was as tough as
nails, and so was I. Zapata was reduced to the position of
spectator as we slugged it out. It was, by the way, a battle
she won. Oh, that happens—but in a sense I was pleased.
Twenty years ago there would have been no woman at the

prosecution table, no woman court reporter. I would have been alone and spiritually dependent on the man at my side. Now I was dependent no longer; sex had definitely taken a back seat, and so had other forms of prejudice, as witness the black judge on the bench, one of the most respected and fairest judges in Brooklyn.

During a lunch recess, I had another case of déjà vu when I walked over to a new building, vaguely Grecian in outline; on its facade, bright gold letters identified it as The Brooklyn Law School.

Down the street from the new law school building is the battered brown building which once housed that institution. It was there that I learned the theory of the law. In those days my head was so full of the historic arguments and historic decisions of So-and-so versus So-and-so that I had not really considered the obstacles awaiting me, a woman, when I finally became a lawyer. The fact that there had not been many other women in my situation had not daunted me. I just thought of putting the theories I had learned to use in a practice that would have a place in the legal community. It was only after I passed the bar examination that I found that, as far as most lawyers and judges were concerned, a woman's place in that sequestered community was with a Stenotype machine rather than a brief in her hand. It took me the better part of twenty years to realize the hopes and aspirations I had entertained as I sat in class at Brooklyn Law School. In those twenty years, many changes had taken place in the status of women in general in the United States. Consciousness had been raised; rights had been claimed. In view of this, I wondered how the women currently attending law school viewed their future careers. Did they anticipate less opposition than I had faced? Did they expect to be accepted on the strength of their knowledge and ability alone?

I walked through the shining glass doors into the great

square lobby of the new law school building, crossed to the elevators, and rode to the basement, where the cafeteria and bulletin boards are located and where many students congregate. A glance at the tables in the cafeteria confirmed that there were many more women attending law school than there had been in my day.

I stopped a group of young women and learned from them that the student body was 40 percent female, with 50 percent expected to be enrolled the following year. The women to whom I spoke were full of hope. They told me about how many young women lawyers there were in Family Court, in Legal Aid, how many worked in the D.A.'s office —and, of course, how many were judges.

I was very happy as I left the school and walked back to the courthouse. More than ever, I felt like a pioneer who, on returning to the wild frontier of twenty years back, finds it has changed into a metropolis.

Oh, it's not entirely perfect, not even now. Occasionally there are little pinpricks that remind you that while women are being liberated in their thinking, the male ego is not adjusting as quickly as one would like. This happened to me very recently. I had an appointment with a judge, and, while waiting in the "Lawyers Only" section of the courtroom, I heard a voice ask, "Is this seat taken?"

I looked up and saw a tall young man, briefcase in hand, standing over me. I glanced at the seat next to mine, where someone had dropped an overcoat. "I don't know whether it's taken or not," I said, "but he left his coat here."

He shook his head. "I wasn't asking about *that* seat," he said. "I meant your seat. This section's reserved for lawyers only."

I saw red. "What do you think I am?" I demanded hotly. "I am a lawyer, my dear sir, and I have as much right as any smug jackass of a male lawyer to sit where I am sitting."

He looked most discomfited, and a male colleague of

mine, who had witnessed the exchange, laughed and said to him, "Boy, you should never have gotten up this morning." The young man beat a hasty and red-faced retreat.

I could laugh at his embarrassment, but there is nothing funny about the male chauvinism that still pervades our courts. It has to change, and it will change, but it is going to take more time. However, it could happen sooner rather than later if we women had the support of the media, by which I mean newspapers and television. Thus far, television shows have tended to glamorize the image of the female lawyer; she is pictured as svelte and lovely, a sexy lady who also happens to be a lawyer. Generally she has a large, supportive male staff who applaud her every victory, or, if she is alone, she uses her sex rather than her legal knowledge to win cases. I've had to do this myself, but I resent the necessity. Come on, ladies, let's challenge the producers who disseminate this sort of unrealistic claptrap—we don't need it! A woman lawyer, in common with her male counterpart, puts in a lot of grueling work on numerous unglamorous cases. She depends on the same solid background of experience to win those cases, and she is entitled to the same respect.

My friends and my family, looking at the bronze plaque on my office door, the plaque that reads "Sara Halbert" and heads a series of similar bronze plaques stamped with the names of my male associates, say, "Well, Sara, you top the list, you've really made it." I agree—but with qualifications. They are not mine; they are inherent in the newspaper articles that insist upon stating that such and such a client had a woman lawyer. That qualifying word should be dropped. I am not a woman lawyer, I am a lawyer; and I shall feel I have really made it when every newspaper omits the sex reference and every judge eschews the "madam" and calls me "Counselor."

6

Kettering / Jackson

Romanse
ingen naturism
Jordan

Piracco 21
26 3 DAVIDA

JUNE

LOUIS 14 20 65
MIKE 17 RAY
Kathy 1 11 55 8 1955